THE DECISION TO
DIVIDE GERMANY

AMERICAN FOREIGN POLICY
IN TRANSITION

JOHN H. BACKER

DUKE UNIVERSITY PRESS
DURHAM, N.C., 1978

Printed in the United States of
America by Kingsport Press, Inc.

THE DECISION TO DIVIDE GERMANY

TO THE MEMORY OF
PHILIP E. MOSELY

Contents

PREFACE

This book deals with the circumstances which prompted the decision to divide Germany along the present borders separating the Federal and Democratic Republics. It does not concern itself with the eastern boundaries of the latter nor with the annexation of East Prussia and Silesia by the Soviet Union and Poland. In other words, the subject of this inquiry is the de facto reversal of the Potsdam agreement to establish a unified Germany and the developments which led to this fundamental change of policy.

There is a widely held belief in this country that the behavior of the Soviet Union in Eastern Europe and particularly its ruthless exploitation of the Russian Zone of occupation made the decision to divide Germany unavoidable. Traditionalist historians like Herbert Feis and Arthur Schlesinger supported this conclusion. In their writings they emphasized Russia's expansionist aims and cited Soviet disregard for the Yalta and Potsdam agreements as well as repeated refusals in 1945 and 1946 to proceed with the economic unification of Germany. More recently the revisionist school of historiography represented by William A. Williams, Bruce Kuklick, and others has placed the blame for the division of Europe on the doorstep of the United States. American economic imperialism, so the revisionists assert, demanded an aggressive "open-door" policy and free-market economies abroad in order to make the world safe for the American brand of capitalism.

The common denominator of these two interpretations—a governing grand design—will be challenged. Undoubtedly, similar long-range schemes were in the minds of some leaders on both sides of the Iron Curtain. But in the United States there were also other schemes canceling out the former and it is safe to assume that a similar process took place inside the Politburo of the Soviet Union. The result then was a series of small, incremental decisions, sometimes taken at the lower levels of government and often prompted by expediency rather than by long-term considerations. The pervasive influence of congressional appropriations committees is a case in point. The primary constant policy element was the evaluation of the past. Since only two decades separated the two wars and the correlation of forces in the European Theater was quite similar, America's leaders endeavored to learn from past mistakes. However—as will be shown—to the extent that the perceptual heritage of the nation was fallacious, new and fateful errors arose.

On the other hand, the long-range question of whether the partition of Germany ought to be seen in a positive or negative light will not be raised or discussed. This generation has been a witness to the problems which resulted from the division, whereas a discussion of the perils of an alternative solution merely would take us into an area of speculation. The purpose of this study then is to appraise the causes and the rationale of American policies at the national and military government levels, as well as the resulting failure to unify the Eastern and Western Zones of occupation.

Most of the unpublished documents referred to here are stored in the National Archives in Washington, D.C. I should like to express my gratitude to Milton Gustavson and Patricia Dowling for facilitating access to the files of the Department of State, to Thomas E. Hohmann for expediting declassification of War Department documents; and to John Taylor for making the research papers of the United States Office of Strategic Services speedily available. Moreover, I am indebted to Gordon Stewart, Adam Ulam, Barbara Chotiner, Martha and Karl Mautner, Douglas Hodgson, Roy Bullock, and William I. Parker, who read all or parts of the manuscript. William Diebold, Jr. and Herbert Block were most helpful in their scrutiny of the fourth chapter; so was Wynfried Jones in our discussions of the first. Otto Nuebel's incisive comments on the reparations issue were equally beneficial. Finally, I want to thank my wife Evelyn without whose enduring patience this book could not have been completed. Needless to say, the entire responsibility for the contents of this study remains mine.

THE DECISION TO DIVIDE GERMANY

CHAPTER ONE

HISTORICAL PERCEPTIONS AND AMERICAN POSTWAR PLANNING

*In this history-conscious era what men think about the past is fre-
quently more important than the past itself.*
                                        —Robert Endicott Osgood

During recent years American scholars have been scrutinizing the processes of political decision making on an increasing scale. To the extent
that foreign policy was the object, their efforts were reflected in a great
variety of interdisciplinary approaches such as theoretical models, in-
quiries which searched for regularities in the behavior of political actors,
studies which combined several levels of analysis, investigations of
individual or national belief systems, and others. While most of the
papers recognized the significance of historical perceptions, it was not
always spelled out whose "stored memories" were considered relevant
nor how they had come about. On the other hand, the insidious perils
of faulty perceptions—they will be stressed in this book and illustrated
below by some excerpts from the literature—were brought out very
clearly.

One of the frequently discussed models of decision making which oc-
cupies a chapter in Andrew Scott's *The Functioning of the International
Political System* [1] refers in great detail to the role of historical perceptions. Scott's decision makers maintain close relations with an attentive
domestic public and there are continued interchanges between the value
and image systems of the two. Scott defines the value and image systems of an individual as "ideology which should be thought of as part
of a perceptual screen through which the individual views the world."
It influences his perceptions of what is, what was, what may and what

---

1. Pp. 80–105.

should be. Scott deals extensively with the "learning and forgetting" processes of the decision makers. As he points out, decision makers are able to make images of their environment only because of the stored memories of the political system in which they operate. Such stored memories may or may not represent an accurate interpretation of past events and may or may not offer an accurate picture of the existing situation. In a similar vein, the decision-making systems will normally have the capacity to remember and *will almost certainly have the capacity to forget*.[2] Scott concludes that forgetting is a selective process. Each system will develop patterns regarding the material that it chooses to remember or chooses to forget.

Karl Deutsch's *Analysis of International Relations* offers some empirical examples applicable to Scott's theory of "learning and forgetting." In the relevant chapter, appropriately labeled "Decision-making: Combining New Information with Old Memories," [3] Deutsch analyzes the historical perceptions of America's political and military leaders which influenced how the leaders reacted to North Korea's surprise attack on the night of June 25, 1950. Among the perceptual heritage Americans then had were the awareness of the failure of Western powers to resist Japanese aggression against Manchuria and China in the thirties, the Nazi military moves in Europe, the cold war with the Soviet Union, the widely held view that Stalin was testing the resolve of the United States, the indignation of a substantial part of the American public at the Communist victory in the Chinese civil war, and the limited character of American aid to the defeated Nationalists. By contrast some of the memories pointed in a different direction, such as a speech by then Secretary of State Dean Acheson that failed to list South Korea as inside the perimeter of major American national defense interests, and contemporary Pentagon statements describing an American military engagement in Korea as highly undesirable. Another important historical experience in the living memory of most participants, however, was entirely "forgotten" during that night in June: the memories of August 1914, when a local conflict between two secondary powers quickly escalated into the First World War. As Deutsch writes, "none of the officials is recorded as having brought that incident to the attention of others." [4]

Two more studies of decision making have attracted considerable attention among theoreticians as well as among practitioners of political

2. Italics added.   3. Pp. 75ff.
4. Ibid., p. 76.

science: Richard E. Neustadt's *Alliance Politics* and Graham Allison's *Essence of Decision*. Neustadt's study is a multilevel analysis of the Suez and Skybolt crises examining the misconceptions of prominent leaders on both sides of the ocean. The British perception of Truman's actions at the time of Israel's creation let the London government assume that the Jewish influence in America would be decisive in winning American acceptance of a military attack on Egypt.[5] The British regarded the Suez Canal as important as did the United States the Panama Canal [6] and expected a similar view to prevail in Washington. On the American side there were the customary emotional reactions to "other people's empires . . . especially the English—reminiscent of George III —the more so since [America's] Communist competitors played 'anti-imperialist' to the Third World." [7] Furthermore, in the case of the Suez and Skybolt affairs there was the recollection of English parliamentary procedures, as described in textbooks which were no longer valid.

The sometimes pivotal significance of historical perceptions is also demonstrated in Allison's *Essence of Decision,* a three-model analysis of the Cuban missile crisis conducted at the "classical" level as well as on a second plane of "organizational processes" and a third of "bureaucratic politics." According to the conventional view, supported by the writings of Robert Kennedy [8] and Theodore Sorensen,[9] the decision to proceed with a blockade rather than with a surprise air strike was the result of the attorney general's warning that the latter would be "a Pearl Harbor in reverse" and therefore unacceptable to the American people.[10] Although Allison suggests that moral inhibitions were not a crucial factor in the final decision to try a blockade,[11] it is relevant that, as Dean Acheson saw it, Robert Kennedy "seemed to obfuscate rather than clarify thought by a thoroughly false and pejorative analogy." [12]

Each of the four studies mentioned here contained some comments on the role of historical perception, although the respective origin and genesis of these perceptions have hardly come into focus. Deutsch, in his *Analysis of International Relations,* tried to deal with the subject by referring to popular memories as "stored in papers, books, and files; in maps, pictures, monuments and libraries; in diplomatic reports and policy memoranda; in staff plans for war; in the records of government

5. *Alliance Politics*, p. 84.
6. Ibid., p. 61.
7. Ibid., p. 13.
8. *Thirteen Days.*
9. *Kennedy.*
10. Allison, *Essence of Decision*, p. 60.
11. Ibid., pp. 248–249.
12. "Homage to Plain Dumb Luck," *Esquire*, February 1969, p. 76.

bureaus and of business organizations; in laws and in treaties,"—in other words the traditional sources of the scholar.[13] To the extent that these are unedited primary sources, however, the element of time alone would curtail, if not eliminate, any direct impact on the political leaders. Inasmuch as this fact underlines the importance of secondary sources, one is left with these questions: What papers—what books? How do they relate to the biographical experiences of the decision makers? Can their respective influence be traced?

As far as American history is concerned, there is no period which has not been interpreted in several highly divergent fashions. The vigorously contested debate about the origins of the cold war is paralleled by differing appraisals of Pearl Harbor, the interwar period, Versailles, the First World War, the Spanish-American War, the "Open Door" policy, and the War between the States. Even if one puts aside conspiratorial interpretations of history, there remain a great number of contradictory and scholarly analyses which are usually classified as being either traditionalist or revisionist.

To what extent are the historical perceptions of America's attentive public shaped by these varied approaches? Will the foreign policy of the United States in the year 2000 be influenced by the traditionalist interpretation that the Soviet Union in the forties and fifties aimed at conquering for communism as much territory as possible without involving Russia in a third World War? Or will the revisionist analysis of a William A. Williams shape the next generation's "stored" memories by conveying the view that Stalin was interested only in Russia's own recovery and security and that America's economic imperialism was responsible for the cold war? Naturally, we do not know the answer. Nor is it yet possible to determine whether the current policy of "detente" is the consequence of a corrected perception of the postwar situation or simply the result of the "logic of the situation"[14] which evolved from the disclosure that monolithic communism was not a valid concept any longer. It may be easier to find an answer to our question by facing the past and turning to the three American policies which were of fundamental significance for the postwar world: the demand for unconditional surrender, the plans for the division of Germany, and the position on the problems of reparations. Evidently these policies grew out of a widespread belief that Germany was a permanent threat to world peace.

13. Karl Deutsch, *The Analysis of International Relations*, p. 75.
14. A term coined by Sidney Verba.

What was the role of American historiography in promoting these anti-German sentiments?

That the First World War and the events of the interwar period played an important role in shaping these perceptions is generally recognized. Earlier positive or negative reactions of American public opinion with regard to Germany are less well remembered. President Wilson in his Fourteen Points had taken the position that "the wrong done to France by Germany in 1871 in the matter of Alsace-Lorraine should be righted in order that peace may once more be made secure in the interest of all." At the time the statement was made, American public opinion was generally in agreement with Wilson's recommendation, but fifty years earlier Americans had seen the Franco-Prussian war in a very different light. Having just emerged from a fratricidal struggle for unity, it seemed only natural that Americans in general sympathized with German attempts at national unification. Moreover, in contrast to Napoleon III, whose imperialistic ambitions were notorious, Prussia and the other German states had supported the case of the Union during the Civil War. In short, the American public by and large considered France the aggressor and thought that no wrong had been done by the taking of Alsace-Lorraine.[15]

The pro-German attitude in America did not last very long, however. A number of factors were responsible: first, there was the rapid industrial development of the Second Reich, which created a need for new markets and colonies; second, Bismarck succeeded in putting his autocratic stamp on the new empire while curtailing the influence of the liberals; and third, there was the unattractive personality of the young kaiser, who after Bismarck's departure took German foreign policy into his own hands and whose public statements all too often caused resentment among rank-and-file Americans.[16] The fact that the United States at the turn of the century began to pursue its own policies of expansionism was of course an aggravating element. The result was a series of American-German diplomatic conflicts.

The first conflict, which occupied the attention of America's Department of State and the British and German foreign offices from 1889 to 1899, was an international dispute growing out of the Samoan question. Although it came close to involving the three nations in an armed

15. Clara Eve Schieber, *The Transformation of American Sentiment Toward Germany, 1870–1914*, p. 3.
16. Ibid., p. 39.

conflict, their governments were wise enough to realize that the small group of islands in the Pacific did not justify any dramatic action. Consequently, after a decade of civil war on the islands, international jealousies, consular disputes, and official blunders, the Samoan question was settled by the Treaty of Washington (December 2, 1899). American sentiment was practically unanimous in condemning Germany's arrogant and provocative methods and in justifying the State Department's position.[17] While the dispute passed without serious repercussions, it caused friction between the two countries and was responsible for the emergence of an anti-German sentiment of distrust and suspicion.

Later events led to more American-German confrontations. There was the German seizure of Kiao Chau, prompted by the murder of two German missionaries which offered the imperial government a convenient but transparent alibi. "The massacre could not have come at a more suitable time for the Emperor William's plans." [18] ". . . it was made a pretext for gaining a permanent foothold in the Celestial Empire," [19] wrote an American diplomat. There was the Boxer Rebellion, the murder of the German minister, Baron von Ketteler, at the hands of the Chinese, and brutal German reactions which suggested to the American press the term "Hun." And there was the provocative arrival of Germany's Asiatic Fleet in Manila Bay during Commodore Dewey's operations—a move widely interpreted as a preliminary to seizing some islands if the opportunity presented itself.[20]

The United States had interfered with German plans in the Far East, so at the beginning of the twentieth century Germany turned its attention toward the West—only to encounter an even stronger American opposition. In addition to minor attempts in Haiti and San Domingo to utilize unpaid debts as a means of gaining a permanent territorial foothold in the Caribbean, Germany joined forces with Great Britain and Italy in a blockade of Venezuelan ports, in bombarding two forts, and in seizing several Venezuelan gunboats. Despite the joint responsibility of the three powers, the Department of State as well as American public opinion were most suspicious of the real intentions and designs of the Germans.[21] The incident was eventually settled through arbitration to which Great Britain promptly and Germany only hesi-

17. Ibid., p. 88.
18. Paul S. Reinsch, *World Politics at the End of the Nineteenth Century as Influenced by the Oriental Situation*, p. 270.
19. Ibid., p. 33.
20. Schieber, *Transformation . . .* , pp. 106–136.
21. Samuel Flagg Bemis, *A Diplomatic History of the United States*, p. 523.

tatingly agreed. Although the German government never challenged the Monroe Doctrine openly, its actions in the Caribbean and in South America could be interpreted only as a testing of the American will to defend this fundamental concept. It is not surprising then that the American press in general was skeptical as to the good faith of German policies in Latin America.[22] Furthermore, in the United States the kaiser's conduct and public utterances appeared obnoxious and repulsive to the average citizen. Thus, on the eve of Sarajevo, American public opinion was unfavorably disposed toward Germany.

According to traditionalist historians such as Samuel Flagg Bemis, the First World War resulted from unilateral acts of aggression by the Central Powers. The United States, carefully observing the rules of international law, attempted to remain neutral and entered the conflict only when Germany's naval warfare became indiscriminately ruthless. When Germany surrendered in 1918 on the basis of President Wilson's Fourteen Points, its military defeat was complete and Berlin would have been obliged to accept unconditional surrender had the victors made the demand. The Treaty of Versailles, while harsh in some respects, was not a Carthaginian peace. If, in some areas it twisted Wilsonian principles beyond recognition, it nevertheless granted millions of people self-determination and national identity.[23] Although the other Allies demanded very high reparations, the United States not only did not ask for reparations for itself, but also attempted, alas in vain, to reduce the claims of its Allies. France appeared particularly vengeful in this regard and its efforts to collect reparations forcibly failed. On the other hand, Germany displayed ill will almost from the start and refused to honor its obligations.

The runaway inflation which accompanied the French occupation of the Ruhr was to a considerable extent self-generated; its unfortunate side effect—the financial destruction of the German middle class—laid the ground for the later successes of the National Socialist party and the emergence of a revanchist foreign policy. The United States attempted to put Germany back on its feet by extending long-term financial aid, but Germany soon defaulted, and for all practical purposes American taxpayers paid Germany's reparations. In addition, the gullible victors provided sufficient funds for Germany to build up its armament industries and prepare for a next war.[24] Germany's rearmament

22. Schieber, *Transformation* . . . , p. 153.
23. Bemis, *Diplomatic History* . . . , p. 639.
24. Ibid., p. 724.

—initiated and implemented under Hitler—was made possible because of the divergent policies of the victorious powers. The United States had tried to divorce itself from further involvement in European affairs but Germany's second reach for world power—this time in conjunction with Japanese aggression—made America's military involvement inevitable.

A significant aspect of this interpretation is the emphasis on the ethical and legal causes of America's intervention and a concomitant neglect of the role of national self-interest in the wartime policy of the United States. While the American public at large was indeed unaware that national self-preservation could be involved,[25] the prospect of a future German threat to the security of the United States was foremost in the minds of political leaders such as Secretary Lansing, Colonel House, and Ambassador Page;[26] to a lesser degree it also influenced President Wilson's decisions.[27]

On the other hand, it is understandable that the element of long-range national self-interest had no place in the assessments of revisionist writers such as Harry E. Barnes. Their point of departure was to assert the war guilt of the Entente. As to America, the revisionists argued that from the outset Wilsonian policies favored Great Britain and that legalistic interpretations of the rules of naval warfare actually reduced American neutrality to a hollow theoretical concept. Accordingly, Germany tried as long as possible to avoid a war with the United States but the increasing stream of military supplies reaching Germany's enemies made an eventual military confrontation almost inevitable. Revisionists maintain that there was no justification for the treaty's war-guilt clause, which proved to be a most unfortunate diplomatic instrument. It seriously damaged chances for the growth of a democratic and peaceful Germany, and it soon provided welcome ammunition for nationalist and revanchist elements. With the assertion of Germany's unilateral war guilt in jeopardy, many of the sanctions imposed at Versailles no longer seemed justifiable. This applied especially to reparations, which, with America's active participation, had been set at an impossibly high level.[28] As to self-determination, revisionists mention the questionable moral standing of a doctrine which fifty years earlier had been effectively negated within the confines of the United States. More to the

25. Robert Endicott Osgood, *Ideals and Self-Interest in America's Foreign Relations*, pp. 197, 199, 222, 223.
26. Ibid., p. 170.
27. Henry Cabot Lodge, *The Senate and the League of Nations*, pp. 137–138.
28. Philip Mason Burnett, *Reparation at the Paris Peace Conference*, p. 62.

point, they cite the cases of Austria and of the Sudeten territory, where the implementation of the doctrine was rejected for strategic reasons. The incorporation of these areas into Germany not only would have increased Germany's population but also would have greatly added to the Reich's economic strength. A common German border with Italy, Hungary, and Yugoslavia appeared equally unattractive to the victors. Finally, the projected Czechoslovakian Republic would have been crippled at its birth. The revisionists conclude that the one-sided application of the Wilsonian principles at Versailles destroyed whatever chances there were in Europe for an enduring peace.

Since the two interpretations of history were indeed irreconcilable, it is fortunate that historiography was eventually able to narrow the gap. In 1930 the highly respected historian Bernadotte Schmidt reached the conclusion that a *greater* share of responsibility for the war was on Germany's side,[29] whereas in the same year the equally prominent revisionist Sidney B. Fay made the opposite point.[30] In other words, at an academic level the theory of unilateral German war guilt was abandoned, while in the political arena the verdict remained unchanged. Moreover, with regard to the rules of naval warfare, by the midthirties America had second thoughts as to whether national honor indeed required the protection of citizens who chose to travel on the ships of belligerents. Concurrently, against a background of Japanese and German aggression, increasing credence was given to the factor of self-preservation, with Samuel F. Bemis offering the following rationalization:

> What the United States really gained from the war was the overthrow for a generation of the military German empire, which, victorious, would have been in a position for an inevitable Japanese alliance that would have caught the nations of the New World in the jaws of a crushing vise of Occidental and Oriental military and naval power. The price of temporary immunity, while high, was hardly excessive.[31]

Bemis's interpretation has the advantage of evading the question of war guilt and of confining itself to the *perception* of Germany as a putative aggressor. Actually, in the light of what happened after 1933, Bemis's evaluation would attribute far-sighted statesmanship to America's foreign policy, although this point will have to remain debatable;

29. *The Coming of the War, 1914.*   30. *The Origins of the World War.*
31. *Diplomatic History . . . ,* p. 676.

the inevitability of an aggressive and expansionist Germany after 1918 can never be demonstrated nor can it be disproved. By the same token, if Bemis's thesis is accepted, neither the handling of the war-debts issue nor Versailles and its aftermath could be defended any longer. If the First World War was indeed a preventive war on the part of the United States, the war debts should have been canceled or at least greatly reduced. As to the treaty, there should have been either a lenient peace in an attempt to reeducate the German people and to strengthen the liberal and democratic elements or enforcement machinery to keep the would-be aggressor down. With the wisdom of hindsight one can only regret that none of these measures was adopted.

Turning now to the role of American stored memories at the eve of the Second World War, the influence of revisionist thought was apparent in the neutrality legislation, while the accompanying public debate sharply reflected the divergence of historical perceptions. It would be a mistake, however, to deduce from this controversy that pro-German sentiments had replaced anti-German biases. Nobody saw this more clearly than Hitler's ambassador in Washington, Dr. Hans Heinrich Dieckhoff, who reported to Berlin in 1937 that "the position taken and the stir created by the supporters of the isolationists are to be welcomed . . . but we must clearly understand one thing: the pacifists . . . have their attitude in no way determined by friendship or sympathy for Germany." [32] In other words, the impact of revisionist historiography on American public opinion was essentially negative: the conclusion was that the United States should not have become involved in European affairs but not that Germany had been vindicated. As a Gallup poll in April 1937 disclosed, 64 percent of those questioned regarded America's participation in World War I a mistake.[33]

Revisionist influence can also be detected in an often apathetic attitude toward the taking of Austria and even of the Sudetenland. While some columnists like Dorothy Thompson used the strongest possible language to condemn Germany's action, others felt that Hitler or Germany had a case in nullifying the Paris treaties and some of their unwise territorial provisions.[34] Several commentators maintained that Austria should never have been made a completely independent state; it had voluntarily sought economic union with Germany long before the advent of Hitler and "its government was not a democracy but a form

---

32. Manfred Jonas, *Isolationism in America, 1935–1941*, p. 199.
33. *Public Opinion Quarterly* 5 (Fall 1941): 477.
34. Jonas, *Isolationism* . . . , p. 224; Osgood, *Ideals* . . . , p. 370.

of dictatorship under Italian influence." [35] President Wilson and British Prime Minister Lloyd George, it was pointed out, had opposed giving the Sudetenland to Czechoslovakia in 1919, and "long before the Munich crisis of September 1938 responsible British and even French statesmen were apparently agreed that the incorporation of the Sudetenland into Germany was fair and desirable." [36] Even John Foster Dulles, certainly not a confirmed isolationist, wrote that the status quo was unjust and that the "exponents of force are the inevitable product of a society within which change can occur only through force." [37]

In sum then, the challenge of revisionist thought to the traditional interpretation of the First World War and its aftermath remained strong until Nazi Germany invaded Poland in the fall of 1939. Revisionism receded during the next two years, although it was still reflected in the vocally expressed views of the America First Committee, a strong minority opposing United States entry into the war. As one would expect, after Pearl Harbor and Hitler's declaration of war, the traditionalist appraisal of Germany as an aggressor nation regained its strength. Undoubtedly, one factor favoring this notion in the thirties had been the rise of nationalist and antidemocratic elements whose activities tended to reinforce prevailing anti-German sentiments. Another factor was the short period between the two wars and the continued power of a generation whose biographical experiences were stronger than revisionist analysis. Generally in their fifties and sixties, American political and military leaders had been adults during the First World War and often had occupied positions of considerable responsibility. To name a few, the secretary of the army, Henry Stimson, had held the same position in the Taft Administration. The secretary of the navy, Frank Knox, had served with Theodore Roosevelt's Rough Riders and later in the American Expeditionary Force in Europe. Secretary of State Cordell Hull had been a member of the United States House of Representatives from 1907 to 1921, and in this capacity had supported Wilson's foreign policy to the bitter end. Harry Hopkins had held an executive position with the American Red Cross during World War I. General Marshall had served as General Pershing's senior aide. One of the younger in this group, Secretary of the Treasury Henry Morgenthau, Jr., had held no official position under Wilson, but during his father's tour as American ambassador to Turkey from 1913 to 1916 had acquired a strong anti-German bias as a result of contacts with German officers

35. Jonas, *Isolationism* . . . , p. 225.
36. Ibid.   37. Ibid.

and diplomats. As is well known, Franklin D. Roosevelt had held the position of assistant secretary of the navy under Wilson and had been a proponent of an early declaration of war. In October 1918, when the Germans had asked for an armistice, Roosevelt had shared the widespread objections to an agreement for a cessation of hostilities that resembled a "peace without victory." [38]

It is not surprising then that twenty years later the same Roosevelt told the Senate Foreign Relations Committee that America's first line of defense in the Atlantic was on the Rhine, with that extreme part of the perimeter being protected by the Western opponents of Hitler's Germany. Accordingly, America's foreign policy prior to Pearl Harbor followed Wilson's example of giving maximum help to America's European friends with even less regard for the niceties of international law and with the clearly accepted risk of America's sudden and direct involvement. As to Congress and the majority of the American people, the revisionist critique of America's entry into the First World War had not left enough of an imprint to produce an effective opposition. As Andrew Scott had theorized, ". . . every system develops patterns regarding the material that it chooses to remember or chooses to forget." In this case a deadly threat to the survival of the free world determined the pattern.

A similar selective perception of the past is reflected in the three basic American policies mentioned above. As to the first, the demand for unconditional surrender, the conventional interpretation holds that the Casablanca formula offered the Soviet Union an assurance that the United States was not going to sign a separate peace. Implied was the expectation that Russia would remain an equally dependable ally and the recognition that a split among the Allies virtually would assure Axis success or at least a compromise peace.[39] However, there was a second aspect of the Casablanca Declaration. German leaders of various political persuasions had insisted all along that Germany had not been defeated on the field of battle, that it had surrendered on the basis of Wilson's Fourteen Points, and that neither this understanding nor the armistice agreement limiting the concept of reparations had been honored. During the interwar period, this line of argument had been reflected on an ever-increasing scale in Germany's semiofficial and official governmental statements justifying the gradual destruction of the treaty. As indicated, American revisionists had expressed similar views.

38. Raymond C. O'Connor, *Diplomacy for Victory*, p. 2.
39. Ibid., pp. 100–101.

At Casablanca the American president could have mentioned the revisionist evaluation of Versailles and proclaimed that the next peace settlement would not be guided by a spirit of revenge but be based on the principles of the Atlantic Charter. By taking this course, he would have given encouragement to the democratic elements in Germany and possibly brought the war to an earlier end. However, Roosevelt and the great majority of the American people perceived history in a different light. In their opinion, World War II had to be fought not because of an unwise treaty but because in 1918 there had been a conditional surrender. Wilson had erred by permitting the Germans to negotiate for terms.[40] The error was not going to be repeated—this time it had to be unconditional surrender. As Robert Sherwood put it, "the ghost of Woodrow Wilson had been at Roosevelt's shoulder at Casablanca." [41]

The connection between the traditionalist interpretation of the First World War and the plans for a division of Germany is equally conclusive. Since Germany was seen as an inherently aggressive nation and its economic and military power potentially dangerous for the safety of the United States, a contractual agreement similar to Versailles would not be satisfactory. Security would have to be sought by breaking up the territory of the would-be aggressor. Only when the power vacuum created by unconditional surrender and the four-zonal division of the country demonstrated new realities were these plans shelved.

As to the reparations issue, the economic and social upheaval caused by the Allied claims had demonstrated that the policies of Versailles had been erroneous. Beyond this point, however, the historical perceptions of America's decision makers varied widely. At one end of the spectrum one finds Morgenthau and like-minded groups who saw in Germany a three-time aggressor and who believed that its rapid rearmament for the Second World War had been facilitated by an industrial base developed for the supply of reparations. They consequently favored dismantlement and opposed reparations from production. Moreover, since it was obvious that devastated Russia would have to be rebuilt, it was suggested that the Soviets be bought off with a loan.

On the other end of the scale were political leaders who, fearful of the Soviet Union, rejected a drastic and permanent weakening of Germany's economic strength. They found comfort in revisionist exculpa-

40. National Opinion Research Center, University of Denver, *Germany and the Post-War World,* p. 55.
41. Robert E. Sherwood, *Roosevelt and Hopkins,* p. 697.

tions of imperial Germany and also drew on the writings of tradition-alists who had "forgotten" troublesome facts and in a simplistic shortcut to a complex problem had traced Germany's reparations payments to concurrent American loans. Morgenthau's opponents therefore argued that any kind of reparations should be held to a minimum.

The convergence of these conflicting views caused a hesitant attitude in the United States toward reparations; it also produced an uneasy compromise in the form of an occupational directive which in many respects left it up to the American military governor's ingenuity to find equitable solutions. Unaided by clear policy guidance, he was given the impossible mission of administering without assistance from abroad a geographic area whose cities were in shambles and which by itself was not a viable economic entity. Accordingly he seized on reparations as a suitable issue to bring about Germany's economic unification, or, as an alternative, to provoke a workable political decision at top govern-mental levels.

The Soviets, on the other hand, having had no part in Versailles and having condemned the treaty from the very beginning, were able to evaluate the economic difficulties of the twenties in a more factual man-ner. As a consequence, they saw America's resistance to reparations after the Second World War as callous and hostile.

The Kremlin's disregard for the Yalta agreements, its aggressive poli-cies in Eastern Europe, a stiffening Western response, the dwindling strength of the United States army, Germany's prostrate economy, the problems arising from hermetically separated military zones, the need for American food supplies, the threatening collapse of West European economies, and the growing disenchantment of the American people with their wartime ally were important elements of the emerging power conflict in central Europe. Under these circumstances the question of reparations to the Soviet Union could hardly fail to become a critical and eventually decisive issue.

CHAPTER TWO

EARLY PLANS FOR PARTITION

Russia had been defeated by the military might of imperial Germany in the First World War; only a few decades later it was again involved in deadly struggle against the same enemy. England had been saved from defeat in 1918 only to face the likelihood of a German invasion twenty odd years later. The United States had entered the two wars against a nation which many Americans considered an inveterate aggressor. Under these circumstances it was not surprising that most thinking persons in these countries asked themselves how a repetition of such catastrophes could be avoided in the future. While scholars often traced the causes of the Second World War to an unfortunate treaty, America's leaders usually analyzed history in a more simplistic fashion. As many of them saw it, Versailles had failed not because it was too severe, but because it was not severe enough and its terms had not been enforced. Their logical proposition for the future was the dismemberment of Germany.

This remedy was first brought up by Stalin, whose predecessor, interestingly enough, had referred to Versailles as "a thousand times worse than Brest Litovsk." [1] In December 1941, when talking to Eden, Stalin suggested that the Rhineland should be taken from Prussia and set up as an independent state, that Bavaria should be separated, and that Austria's independence as established at St. Germain should be restored. The Russian leader also indicated that Poland's eastern boundaries should follow the Curzon Line, and that it ought to be compensated for this loss of territory by the acquisition of East Prussia and possibly by a part of Silesia, which might be divided between Poland and Czechoslovakia. [2] The possibility of a French frontier on the Rhine was also mentioned on this occasion. Churchill, who was on shipboard traveling

---

1. Vladimir I. Lenin, *Sochineniya*. Third Edition, 24: 545.
2. "Official Policies and Views of the Soviet, British and American Governments" (National Archives, SDF, Record Group 59, Notter).

to Washington, was kept informed of Eden's conversations in Moscow and presumably passed on their substance to Roosevelt. Neither the American nor the British governments took an official stand on the issue at the time but it appears that Roosevelt brought it to the attention of Under Secretary Sumner Welles as requiring a study by the Department of State.[3] Four subcommittees of the department's Advisory Committee on Post-War Policy accordingly began to scrutinize the problem of Germany's dismemberment and continued to concentrate on the issue for more than a year.

In contrast to some of the president's key advisors, whose memories of the last war had not been affected by critical inquiry, the department's experts on international affairs—often recruited from academe —analyzed the issue in a more sophisticated fashion. As to be expected, a host of multifaceted questions had to be dealt with at their meetings. Would Germany be controlled more easily as a single unit or if broken up into several states? Would it be easier to conduct the military occupation of a unified Germany or of a Germany split into parts? As the committees envisaged it, there would be three consecutive postwar periods: an immediate occupation after the cessation of hostilities, a transitional period of German political reorganization, and probationary years when Germany would be promised an eventual relaxation of dismemberment. Was it not likely that as soon as military control was withdrawn, the separated parts of Germany would try to reunite? If reunion could be expected, should Germany not be held under military control for a generation? It was possible that the whole orientation of the German people would change during that time. On the other hand, if this course of action were decided upon, would public opinion in America support a prolonged occupation?

Was not the dismemberment of Germany an unreal and artificial step which could not be made to stick? Actually it might simply provide all Germans with a permanent grievance around which to rally. Psychologically, it might not only be fatal but also ineffective. Was it preferable to divide Germany into a number of very small states—possibly seven—which would be permitted to join in a loose federation? The political structure of such a federation might be so weak that it would not constitute a military menace. On the other hand, three German states, if reasonably strong and prosperous, might be more likely to remain separated. From the standpoint of security what partition

3. Philip E. Mosely, "Dismemberment of Germany," pp. 487–498.

lines should be chosen? Was a division along religious lines desirable or should economic factors be decisive? Was it not of primary importance to separate the Ruhr and could this not be best accomplished under an international commission? Or would a continued supervision of German industries be preferable?

As to the future of German-Polish frontiers, would a cession of East Prussia to Poland actually increase Polish security? There were no natural barriers in the disputed area. The transfer of the German population from East Prussia might be advisable if the region were ceded. In a less "enlightened" age the wholesale uprooting of people from their traditional homelands would have been considered an unthinkable and shocking act, but Hitler had demonstrated how it could be done even in the heart of Europe; there seemed to be some merit in his approach to a vexing problem. Similar considerations pertained to the German-Czechoslovakian border.

These and other considerations provided the agenda for numerous State Department meetings which took place during the course of 1942 at regular intervals. By the end of January 1943 sufficient consensus had emerged within the department to permit a summing up of two opposed positions at a policy meeting chaired by Under Secretary Sumner Welles and attended among others by such luminaries as Hamilton Fish Armstrong, Isaiah Bowman, and Leo Pasvolsky.[4] A hypothetical map had been drawn up for the occasion which showed a Germany divided into three states: a Northwest Germany with a population of 26,000,-000, a South Germany with 23,000,000 inhabitants, and a Northeast Germany, as it was called, with a population of 18,200,000. A plan for partition along these lines was discussed at the meeting of January 23. It was explained that, while there had been an attempt to create three fairly equal divisions in terms of resources, production, and population, the Prussian part was made somewhat smaller than the others. The southern unit was largely Catholic, whereas the two others were Protestant; furthermore, where the two lines of division did not follow the Rhine or the Elbe, they coincided with established administrative boundaries.

The basic rationale for partition, as presented at the meeting, was that militarism in Germany was two hundred years old and that, if Germany were not weakened by partition, recrudescence of militarism would present a danger to the world. If Germany were partitioned and

4. Policy Minutes 42 (National Archives, SDF, Record Group 59, Notter Files).

the other states again became "easy-going," Germany would first have to reunite and then rearm. On the other hand, a Germany already united would have to take only one step toward aggression.

The opposition view, as expressed at the meeting, was based on the recognition that if Germany were divided as suggested, reunification would become a great political issue in the three newly created states. The durability of the partition, therefore, seemed quite questionable, especially since the American people could hardly be expected—maybe fifteen years after the war—to approve the use of force to prevent the German people from achieving unity. Actually, a tripartite division of Germany might develop, in case of a later unification, in such a way as to create a state that might be economically stronger than that of 1939.

Another discussion of the issue took place at the highest governmental level when Eden visited Washington in March 1943. On this occasion the foreign secretary raised the question of whether the "Allies were going to insist that Germany be broken up into several states after the war?" The president's reply was somewhat ambiguous. On one hand, Roosevelt and Eden agreed on the necessity of partition, and especially on the separation of Prussia. On the other hand, the president hoped that "we would not use the methods discussed at Versailles and also promoted by Clemenceau to arbitrarily divide Germany," but thought that "we should encourage the differences and diversities that will spring up within Germany for a separatist movement and, in effect, approve a division which represents German public opinion." [5]

Within the Department of State the upshot of the prolonged deliberations was a fifty-page policy summary of July 27, 1943, a document labeled "H-24 Germany: Partition." [6] It was accompanied by a great number of maps which showed various possible partition lines as well as economic, political, and religious boundaries. The drafters of the document considered the arguments for and against partition and proceeded by analyzing the envisaged political and economic relations between the partite states as well as the respective advantages of bipartite, tripartite, fourfold, or multiple divisions. They concluded by discussing the likely duration of partition. The argument advanced in favor of division was that world security demanded that Germany should never again become a menace to peace. Consequently, the means to that end were the destruction of power concentrated in Berlin and the "decen-

5. Mosely, "Dismemberment . . . ," pp. 487–498.
6. (National Archives, SDF, Record Group 59, Notter Files).

tralization of Germany's energies by a division that would split across the political and moral forces of the land."

The basic argument against partition, on the other hand, was that it would not take root but would create a bitter hostility among the German people and jeopardize eventual German reconciliation with the peace settlement and German cooperation within a society of law-abiding nations. As to the duration of partition, the document juxtaposed the views of those who recommended permanent division because of its great utility in weakening Germany with the opinion of those who argued that partition should be maintained only until the ultimate conversion of the Germans was clear. The drafters of H-24 did not attempt to decide on the respective merits of the two positions nor did they offer a final recommendation. Nevertheless, the document shows a definite bias in favor of unity, reflecting the combined judgments of dispassionate and informed experts.

Whether President Roosevelt was given the opportunity to read H-24 is not clear. One incident suggests otherwise. On September 3, 1943, the *New York Times,* under the heading "Control of the Reich Required," published a letter to the editor from Gerard Swope, a prominent New Dealer, a friend of FDR's, and also a well-known industrialist. Evoking the popular "black-top image" [7] of a military clique which "has always dominated Prussia and for the last 75 years all Germany," Swope asserted that this clique had been the source of the trouble in Europe for the last two hundred years. With the support of a one-sided analysis of Germany's political and economic development during the nineteenth and twentieth centuries, Swope suggested that after the war German heavy industries and power development be controlled by the United Nations. If this were done, he wrote, "Germany cannot initiate war while such control continues." In Swope's opinion some of the essential factors of continuing peace were (1) the breaking up of the German Reich into the original states, (2) the entire disruption and wide emigration of the Prussian military caste, (3) placement of the voting control of German heavy industry in the hands of the United Nations, and (4) the rebuilding of invaded and destroyed territories by a demobilized German army.

The most surprising aspects of these somewhat naive proposals were not that they attracted FDR's attention but that he considered them

---

7. A term coined by Ralph K. White in *Nobody Wanted War,* p. 24. It refers to the tendency to regard all enemy leaders as distinguished from the population as "evil."

important enough to send them to Cordell Hull for his comments. The State Department's reply, as well as Secretary Hull's covering letter, repeated the principal antipartition arguments of H-24 and indicated that there would be much less difficulty and greater certainty of obtaining security against future German aggression if Germany were left unified. The detachment of East Prussia and other changes of frontiers were considered advisable and the same applied to military and economic restrictions. Hull concluded that "imposed partition would be little short of a disaster both for Germany and for us." The department's reactions to Swope's other proposals were equally negative.[8] It was hardly a coincidence that the definite antipartition stance reflected in this reply, as well as unanimous recommendation of the Interdivisional Committee against Partition, surfaced at a time when Under Secretary Sumner Welles was leaving government service.

Apparently the department's negative reaction to Swope's proposal made at least a temporary impression on the president. Hull wrote that in conversations with Roosevelt prior to the secretary's departure for Moscow, the president continued to favor the partition of Germany while admitting that the "whole transitional period would have to be one of trial and error and that it might well happen . . . that partition . . . would have to be abandoned."[9] As to the subsequent Foreign Ministers Conference, Hull's colleagues evidently shared his reservations about the benefits of dismemberment: there was an "increasing disposition to keep an open mind on this point."[10] The gap between the top and lower governmental levels, nevertheless, becomes apparent when one examines the record of the Teheran Conference which followed. It also exemplifies Richard Snyder's observation that "factors objectively identifiable by an observer may be ignored by decision-makers. . . ."[11]

On November 19, 1943, at a meeting of the Joint Chiefs of Staff in the Admiral's cabin of the USS *Iowa* en route to Teheran, the president expressed the belief that a tripartite division was a logical basis for splitting up Germany.[12] The southern state would be largely Roman Catholic, he remarked, and the northwest Protestant, whereas "it might

8. CAC 13 (National Archives, SDF, Record Group 59).
9. Hull, Memoirs, pp. 1265–1266.
10. Ibid., p. 1287; Mosely, "Dismemberment . . . ," p. 489.
11. Richard Snyder, H. W. Bruck, and Burton Sapin, *Decision-Making as an Approach to the Study of International Politics,* p. 66.
12. U.S. Department of State, *Foreign Relations of the United States . . . The Conferences at Cairo and Teheran, 1943,* p. 253.

be said that the religion of the Northeastern part is Prussianism." He felt that Stalin would "okay" such a division. The president then proceeded by tying the likely zones of occupation to the suggested pattern of partition. Ten days later he had the opportunity to outline his plans for dismemberment to Stalin and Churchill, who both had previously indicated that they considered partition a desirable goal. On this occasion Roosevelt mentioned a fivefold division: Prussia, all of which was to be rendered as small and weak as possible; Hannover and a northwest section; Saxony and the Leipzig area; Hesse-Darmstadt, Hesse-Kassel, and the area south of the Rhine; and finally Bavaria with Baden and Württemberg. The president also said that there should be two additional regions under the United Nations or some other form of control, namely Hamburg, including the area of the Kiel Canal, as well as the Ruhr and Saar.[13] In reply Churchill made the perceptive comment that "the President had said a mouthful" and suggested an alternative scheme. Prussia would be separated from the Reich, and so would Bavaria, Baden, Württemberg, and the Palatinate. The four southern states would be brought into a confederation of the Danube. Stalin, while expressing agreement with the principle of dismemberment, remained noncommital as to specifics. He agreed that Prussian officers and staffs should be eliminated but he failed to subscribe to the simplistic indictment of the German General Staff by his two partners. To him there was no difference among Germans: "all German soldiers fought like devils and the only exception was the Austrians." [14] Not surprisingly he preferred Roosevelt's to Churchill's plan, which seemed to imply a restoration of Austria-Hungary. It would be a mistake, he said, to unite Hungary with the Germans, since the latter would only control the Hungarians. To create a large framework within which the Germans could operate, he said, would be very dangerous. The three leaders then agreed that the newly created European Advisory Commission in London was the appropriate body to study the question of German dismemberment.[15]

Sumner Welles's departure from the government in the fall of 1943 gave him an opportunity to present his views on a future peace settlement to the American people. His *Time for Decision,* published in the spring of 1944, in addition to offering an outline for partition, also revealed a highly slanted perception of German history which the author

13. Ibid., pp. 600, 602.   14. Ibid., p. 602.
15. Ibid., p. 604.

shared with other political leaders. As Welles saw it, during the last hundred years Germany had been "the bane of Europe," and he supported this indictment by a bill of particulars.[16] He listed "wars of aggression" against Denmark, Austria, and France, the latter being based on "falsehood and misrepresentation," as well as another attempt to wage war against France in 1875, "averted only through joint British and Russian pressure."[17] Repeating a widely disseminated "Devil's theory of history," Welles assigned the guilt for the two world wars to the German General Staff. There was little in his presentation that differed from the World War I output of Creel's notorious Committee on Public Information. As far as the former under secretary was concerned, the invalidation of Article 231 by American scholarship had never taken place. Proceeding from this one-sided analysis, Welles then asserted that the German menace could be ended. His conviction that "German unity means a continuing threat to the peace of the world" he said had brought him to the conclusion that "partition is the only way of off-setting the German menace in the future." Welles denied that the so-called "centripetal urge" on the part of the German people was the powerful force that many claimed. The demand for the reconstruction of the German Reich and the unification of all Germans had been largely created by the German General Staff. A unified Germany was by no means a prerequisite for prosperity or individual happiness, as the history of the nineteenth century had demonstrated. Opponents of partition were inclined to disregard the brief span of time which had elapsed since the establishment of the Reich. Welles also denied that the economic prospects of the German people would be irreparably damaged by partition and said that "the greatest safeguard against future German military aggression would be measures giving every German equality of economic opportunity with the citizens of other European countries." Consequently any partition of the German Reich would have to be accompanied by economic arrangements insuring the eventual prosperity of the German people. The plan Welles then outlined for setting up three German states was a replica of the relevant section of H-24, with the exception that he proposed the cession of East Prussia to Poland to compensate for some of the eastern Polish territories, which "undoubtedly would have to be ceded to Russia."

Welles's views of history were quite similar to those of Henry Morgen-

16. Sumner Welles, *The Time for Decision*, p. 337.
17. Ibid., p. 338.

thau, who presented his postwar plans for Germany a few months later and provoked an extensive controversy in this country and abroad. As pointed out elsewhere by the present writer,[18] there were substantial differences between some of the so-called Morgenthau plans. The secretary's memorandum to the president submitted on the eve of Roosevelt's departure for Quebec [19] recommended the partition of Germany into three states. These included a South German state in customs union with Austria, with the Main river as the northern boundary; a North German state encompassing Prussia, Saxony, and Thuringia; and most significantly, an international zone reaching from the Danish border to the Main. The last part was to include the Ruhr, surrounding industrial areas, and the Rhineland. France was to receive the Saar and the adjacent territories bounded by the Rhine and Moselle rivers. The difference between this proposal and the three-Germany plan suggested in H-24 will be readily recognized. Another "Morgenthau plan" was occasionally referred to within the bureaucracy as the "pastoral letter." [20] Initialed by Roosevelt and Churchill at Quebec, it differed in several important respects from Morgenthau's "Program to Prevent Germany from Starting a World War III" described above. It did not mention the suggested permanent division of Germany into three states or the customs union of Southern Germany with Austria. Furthermore, rather than confirming the recommended annexation of the Saar by France, it put this area, as well as the Ruhr, under international supervision. On the other hand, it spelled out Morgenthau's aim of making Germany "a country primarily agricultural and pastoral in its character," a proposal not mentioned in the secretary's top-secret memorandum to the president.

The fate and the indirect impact of the Morgenthau plan or plans having been analyzed before,[21] we can turn again to the drafting processes at the Department of State and the simultaneous work of the European Advisory Commission in London. As Philip Mosely, who served as Ambassador Winant's political advisor, indicated,[22] the department continued its deliberations on postwar policy toward Germany during the first months of 1944, the final result of which was a basic memorandum that was approved by Secretary Hull in July. The document reiterated

18. *Priming the German Economy*, p. 16.
19. Henry Morgenthau, Photographic copy of Memorandum to the President, *Germany Is Our Problem*, pp. 1–4.
20. Backer, *Priming . . .*, p. 16.   21. Ibid., passim.
22. Mosely, "Dismemberment . . . ," p. 490.

the arguments for and against dismemberment mentioned in H-24 and added a warning against a de facto division of Germany through the creation of three zones of occupation. As the memorandum predicted, in this manner the individual parts would fall under the control of the Great Powers, which would "find themselves bidding for German support by promising to work for the reunification of Germany." On September 29, in a move to table the issue temporarily, Hull suggested to the president that "no decision should be taken on the possible partition of Germany until we see what the internal situation is and what is the attitude of our principal Allies on this question," [23] a proposal approved by the president on October 20.[24] The concurrent tripartite meetings in London naturally produced no decision on the issue, since the commission, as its name indicated, had only an advisory role.

The reluctance of lower governmental levels to endorse partition may have had some effect on the views of the Big Three, whose relevant comments from here on appear quite vacillating. Stalin, an early proponent of dismemberment, reversed himself on the occasion of Churchill's visit in October, abandoning his former opposition to a Danubian federation.[25] A few months later at Yalta he emphasized that he considered earlier discussions of the subject "only an exchange of views." [26] Also there is little in the now fully available Yalta record to substantiate Philip Mosely's earlier interpretation (1950) that Yalta "turned the interest [of the Big Three in partition] into an intention." [27] Actually in spite of Stalin's admonishment to reach a decision, one gains the impression that the three leaders shied away from the issue. They agreed only that dismemberment should be mentioned in the document of surrender and that a committee consisting of Gusev, Eden, and Winant should "study the question of partition but not prepare plans for partition." [28] It was a significant distinction obliquely referred to by "Doc" Matthews, a key witness at Yalta, in a transatlantic conversation with Winant:

> Well, I can give you the background. That word [dismemberment] was put in there, not as mandatory on the four governments, but mandatory upon the Germans, if the four governments decided to

23. U.S. Department of State, *Foreign Relations of the United States . . . The Conferences at Malta and Yalta, 1945,* p. 159.
24. Hull, *Memoirs,* p. 1622.
25. *Foreign Relations . . . Malta and Yalta, 1945,* pp. 159–160.
26. Ibid., p. 612.
27. Mosely, "Dismemberment . . . , p. 492.
28. *Foreign Relations . . . Malta and Yalta, 1945,* p. 626, 709.

dismember. And it was put in there by formal agreement of the three governments. I don't think we can go back and change it.[29]

As Mosely pointed out, the entire question had been referred to London in a "nebulous form." [30] The Committee on Dismemberment therefore held only two formal meetings and never arrived at a discussion of the substantive questions.[31] At the same time the course of military operations in Europe began to take care of the issue. As indicated, the planners at the State Department had recognized at an early date the likely consequences of a "temporary" zonal division. A final effort on their part, however, to forestall the seemingly inevitable by curtailing the independence of the zone commanders collapsed in the face of opposition from the Treasury and War Departments.[32]

When the Allied armies of occupation, by moving into their positions, executed a de facto division of Germany, the interest of the leaders in long-range plans for dismemberment waned. Churchill expressed this feeling quite bluntly only six weeks after Yalta: "I hardly like to consider dismemberment until my doubts about Russia's intentions have been cleared away." [33] In a similar vein Ambassador Gusev wrote to Eden in March that according to the Soviet understanding of Yalta, Germany's dismemberment was not an obligatory plan but a possibility of exercising pressure on Germany to make it harmless if other means should prove inadequate.[34] With the common enemy out of the way, the reality of a new opponent provided the spark for a new "learning and forgetting process." The early reaction of Eastern and Western diplomats to the new situation was initially subdued, but soon became an increasing effort to revive the power of a unified Germany and to enlist it in the contest with the new adversary. The struggle for Germany had begun.

29. U.S. Department of State, *Foreign Relations of the United States . . . European Advisory Commission; Austria; Germany, 1945,* 3: 269–270.
30. Mosely, "Dismemberment . . . ," p. 492.
31. Ibid., p. 494.
32. *Foreign Relations . . . European Advisory Commission . . . 1945,* 3: 434–438, 460–464.
33. Winston Churchill, *Triumph and Tragedy,* p. 443.
34. *Foreign Relations . . . European Advisory Commission . . . 1945,* 3: 205–206.

CHAPTER THREE

THE REPARATIONS ISSUE BEFORE POTSDAM

Roosevelt's demand for unconditional surrender was greatly influenced by his interpretation of the Versailles treaty and its consequences. The president's rationale for a partition of Germany was based on similar considerations. Both policies had a short-term impact but did not cause any lasting damage. The Casablanca statement possibly stiffened Germany's resistance and prolonged the war unnecessarily. However, this view has been challenged by others [1] and the counterargument is that a less intransigent attitude on the part of America toward the common enemy might have sparked Soviet moves toward a separate peace. As to FDR's plans for Germany's dismemberment, they were, as shown, superseded by occupational arrangements which divided Germany into four zones, while authorizing the zone commanders in case of need to act independently from the quadripartite Control Council.

By contrast, American historial perceptions about the third policy issue, reparations, had a long-range detrimental effect. Keynes had exposed the economic blunders of Allied reparations policy at an early date [2] and subsequent events had borne out his dire predictions. The moral underpinnings of the reparations claim, the war-guilt clause, and the legally questionable methods of computation [3] had been equally fallacious. No wonder then that the reparations issue had poisoned the political atmosphere between the two wars, a development which even a stalwart defender of the reparations claim, the young Frenchman Etienne Mantoux, was obliged to recognize. [4]

American decision makers during the Second World War were, of course, aware of the calamitous results of the reparations policy. However, viewing the past through the selective screen of their society's

---

1. O'Connor, *Diplomacy for Victory*, pp. 61, 100–104.
2. *The Economic Consequences of the Peace.*
3. See Chapter Four.
4. *The Carthaginian Peace*, p. 157.

value and image system, they did not face up to the disturbing truth that the claim's revanchist foundations had been at the roots of the evil. The ill effects of reparations thus were traced to deliveries from current production, although it had been demonstrated that payments in kind could solve the reparations problem as long as creditor countries were willing to accept German products. Moreover, reparations were seen as a putative burden on the American taxpayer, who allegedly had paid most or all of Germany's reparations after the First World War. As one would expect, though, at the working level of the Department of State a more objective and professional approach prevailed. One of the department's early papers on reparations accordingly cautioned that no useful purpose would be served by linking Germany's responsibility for compensation with general responsibility for the war. It did not seem wise, the paper said, "to raise in this connection the exacerbating issue of war guilt." The document cited was the final report of an Interdivisional Committee on Reparations, Restitution and Property Rights,[5] whose six subcommittees had begun to deal with the subject in November 1943. The subcommittees had the benefit of two earlier studies, one conducted under the auspices of the Council on Foreign Relations,[6] the other completed by a British Interdepartmental Committee on Reparations and Economic Security [7] under the chairmanship of a senior civil servant, Sir William Malkin. The first paper, written by the distinguished economists Alvin H. Hansen, Jacob Viner, and William Diebold, Jr., recommended that reparations should be imposed only to the extent that they would contribute to strengthening the postwar economic and social order and not as a major instrument of control over Germany's military power; they should be stated in terms of specific amounts of goods or services that the creditor countries would be willing to accept and should be limited to a few years after the cessation of hostilities. As the three economists stressed, "the unwillingness of the Allies and of the United States to accept large amounts of German goods was one of the chief reasons for the breakdown of the reparations settlement after Versailles."

The Malkin report was the basis for a Washington briefing of Dean Acheson, Averell Harriman, and others by John Maynard Keynes in September 1943.[8] Keynes mentioned on this occasion the widely entertained "false conclusion" that any attempt to exact payments from Ger-

5. (National Archives, SDF, Record Group 59, Notter Files).
6. Ibid.   7. Ibid.
8. Ibid.

many after the war was fruitless and he referred to Germany's "immensely efficient industrial organization capable of vast and sustained output." If the skill and industry and determination which Germany had devoted to evil purposes could be diverted to works of peace, he said, its capacity over a period of years should be very great. In their conclusions the authors of the Malkin Report opposed total deindustrialization of Germany and suggested an elastic formula to be automatically adjusted to the facts of the future as they disclosed themselves.

The State Department's Interdivisional Committee, in addition to covering a number of tangential issues such as restitution, replacement, priorities of recipient countries, and resettlement aid, addressed itself to such key aspects as purpose, time period, form and amount of indemnity payments. Its final report indicated that reparation settlements should serve primarily as a means of speeding the physical reconstruction of devastated countries, "although the payments need not be narrowly confined to this purpose." Payments should not continue for longer than necessary to permit Germany to make a substantial contribution to reconstruction, it said, and a period of ten to twelve years was envisaged as satisfying this condition. The committee also recognized one of the detrimental factors of World War I reparations, namely, the unwillingness of the claimant countries to accept payment in the form of goods and services, and concluded that "to facilitate prompt and predictable transfer of reparations considerable use should be made of deliveries in kind, particularly where they can be clearly related to the reconstruction and rehabilitation programs of recipient countries." The committee, however, was careful not to venture too far beyond the perceptual heritage of the nation. A subcommittee report challenging some popular myths,[9] which also will be discussed below, was "ordered to be withdrawn." [10]

The report included, on the other hand, a study conducted under the auspices of the Federal Reserve [11] which had examined Germany's net national output and its uses from 1925 to 1938 as a starting point. On the basis of these data an estimate of Germany's capacity to pay reparations was prepared which envisaged two initial "fallow years" to be followed by a reparations annuity of 1.5 billion marks in the third postwar year; in the subsequent five years reparations were expected to rise to an

9. Reparation 17, L-105, 25 February 1944, "The German Case Against Reparations 1918–1932" (National Archives, Notter Files).
10. Staff Memorandum, Interdivisional Committee on Reparation, Restitution and Property Rights, 15 June, 1944 (National Archives, Notter Files).
11. Ibid.

annual obligation of 16 billion marks. The total reparations bill, according to this estimate, would be 120 billion marks to be collected during twelve years. The calculations were based on 1938 prices and a conversion rate of four marks to the dollar. In conclusion the Federal Reserve document asserted that the final amount was "a realistic and not merely an ideal figure." The Interdivisional Committee, however, refrained from committing itself to a definite sum.

In August 1944 American planners began to examine the reparations problem within the broader framework of United States economic policies. The resulting staff papers of an Executive Committee on Foreign Economic Policy, chaired by Dean Acheson and composed of representatives of the Departments of State, Treasury, Agriculture, Commerce, and Labor; of the United States Tariff Commission; and of the Foreign Economic Administration,[12] reached another conclusion. They decided that an indefinitely continued coercion of more than sixty million technically advanced people would be an expensive undertaking at best and would offer the world little sense of security. After the end of the war Germany should make prompt contributions to the relief and rehabilitation of other countries and for this reason Germany should be required initially to retain the existing administrative machinery of its economy and place it under the control of the occupational authorities. The overriding principle with regard to reparations was that reparations policy should conform to the long-range objectives of the American government regarding the world at large. The Executive Committee emphasized that the great bulk of reparation deliveries had to come from current production, "since the reparations which could be derived from the transfer of capital equipment would in any case be relatively small compared to that available from current production." The committee did not reach any final conclusion regarding labor services, confining itself to the statement that "under appropriate conditions and to a limited extent labor services can be a useful form of reparations."[13]

In sum then, most of the policy recommendations before September 1944 were based on the recognition that monetary transfers were undesirable, that reparations should be paid primarily by shipments from current production, that the willingness of Allied and neutral countries to accept German products would be decisive, and that there should be a reasonable time limit.

12. U.S. Department of State, *Foreign Relations of the United States . . . General, 1944,* 1: 277.
    13. Ibid., 1: 279–295.

The subsequent celebrated debate [14] between the secretaries of state, war, and treasury initiated by the president and chaired by Harry Hopkins marked an important turning point in postwar planning, since it prompted Henry Morgenthau to introduce his proposal for a "pastoral" Germany. As far as reparations were concerned, its two cardinal points were the proposed dismantlement and exportation of Germany's heavy industrial equipment and the recommendation to preclude payments through exports from current production. While the two provisions were mutually supporting, the absurd basic concept of Germany's agrarianization encountered vehement opposition at the secretarial level; with the assistance of an aroused public press and in spite of Roosevelt's tentative concurrence at Quebec, the idea was soon abandoned in favor of a presidential policy of postponement. As FDR put it, "It is all very well for us to make all kinds of preparations for the treatment of Germany but there are some matters in regard to such treatment that lead me to believe that speed in these matters is not an essential at the present moment. . . . I dislike making detailed plans for a country which we do not yet occupy." The question of the economic treatment of Germany, nevertheless, did not remain submerged for long. By November 10 the acting secretary of state, Stettinius, returned to the subject of reparations by reporting to the president [15] that the British were more interested in reducing future German competition with British exports than in collecting large reparations. The Russians, on the other hand, as he surmised, intended to extract from the German economy large contributions to the reconstruction of the USSR and these contributions were expected to come primarily from current German production. As far as the United States was concerned, the State Department recommended at this juncture "a short program of heavy reparations payments derived largely from current German production. However, reparations should not be allowed to provide a pretext for building up Germany's productive power as a means of increasing her capacity to pay." The president, nevertheless, continued to vacillate.[16] He thought that Germany should be permitted to come back industrially to meet its own needs but "not do any exporting for some time and we know better how things are going to work out." And he added, "we are against reparations."

14. Hull, *Memoirs,* pp. 1604–1621. Herbert Feis, *Churchill, Roosevelt, Stalin,* pp. 366–373. Henry L. Stimson, *On Active Service in Peace and War,* pp. 567 et sequ. Backer, *Priming . . . ,* pp. 10–16.
15. *Foreign Relations . . . General, 1944,* 1: 398–403.
16. Ibid., 1: 414.

As far as the U.S. Treasury was concerned, the initial setback after the Quebec conference was not accepted as a final answer. During the rest of Morgenthau's incumbency, he continued his efforts to introduce the essential elements of his "plan" into the directives which were to govern the military occupation of Germany. The questions of dismantlement and of reparations from current production, therefore, remained on the agenda of innumerable high-level meetings. There was, of course, general agreement that Germany should be disarmed but the views regarding the extent of the dismantlement process varied. The opponents of Morgenthau favored moderate reparations from current production rather than dismantlement, in part on economic grounds and in part because of the political consideration that a healthy Germany was essential for Europe's stability. The Morgenthau plan, by contrast, had the advantage of internal consistency: if the German economy at the time of surrender was prostrate, the United States should follow a "hands off" policy; Germany's heavy industry should be completely dismantled in order to reduce the country to a second rate power; and there should be no reparations from current production, precluding an industrial come-back. Within the Treasury, Morgenthau's post-war policy for Germany had been researched by several of his associates who subscribed to the theory that reparations from current production meant the recreation of a powerful Germany: [17]

> If we were to expect Germany to pay recurring reparations, whether in the form of money or goods, we would be forced at the very beginning to start a rehabilitation and reconstruction program for the German economy. . . . When reparations deliveries cease, Germany will be left with a more powerful economy and a larger share of foreign markets than she had in the Thirties.

It is apparent that this kind of reasoning was appropriate mainly as far as Morgenthau's American opposition was concerned. As he himself was well aware, when negotiating with the Russians—who expected extensive reparations from current production—a different approach would have to be used. Accordingly, the Treasury had prepared an auxiliary solution—a Soviet loan, which will be discussed below.

At the beginning of January, probably because of the impending summit meeting, the secretary of the treasury felt that the time had come for another effort to gain the president's support. In a memorandum [18] dated

17. *Morgenthau Diary: Germany*, p. 597.
18. *Foreign Relations . . . European Advisory Commission . . . 1945*, 3: 376.

January 10, 1945, Morgenthau listed as "unassailable premises" that the German people had the will to try it again; that programs for democracy, reeducation, and kindness could not destroy this will within a brief time; and that heavy industry was the core of Germany's warmaking potential. He continued with the assertion that the real motive of those who opposed a weak Germany was the fear of Russia and communism. In his opinion it was "the twenty-year-old idea of a bulwark against Bolshevism which was one of the factors that brought this present war down on us." According to Morgenthau, all kinds of smoke screens were thrown up to support the proposition that Germany must be rebuilt and he mentioned as examples:

(1) The fallacy that Europe needed a strong industrial Germany.
(2) The contention that recurring reparations (which would require immediate reconstruction of the German economy) were necessary so that Germany might be made to pay for the destruction she had caused.
(3) The naive belief that the removal or destruction of all German war materials and the German armament industry would in itself prevent Germany from waging another war.
(4) The illogical assumption that a "soft" peace would facilitate the growth of democracy in Germany.
(5) The fallacy that making Germany a predominantly agricultural country, with light industries but no heavy industries, would mean starving Germans.

Morgenthau's concluding offer to submit studies demonstrating that these propositions were false was not taken up by the president; with the conferences of Malta and Yalta impending, it is likely that other issues had priority on Roosevelt's time.

As it turned out, Yalta provided the State Department with an opportunity to take a leading hand again in shaping America's reparations policy. The economic part of the briefing book, prepared by the advisor on German economic affairs, Emile Despres,[19] reiterated most of the State Department's previously mentioned positions. While emphasizing that the reparations settlement with Germany was an issue of major importance to the United States, the paper advised against establishing a definite monetary amount in order "to avoid difficulties with public opinion in Allied countries."[20] It recommended payment in goods and

19. Ibid., 3: 424.
20. *Foreign Relations . . . Malta and Yalta, 1945*, pp. 190–197.

services and suggested a program of short duration because transfers of reparation goods from Germany must necessarily interfere with the export trade of other countries. The briefing book then introduced an important new element by suggesting that the other interested powers should be notified "that the United States will not finance the transfer of reparations either directly by extending loans or credits to Germany or indirectly by assuming the burden of supplying at its own expense essential goods or equipment to Germany." The Treasury's dire predictions evoking the danger of a revitalized Germany had played a role in the deliberations of American decision makers. The State Department's reference to a possible financial involvement of the United States, on the other hand, touched on an even more sensitive chord, since it introduced the element of American domestic politics into the decision-making process. Considering the psychological makeup of American elected officials, it is not surprising then that this caveat became one of the most important factors in shaping American reparations policy from this point on—overshadowing all economic studies which testified to Germany's capacity to pay.

One of the scholarly papers among the latter, a forty-page document of the Office of Strategic Services, was completed by its Research and Analysis Branch on the eve of the Yalta conference and disseminated under the heading "Problems of German Reparations." [21] Similar to the earlier study of the Federal Reserve, the OSS had reached the conclusion that "contrary to general belief, experience does not indicate that the payment of large sums by Germany is impossible." It denied that the transfer problem as such had to be serious as long as "the underlying policy was clarified," and it stressed that the value of imported raw materials was small in relation to that of finished export goods. As to specifics, the document mentioned the German 1938 GNP of 110 billion marks, which had included 26 billion of military expenditures, and it concluded that "under favorable assumptions with regard to boundary changes, social disorganization, etc., Germany might be able to make annual contributions of about 26 billion marks at 1938 prices—or roughly 6.5 billion dollars." This figure pertained solely to reparations from current production and was even in excess of the sum suggested by the Federal Reserve.

The summaries of the relevant discussions at Yalta, Moscow, and Potsdam below, however, will show that neither the OSS paper nor

21. U.S. Office of Strategic Services, "Research and Analysis Report 2350" (National Archives).

similar economic studies were taken into active consideration at the top level. Whereas some writers [22] in their respective analyses have blamed inadequate staff briefings for the lacunae, it is suggested here that the all-pervasive process of cognitive dissonance [23] was again at work. As will be discussed later in some detail, any information which did not conform to the historical perceptions of the decision makers was promptly discarded.

At Yalta the reparations issue was on the agenda of the Second Plenary Meeting on February 5. [24] The discussion began with a presentation of the Soviet reparations plan by Ambassador Maisky, who indicated that it consisted of two parts: the "removal" of plants and equipment from Germany's national wealth to be completed within two years and deliveries from current production over a period of ten years. The Soviet representative asserted that 80 percent of Germany's heavy industry could be removed and that the remaining 20 percent would take care of the country's economic needs. In the interest of Europe's security the German economy should remain under Anglo-Soviet-American control even beyond the period of reparations payments. The reparations should be divided among the victorious powers on a priority basis in accordance with the individual contributions to the winning of the war, as well as according to their respective material damages. He suggested that a special tripartite reparations committee should be set up in Moscow and he concluded his remarks by presenting a Soviet reparations claim of $10 billion. Churchill, in reply, expressed doubts as to whether the Soviet Union would get anywhere near the sum which Maisky had mentioned. As the prime minister remembered, only £2 billion ($8 billion) had been extracted from Germany in the form of reparations after the First World War and even this would not have been possible had not the United States given Germany credits. Evoking the specter of German commercial competition, Churchill also cited the example of old Atlantic liners which were taken as reparations with the result that the Germans promptly built new and better ships. As he saw it, there was no point in repeating the mistakes of the First World War when the Allies had indulged themselves with fantastic figures. Roosevelt, who was the next one to speak, took his cue from the briefing book and remarked that after the last war the United States had lost a great deal of money. He then cited a fanciful sum of "over ten billion

22. E. F. Penrose, *Economic Planning for the Peace*, pp. 264–265; Richard D. Hughes, "Soviet Foreign Policy and Germany, 1945–1948," p. 74.
23. Leon Festinger, *A Theory of Cognitive Dissonance*.
24. *Foreign Relations . . . Malta and Yalta, 1945*, pp. 611–623.

dollars lent to Germany," adding that this time the United States would not repeat its past mistakes. He said that the Germans had no plants or equipment that the United States needed and he also did not want to contemplate the necessity of helping to keep the Germans from starving. However, he would willingly support any claims for Soviet reparations because the German standard of living should not be higher than that of the Soviet Union. His conclusion was that the maximum amount of reparations should be extracted from Germany but not to the extent that people should starve. The Russians retorted that the reparations problem after the First World War was not the sum demanded but the monetary settlement required. Reiterating the economist Varga's thesis,[25] they asserted that the transfer problem had been the cause of the failure of the reparations policy; in the case of the Soviet Union this problem did not exist because Russia would accept payments in kind. The meeting ended with the understanding that a reparations commission would be established to sit in Moscow and that the three foreign ministers would promptly work out the necessary directives. Accordingly, Eden, Molotov, and Stettinius met on February 7 [26] to examine a Soviet paper which in general followed Maisky's oral presentation. The paper again mentioned the Soviet claim for $10 billion, adding $8 billion for Great Britain and the United States, as well as $2 billion for all other countries. In an effort to substantiate these figures, the Soviets quoted an estimated German national wealth of $125 billion at the beginning of the war, reduced by 40 percent as a result of the hostilities. A Russian analysis of the national wealth of the more highly industrialized nations had contended that about 30 percent was movable. Accordingly, it was estimated that about $22 billion or $23 billion worth of German capital was transferable. The Soviet government proposed to remove $10 billion and to leave the remainder in Germany to secure a living standard comparable to other Central European countries. The national income of Germany before the war amounted to $30 billion annually, the Russians said. As a result of the war it probably had been reduced to about $18 billion to $20 billion. The Soviet government proposed to take $1 billion annually, or 5 to 6 percent, from Germany's national income. This amount could be raised by Germany, Moscow said. The Western representatives merely replied that they were going to examine the Soviet data carefully.

On February 9, when reparations were again on the foreign ministers'

25. "Reparations by Hitler's Germany and its Accomplices."
26. *Foreign Relations . . . Malta and Yalta, 1945*, pp. 609–704.

agenda,[27] Stettinius concurred in principle with the Soviet plan but suggested that the final sum should be decided by the reparations commission in Moscow.[28] Molotov, in reply, demanded that the sum of $20 billion should be referred to the commission as the basis for negotiations, adding that his figure was based on 1938 prices and that possibly the final amount might be 15 to 20 percent higher. After some discussion American and Soviet delegates reached an agreement on this point, but Eden demurred, indicating that he would have to wait for instructions from London. The negotiations were resumed the following day,[29] with Eden now taking a definite stand against the establishment of a fixed reparations amount. He suggested, on the other hand, that reparations in the form of labor should be incorporated in the final protocol. Since no agreement could be reached at the foreign ministers' level, the issue was shifted to the next Plenary Meeting [30] where Stalin, after listening to Churchill's comments, angrily remarked that if the British felt the Russians should receive no reparations, it would be better if they said so frankly. Eden then read a telegram from the War Cabinet which objected to stating a definite figure and questioned the possibility of extracting $20 billion, the equivalent of Germany's annual export trade in time of peace. Germany also had to pay for its imports and these should be given a priority over reparations. Otherwise other countries would be paying reparations to the nations receiving them. Eden concluded that the British government felt, rightly or wrongly, that even the naming of a sum as a basis of discussion would be a commitment. Accordingly, the British position was recorded separately in the final reparations protocol which the three leaders of the alliance signed.

Prompted by the Yalta deliberations, Roosevelt decided that the time had come to accelerate the planning process and he instructed the secretary of state to assume responsibility.[31] The result was the creation of an Informal Policy Committee on Germany under the chairmanship of Stettinius which also included representatives of the Departments of War, the Navy, and the Treasury, as well as of the Foreign Economic Administration. This development also provided the State Department with an opportunity to make a strong and final effort for a modification of the draft directives which in its judgment tended to promote a de

27. Ibid., pp. 802–811.
28. Stettinius's compassionate reaction may have been prompted by an OSS study (Research and Analysis Report 1899) which anticipated a Soviet reparations claim of $35 billion.
29. *Foreign Relations . . . Malta and Yalta, 1945*, pp. 874–875.
30. Ibid., pp. 901–903.
31. *Foreign Relations . . . European Advisory Commission . . . 1945*, 3: 433.

facto division of Germany. The department's proposals of March 10 [32] centered on the far-reaching provision that "the authority of the Control Council shall be paramount throughout Germany. The zone of occupation shall be areas for the enforcement of the Council's decisions rather than regions in which the zone commanders possess a wide latitude of autonomous power." According to this draft, the Control Council should utilize centralized instrumentalities for the execution of its policies as much as possible, subject to the supervision of the occupying force. "Whenever central German agencies or administrative services which are needed for adequate performance of such tasks have ceased to function," the paper said, "they shall be revived or replaced as rapidly as possible." With regard to reparations the State Department listed the categories agreed upon at Yalta and mentioned the need to eliminate contradictions. Germany should be able to pay its way as soon as possible. There should be no simultaneous payment of reparations and extension of credits to Germany; moreover, payments for imports should be a first charge upon German exports. The document closed with the ingenious suggestion that "if Germany is unable to export sufficient goods in excess of reparations deliveries to pay for authorized imports, reparations recipients should be required to shoulder this deficit in proportion to their respective receipts from reparations."

A few days later,[33] at a State Department meeting, the secretaries of war and of the treasury as well as other key officials were given the opportunity to study the Yalta reparations protocol, as well as the State Department's recent draft. As to be expected, Stimson and Morgenthau promptly objected to the suggested strengthening of the Control Council's authority. As far as the War Department was concerned, its opposition was simply a matter of administrative expediency. On the eve of completing its wartime mission in Europe, the army was determined to be equally effective in its forthcoming assignment. Understandably, the prospect of an American zone commander unable to make vital decisions because a quadripartite body could not reach an agreement was a veritable nightmare for the planners in the Pentagon and at SHAEF (Supreme Headquarters Allied Expeditionary Force). The secretary of the treasury, on the other hand, saw his scheme for the destruction of Germany's military and economic power in jeopardy, and he inquired incredulously whether it had been definitely settled at Yalta that Germany should be treated as one nation. Stettinius's somewhat evasive reply that such a decision had been reached for the immediate period of

32. Ibid., 3: 433–442.   33. Ibid., 3: 452–457.

military occupation provoked an angry outburst. The recommended policy seemed to be to continue and reconstruct the power of the German empire through the medium of a central unit in Berlin, Morgenthau exclaimed, and he demanded a direct answer. Stettinius merely reiterated that the present plan was only for the immediate period of occupation and that at a later stage further consideration would be given to the problem of decentralization and partition.

Morgenthau's counterattack came in the form of a memorandum to the secretary of state [34] which tried to demonstrate that the State Department's recommendations were not "even implied in the Yalta decisions." He said the recommendations were "opposed in their most important implications to the views which I understand the President holds on Germany." The secretary especially questioned the concept that it was necessary to control and administer the German internal economy in order to collect reparations. The Yalta decision, he wrote, clearly did not contemplate that the collection of reparations would require the Allies to take steps designed to rehabilitate the German economy. His concluding points were that the United States should avoid assuming responsibility for the functioning of Germany's internal economy, that it should aim at the greatest possible "contraction" of Germany's heavy industry and that the actual administration of affairs in Germany should be directed toward the decentralization of its political structure.

President Roosevelt, after first concurring with the State Department's draft, reversed himself and the oppositional views of the Pentagon and of the Treasury prevailed. As a result, the War Department's occupational directive, JCS# 1067, which reflected Henry Morgenthau's influence, remained the governing document. Approved by President Truman in May, it was the guiding instrument of United States occupation policies for two months until some of its principal provisions were superseded in August by the Potsdam protocol.[35]

In an additional move to implement the Yalta decisions, on March 12 President Roosevelt had appointed Dr. Isador Lubin from the Bureau of Labor Statistics to head the American delegation to the Moscow Reparations Commission.[36] Lubin, although suggested for this assignment by Stettinius, was most sympathetic to the Treasury's position. His draft of instructions [37] regarding reparations policy submitted to the

34. Ibid., 3: 460–464.   35. Backer, *Priming* . . . , p. 27.
36. *Foreign Relations* . . . *European Advisory Commission* . . . *1945*, 3: 1179.
37. Ibid., 3: 1179–1181.

White House on March 22 listed as primary objectives the elimination of Germany's military potential, the weakening of its economy, and the reduction of Germany's living standard to the average European level. Reparations should primarily consist of dismantled German plants and equipment, whereas deliveries from current production should include shipments of products such as coal, timber, and potash, but should not be made in the form of manufactured goods. "We are opposed," the draft said, "to any reparations program which . . . would require the United Nations . . . to take responsibility for the efficient running of the German economic and financial system." Lubin's paper ended with a detailed list of industries which would remain after completion of economic disarmament; it excluded all heavy industry. At the State Department Lubin's draft was considered "the most extreme statement regarding the economic treatment of Germany" [38] and Lubin commented to a Treasury representative that "he would battle the matter out with State and that unless he got 95 percent of what he wanted he would not take the assignment." [39] As it turned out, however, fate in the form of Roosevelt's death intervened: the new president promptly appointed one of his close companions, Edwin W. Pauley, to head the American delegation with the rank of ambassador. Lubin was moved to the number two position.

In the weeks which followed, the Informal Policy Committee on Germany [40] went over the final drafts of JSC# 1067 and of the "Instructions for the United States Representative on the Allied Commission on Reparations." [41] It appears that the latter eventually incorporated all of the Treasury's terms. In addition to assisting in the elimination of German industrial capacity considered to be dangerous to the security of the United Nations, Pauley's instructions called for a reparations plan which would not entail any direct or indirect financing on the part of the United States. It should not maintain or foster the dependence of other countries on the German economy; it should not put the United States into a position where it would have to assume responsibility for sustained relief of the German people. A first charge of all exports should be a sum necessary to pay for approved imports; deliveries from current production should be as small as possible in relation to reparations in the form of dismantled equipment; and these deliveries should consist

38. Ibid., 3: 1181.
39. *Morgenthau Diary: Germany*, pp. 1095–1096.
40. Ibid., pp. 1337–1368, 1371–1406.
41. *Foreign Relations . . . European Advisory Commission . . . 1945*, 3: 1222–1227.

primarily of raw materials and "to the smallest extent possible . . . of manufactured products." A peculiar aspect of the document was that it represented the joint efforts of those who favored a strong Germany and of the influential Morgenthau group who wanted to see Germany's industrial potential eliminated. Both sides supported a curtailment of reparations from current production, the former in order to protect the German economy, the latter in order to remove any pretext which might be used to leave significant parts of Germany's industry intact. Obviously, the rationale of the Treasury would become invalidated if and when the dismantlement process had to be abandoned. Since this was soon the case in West Germany, the ironic consequence of Henry Morgenthau's dabbling in foreign affairs was the practical freeing of the Federal Republic from any significant reparations burden. Oddly, some Treasury officials who were sympathetic to the Soviet Union had also mentioned that their protagonists at the State Department who opposed Morgenthau's reparations policy merely wanted a healthy German economy as a bulwark against Soviet expansion.[42] They apparently failed to recognize that their own contribution to the directive made it an anti-Soviet instrument in its ultimate effects. Since Russia was anxious to rebuild its devastated economy with the help of German industrial products, the practical exclusion of reparations in the form of newly manufactured goods and the caveat against a "dependence of other countries on Germany" made it quite certain that the United States would not be able to reach agreement with the Soviet Union at the Moscow Reparations Commission meeting.

As to the qualifications of Edwin Pauley, Truman's choice followed the familiar pattern of political appointments. A self-made man who had acquired a great fortune in the oil business, Pauley satisfied the cherished American dogma wherby a man with the mythical distinction of having met large payrolls is able to tackle almost any government task entrusted to him. Moreover, as former treasurer of the Democratic National Committee and one of the most important individuals in promoting the nomination of Truman for vice president at the 1944 Democratic Convention, Pauley had established the necessary "rapport" at the White House.[43] While the new ambassador's diplomatic qualifications were debatable, he performed most effectively as his own press agent, claiming credit for a success story at the Moscow preliminary

42. *Morgenthau Diary: Germany,* p. 1179.
43. "Summary of Procedure of Allied Commission on Reparations" (August 1945, Scandrett Papers, Cornell University).

talks and in the subsequent Potsdam reparations agreement. By contrast, as some of Pauley's associates pointed out, only wishful thinkers could deceive themselves into believing that anything had been accomplished in Moscow by the activities of the American delegation. "Pauley and his advisors found an out for themselves," one of their reports read, "in ascribing the failure of the negotiations to the dilatory tactics of the Soviets. The more plausible explanation for the failure is that the United States section was not organized properly; that Ambassador Pauley did not understand the operational habits or practices of the Soviets; that his initial move clearly indicated to the Soviets that what he really proposed was to renegotiate the Yalta agreement and that the Soviets came to a conclusion soon after the initial meeting that they preferred to have the Big Three make the decision in Potsdam. It was evident that the Russians clearly understood at the outset what they themselves wanted, but that Pauley, quite evidently, did not understand what the United States wanted in respect to the European situation." [44] While this may or may not have been a fair evaluation of Pauley's performance, the concluding comment requires correction. Actually, it was the United States which was uncertain about its reparations policy at the time, except for its aversion to financial commitments and its desire to avoid an open break with the Soviet Union.[45]

Reportedly,[46] the attitude of the American delegation toward reparations was influenced by the recollection of John Maynard Keynes's unheeded warnings in 1919; on the other hand, Sir John's recent emphasis on Germany's economic potential had already been "forgotten." Moreover, the negative spirit of the instructions to Pauley was reflected in the ambassador's behavior toward his Moscow hosts. He promptly began to challenge Russian seizures of German property, apparently unaware that Marshall Zhukov had just reported to Stalin similar misdeeds committed by the American and British troops prior "to their withdrawal from the temporarily occupied Russian Zone." [47] When Ambassador Maisky in the first and only plenary session of the Reparations

44. Ibid.
45. According to E. F. Penrose, "Pauley showed no evidence of any strong convictions of what ought to be done; he seems to have taken over an essentially negative, sketchy, hastily conceived and imprecise plan to combine reparations with partial de-industrialization of Germany." *Economic Planning . . . ,* pp. 282–283. In fairness to Pauley, his performance in Moscow ought to be judged in the light of his very specific instructions. Whatever their shortcomings were, they were not "hastily conceived."
46. Interview with Seymour Rubin, a member of Pauley's staff, 23 January 1975.
47. (National Archives, SDF, Records Group 59./740.00119/E.W. 7–3045.CS/E).

Commission presented a Soviet reparations proposal of $10 billion in the form of dismantled equipment and $10 billion from current production—which had been accepted at Yalta as a basis for discussion—he was faced with Pauley's request for supporting data. The members of the American delegation then sat back [48] and waited for a few weeks. When the information was not forthcoming after repeated requests, they began packing their bags. While the American attitude was justifiable in a strictly formal sense, it also ought to be viewed in the light of the fact that it subsequently took a quadripartite Level of Industry Committee more than seven months to prepare a theoretical basis for the dismantlement process. The Soviet delegation had provided a breakdown of capital removals according to individual industries in its initial document and it had submitted a list of industrial products to be supplied as reparations from current production. The American delegation, moreover, had among its records two scholarly studies analyzing Germany's capacity to pay—one prepared by the Federal Reserve, the other by the Office of Strategic Services. As indicated, both exceeded by far the Soviet reparations claim. In other words, had there been a genuine desire to negotiate, sufficient statistical data were on hand.

As it turned out, however, the Reparations Commission, during its three weeks of operations, even failed to clarify the conflicting interpretations of terms such as "restitution," "war booty," and "external German assets," and actually produced only one tentative agreement of any significance. Upon Pauley's initiative, the Yalta proposal of 50 percent reparations to the Soviet Union, 20 percent respectively to the United States and Great Britain and 10 percent to the smaller nations was changed to a 56–22–22 formula with the understanding that reparations for France and the smaller nations would come proportionally from the percentage allotted to the Big Three. The percentage agreement itself was voided at Potsdam, but the principle of the United States, Great Britain, and the Soviet Union taking care of their smaller friends was retained. On the other hand, Pauley failed [49] to convince his Soviet counterpart of the logic of his mathematical formula

$$R = P - (O + C + I),$$

i.e., reparations equals current production less the sum of occupation costs, essential German consumption, and authorized imports. The

48. Interview with Professor Abram Bergson, one of Pauley's advisors, Harvard University, October 1974.
49. "A Report on German Reparations to the President of the United States," Part 4, pp. 7–8 (National Archives, 740.00119/Germany).

crucial "first charge" principle for essential imports over reparations thus had to be left in abeyance.

By the middle of July it had become clear that no progress was being made and, since the Potsdam conference was about to start, the commission decided to transfer its activities to Berlin.

Chapter Four

The American Taxpayer and
German Reparations

The debate among American writers about the origins of the cold war continues unabated. Traditionalist and revisionist interpretations of almost every aspect of the issue differ, but there appears to be general agreement on the critical role of the reparations question in providing the straw that eventually broke the alliance's back.

As mentioned, the Briefing Book for the Yalta Conference had recommended a statement to the other interested powers that the United States was not willing to finance the transfer of reparations from Germany directly or indirectly. At Yalta Roosevelt, always anxious to avoid the perceived errors of the twenties, complied with that recommendation, although the record seems to indicate that he was less concerned with the intricate problem itself than with the anticipated reactions of the American electorate. His statement that after the last war the United States had lent over $10 billion to Germany but that this time America would not repeat its mistakes would have pleased the American voters. Moreover, the reference to an imaginary sum, as well as Roosevelt's insistence that the word "reparations" ought to be replaced by another term,[1] indicated which audience was foremost in the president's mind.

At Potsdam the American position on reparations was presented even more forcefully by Truman, who, in contrast to the Allied policy makers twenty-six years earlier, opposed "a conqueror's approach to victory." The United States did not intend to pay the reparations bill "which it had done so largely after World War I," he declared.[2] As Admiral Leahy described it, "Truman stood up to Stalin in a manner calculated to warm the heart of every patriotic American. He refused to be bulldozed into

1. *Foreign Relations . . . Malta and Yalta, 1945*, p. 915.
2. Harry S. Truman, *Memoirs*, 2: 111.

a reparations agreement that would repeat the history of World War I which found the American taxpayer paying for Germany's reparations." [3]

Political theory suggests that the views of the leaders reflect the stored memories of the political system in which they operate. Accordingly they have the support of history texts which—to quote Professor Kenneth E. Boulding—"gave perspective rather than truth and which presented the world as seen from the vantage point of the nation." [4] An independent appraisal of the three elements of the issue—war debts, reparations, and American loans—will therefore be attempted here.

On November 11, 1918, United States government loans to America's Allies totaled about $8 billion. An additional $3 billion was lent in the immediate postwar years. In granting these loans, the United States Treasury acted under the authority of four Liberty Loan Acts, which empowered the secretary of the treasury, with the president's concurrence, to purchase obligations of foreign governments at war with the enemies of the United States for a total amount not to exceed $10 billion. The obligations were purchased at par and, if compared to the terms of the United States Liberty Bonds, were somewhat more onerous to the debtor governments.[5] The great majority of the postarmistice loans were also based on the authority of the Liberty Loan Acts, whereas the remainder were authorized by special legislation. Inter-Allied debates concerning these debts continued throughout the twenties and essentially dealt with three aspects: the question of funding, that is, the conversion of demand obligations into long-term obligations; the connection between debt payments and the receipt of German reparations; and the possibility of an outright cancellation of inter-Allied debts.

Official negotiations regarding the funding of Allied war debts began in 1922, shortly after Congress had passed an act creating the World War Foreign Debt Commission and authorizing it to refund or convert, but not to cancel, the obligations due to the United States. The act stipulated that the new rate of interest was in such a case not to be less than 4 1/2 percent and the time of payment not more than twenty-five years, limitations which were soon abandoned because of their im-

3. *I Was There*, p. 423.
4. "National Images and International Systems," *The Journal of Conflict Resolution*, 3 (1959), 120–131.
5. Allied certificates of indebtedness at the close of the war bore interest of 5 percent. The rate of the First Liberty Loan was 3 1/2 percent; on the fifth or Victory Loan it was 4 4/5 percent. Benjamin H. Williams, *Economic Foreign Policy of the United States*, pp. 218–220.

practicability. The result of the subsequent and often protracted diplomatic negotiations was fifteen bilateral agreements which provided for payment schedules extending up to sixty-two years in some cases and representing a reduction of accrued interest from 5 percent to a maximum of 3.25 percent. While these debt settlements may seem generous, a prominent American economist has pointed out that prices at the time of the settlement were only two-thirds as high as war prices. "If the debtor nations were to repay the full amounts," he wrote, "they would have to send us fifty percent more goods than they received." [6]

As to the second point, that is, the relationship between the reparations of the vanquished and the debts of the victors, there were repeated and persistent efforts, especially on the part of Great Britain and France, to obtain American consent to the establishment of a legal link. All these attempts failed, however, because—economic realities notwithstanding—neither the Wilson Administration nor those which followed were willing to permit the proposed nexus. The tie between war debts and reparations established by the Young Plan's so-called "concurrent memorandum," signed by Germany and its principal creditors, did not have American approval and consequently was not binding on the United States.

A general cancellation of war debts was recommended by the British government to the United States Treasury soon after the armistice [7] and again suggested by Prime Minister Lloyd George in a letter to President Wilson. The British notes mentioned the serious political dangers which the existence of a vast mass of intergovernmental indebtedness created and described it as a great obstacle to the economic recovery of the world. Since Great Britain had lent more money to its Allies than it had borrowed from the United States, it was in a good moral position to recommend a reduction or cancellation of debts, but as Lloyd George emphasized, such an arrangement would have to be "part and parcel of an all-round settlement of inter-Allied indebtedness." The British prime minister did not mention the precedent set by one of his predecessors a hundred years earlier when England had faced a similar situation to that of the United States at the end of the First World War. From 1793 to 1815 the battles against Napoleon had been fought primarily by England's friends and allies, with Great Britain—in accordance with recognized eighteenth-century practices—providing the financial means in the form of subsidies and loans. By 1815 England had expended

6. F. W. Taussig, "The Interallied Debts," as cited in Williams, ibid., p. 226.
7. Williams, ibid., p. 227.

over £61 million, including £53 million in the form of outright subsidies, in this manner.

A good example of this pattern of cooperation can be found in the treaty of Chaumont between Austria, Russia, Prussia, and Great Britain. After specifying the number of infantry and cavalry units to be supplied against the common enemy by each country, the treaty had the following to say about England:

> As the situation of the seat of War, or other circumstances, might render it difficult for Great Britain to furnish the stipulated Succours in English Troops within the term prescribed, and to maintain the same on a War establishment, His Britannic Majesty reserves the right of furnishing his Contingent to the requiring Power in Foreign Troops in his pay, or to pay annually to that Power a sum of money, at the rate of £20 per each man of Infantry, and of £30 for Cavalry, until the stipulated Succour shall be complete.[8]

In other words, while Prussians, Austrians, Russians, Spaniards, and other nationals died for the common cause, Great Britain, because of its wealth and the accident of geography, was able to confine its contributions essentially to the control of the high seas and to financial support. After the danger of renewed French aggression had receded, the British government decided to wipe the slate clean. While the bulk of the military aid had been in the form of subsidies, there still remained the question of the unpaid loans, with an Imperial Austrian loan being the largest. Economic conditions in England at that time were anything but conducive to generosity abroad. Taxes were higher than ever before, the economy was in serious straits, and there was widespread unemployment. Nevertheless, over the protests of the parliamentary opposition, which challenged the government's "expensive and disinterested generosity," the government of Lord Liverpool maintained that "no arrangement could be wise that carried ruin to one of the countries between which it was concluded." [9] This far-sighted policy was applied not only to vanquished France, but also in the handling of the Austrian loan, canceled in 1824 after a nominal payment by the debtor country.

It is not known whether President Wilson had considered such historic precedents, but his answer to the British prime minister could not have been more negative, nor could it have been clearer. "It is highly

8. Edward Vose Gulick. *Europe's Classic Balance of Power,* p. 153.
9. Edwin F. Gay, "War Loans or Subsidies," p. 395.

improbable," he wrote, "that either Congress or popular opinion in this country will ever permit a cancellation of any part of the debt of the British government to the United States in order to induce the British government to remit, in whole or in part, the debt to Great Britain of France or any other Allied governments, or that it would consent to a cancellation or reduction in the debts of any of the Allied governments as an inducement towards a practical settlement of the reparations claim." These comments were undoubtedly valid. The small, attentive public Lord Liverpool had to deal with consisted of the British gentry and nobility traditionally exposed to international affairs. By contrast Wilson had to deal with the American Congress, and, regardless of his skill in handling public opinion, neither he nor any of the three presidents who succeeded him would have been able to obtain the legislation necessary to cancel the war debts fully or even in part. The prewar image of Great Britain and France as financially powerful was still very much alive. Moreover, the American people had entered the war reluctantly; they had been told it was an idealistic crusade and rescue operation;[10] that national self-preservation could be involved was not grasped nor would it have been believed.[11] Accordingly, it would have been a next-to-impossible task to gain concurrence for cancellation.

The opening of the tsarist archives and the proceedings at Versailles jolted the American belief in Germany's unilateral war guilt, only to have it replaced in time by the "merchants of death" hypothesis. Both developments reinforced the impression that the United States had been drawn into a European conflict and that the issues at stake actually did not involve America's national interests. There was little understanding that power meant international responsibilities. Instead, time-honored wisdom of an essentially parochial world prevailed: budgets—whether private or governmental—ought to be balanced; and just debts—private or political—ought to be paid. President Coolidge's comment, "They hired the money, didn't they?" reflected a national belief. It took a learning period of about twenty years and a new generation to reshape the political concepts of the nation. The great depression, the failure of the League, and the emergence of National Socialism were some of the important lessons in this agonizing process.

There were, of course, some early dissenting voices. In a significant

10. Robert Endicott Osgood, *Ideals and Self-interest in America's Foreign Relations*, pp. 256, 259.
11. Ibid., pp. 119, 197, 199, 222.

statement in 1924 General Pershing declared that the war might have been lost if it had not been for the fact that the Allies held the line for fifteen months after the United States' entry. And he added: "We were responsible for their having to hold the line, and we advanced the money which made it possible for them to hold it. But I believe part of that expense should now be borne by the United States." The president of the Illinois Manufacturers' Association criticized a policy of "collecting from Europe, for nearly a third of a century after we have paid off our own debt, large sums of money, not on account of the principal, but on account of the interest on the money we advanced." And Andrew Mellon, the secretary of the treasury, added a practical consideration when he said: "The entire foreign debt is not worth as much to the American people in dollars and cents as a prosperous Europe as a customer." [12]

At that time, however, these were the voices of a small minority capable of independent thought. It required the experience of twenty years of world-shaking events before another American president, in a message to Congress regarding the lend-lease legislation, could state: "By this provision we have affirmatively declared our intention to avoid the political and economic mistakes of international debt experience during the twenties." [13] To conclude, the Allied war debts after the First World War were not canceled. About $2.5 billion were actually paid but eventually—as a by-product of the Great Depression and the ensuing breakdown of German reparations payments—all the Allies of the United States defaulted. They had good reasons to stress on this occasion that the American protective tariff policies had made debt fulfillment for all practical purposes impossible. Naturally, the resulting loss had to be borne by the United States Treasury and consequently by the American taxpayer.

As far as the policy of wartime lending is concerned, America's decision makers demonstrated in 1940 that they had understood the lessons of history. Their attitude toward the reparations problem, however, revealed a very different phenomenon.

The colossal public debt of $33 billion which was imposed on Germany as reparations in May 1921 is generally regarded as the ill-considered result of wartime passion. At the same time the important role of the United States in establishing this sum is often neglected. The

12. Edwin F. Gay, "War Loans . . . ," p. 400.
13. Report of President Roosevelt to Congress, 11 June 1942. House Document #779, 77th Congress, 2nd Sess., pp. 12–23.

relevant paragraph of the prearmistice documents, on the basis of which Germany surrendered, stipulated that "compensation will be made by Germany for all damage done to the civilian population of the Allies and to their property by the aggression of Germany by land, by sea and from the air." It was a provision which was in line with the Wilsonian concept of "no contributions and no punitive damages." Although this wording was clear enough, there were continued efforts on the part of England and France at Versailles to enlarge the meaning of "all damage to the civilian population" by including the costs of separation allowances and war pensions. By contrast, the views of the United States Delegation on the Committee on the Reparation of Damages coincided with those of Keynes, who later wrote that "if words have any meaning or engagement any force, we have no more right to claim for these war expenses . . . than for any other general costs of the war." [14] All the American representatives on the committee opposed the inclusion of these claims, with John Foster Dulles presenting their position most succinctly: ". . . the word civilian in the pre-armistice agreement implied some necessary distinction between military expenditures and non-military damages. Pensions and separation allowances are popularly and legally recognized as government costs of conducting a war. If the Allies expected Germany to understand that she was to repay the costs of these items, I personally do not see how the Allies could have chosen words less apt to convey that meaning." [15] As it turned out, however, President Wilson saw matters differently, and with the extraordinary comment, "I don't care a damn about logic," he included the controversial items in the reparations bill.[16] The result was a more than doubling of the final claim, i.e., an increase from 58.9 billion to 132 billion gold marks.

In order to pay off this debt the German government, according to the Allied ultimatum, was required to deliver to the Reparations Commission interest bearing A and B bonds totaling 50 billion gold marks which the commission could issue at any time; in addition Germany had to deliver 82 billion gold marks in C bonds, which, however, would be issued only when the commission had ascertained that German payments were sufficient to provide for the payment of interest. The reparations schedule stipulated that Germany was to pay annually until the redemption of all the bonds 2 billion gold marks plus 26 percent of the

14. John Maynard Keynes, *A Revision of the Treaty*, p. 70.
15. Philip Mason Burnett, *Reparation at the Paris Peace Conference*, p. 62.
16. Ibid., p. 64.

value of German exports—making the expected annual payments around 3 billion. In retrospect, one cannot help suspecting that this unusual arrangement was prompted by some doubts in the inner sanctum of the commission as to the wisdom of its action—an appraisal strengthened by Keynes's comment that "bonds and guarantees were merely apparatus and incantation. It is probable that sooner or later the C bonds at any rate will not only be postponed but cancelled." [17] It should be added that Germany's official representative at the reparations negotiations. Staatssekretär Carl Bergmann, had arrived at a similar conclusion.[18]

The history of the subsequent events is well known. The reparations plan was presented in the form of an ultimatum which threatened that the Ruhr would be occupied if Germany failed to sign within six days. Thus forced into submission, Germany met the prescribed payments for more than a year. By the summer of 1922, however, economic conditions had deteriorated to such an extent that the German government asked for a moratorium. The request was not granted; instead French and Belgian troops marched into the Ruhr and seized the German mines. Germany's response was a policy of passive resistance financed by the printing press and leading to the complete collapse of a national currency already seriously weakened by the war.

In November 1923 a new currency, the Rentenmark, was introduced. Shortly afterwards a reparations committee under the chairmanship of General Charles D. Dawes worked out a provisional reparations plan which gave Germany a breathing spell, greatly reduced its initial payments, and, in addition, provided it with an international loan of $200 million, including an American tranche of $110 million. One of the fundamental provisions of the Dawes plan relieved the German government of the transfer responsibility since it was recognized as the principal cause of the collapse of reparations payments. The new plan stipulated that "all payments for account will be paid in gold marks or their equivalent in German currency into the Bank of Issue to the Credit of the Agent for Reparations Payments. This payment is the definite act of the German government in meeting its financial obligations under the Plan." The actual transfer thus became the responsibility of an Allied committee which could authorize the acquisition of foreign exchange only to the extent that it did not endanger the stability of the German currency.

17. Keynes, *Revision* . . . , p. 70.   18. *History of Reparations*, p. 77.

Germany punctually fulfilled all its obligations under the Dawes plan. Moreover, the unexpected influx of foreign capital, about which more will be said below, enabled the Transfer Committee to obtain without difficulty the foreign currencies required by the cash transfer of 1,733.6 million gold marks under the Dawes plan. A significant aftereffect of the resulting euphoria, influencing diplomats and economists alike, was the abandonment of the Dawes plan and its replacement by the Young plan of 1929 establishing a reduced and final German reparations debt of 47 billion gold marks [19] ($10.2 billion) while placing the transfer responsibility again on German shoulders. As we know, the active implementation of the Young plan was of short duration, and in 1931 Germany's reparations payments came to a halt.

We can now turn to the question of Germany's actual reparations fulfillment. As far as the payments after 1924 are concerned, the record is clear and duly presented in Table 1 below. The controversial aspects

TABLE 1. German reparations payments, 1925–1931 (in millions of gold marks)

Category	Under the Dawes Plan	Under the Young Plan	Total
Cash transfers in foreign currencies	1,733.6	1,611.0	3,344.6
Collection under Reparations Recovery Acts [a]	1,510.1	350.0	1,860.1
Deliveries in kind and other payments in marks	4,257.2	990.0	5,247.2
Total	7,500.9	2,951.0	10,451.9

Source: Moulton and Pasvolsky, *War Debts and World Prosperity*, p. 279.
a. Under the British Recovery Act 26 percent of receipts from German exports to Great Britain were collected as reparations.

of Germany's reparations payments pertain almost exclusively to the period 1919–1924, and here the gap between the incomplete Allied figure of 10,420 million gold marks and the inflated German claim of 56,577 million gold marks is tremendous. Fortunately, we have two independently arrived at and scholarly appraisals, one by Keynes and the other by Moulton and McGuire, which gave an approximate total of 25 to 26 billion gold marks for the period under investigation. This figure was obtained by taking into account the incompleteness of the Allied data, by eliminating the merely propagandistic German items such as the scuttled warships and the costs of industrial disarmament and—most important—by affixing an objective evaluation on German

19. Richard Castillon, *Les Reparations Allemandes*, p. 66.

deliveries in kind, as, for instance, on the shipments of coal and surrendered ocean shipping. (In this connection Moulton and McGuire
made corrections for some of the Reparations Commission's practices,
such as charging German-caused losses at wartime prices while crediting
deliveries in kind on the basis of forced sales at the bottom of a depression.) [20] If one takes the impartial analysis by independent scholars
into account, one will arrive at a final figure of about 36 billion gold
marks or $9 billion, which represent all the tangible values surrendered
by Germany to the Reparations Commission from 1919 to 1931. (A
State Department study of February 25, 1944, provides an identical
estimate.) [21]

Before listing data on the concurrent influx of American money into
Germany, some key factors responsible for this development have to
be mentioned. First was the availability of surplus capital, which concentrated on Latin America, Eastern Europe, and Germany in its search
for attractive investment opportunities. Second was the reputation of
the German people for industriousness, thrift, and commercial compe-
tence. The influence of this factor was reinforced by a widespread ig-
norance of some fundamentals of economics which prompted foreign
investors to purchase substantial amounts of the rapidly deteriorating
German currency in the expectation that it would eventually return to
its old parity. (The almost mythical belief in Germany's economic
strength was particularly prevalent among the ethnic German minorities
in Europe.) Since unsophisticated investors, for reasons of their own,
were willing to gamble on Germany's future at a time when the economy
of the Reich was about to collapse, it is hardly surprising that after the
basic structure of the country had been reorganized, an international
loan secured, and an American banker, Gilbert Parker, put in charge
of the Reparations Commission, German bonds appeared a sure bet to
the more sophisticated members of the financial community. Third was
the fact that the German bonds paid an interest rate of about 7 percent
—as compared to 4 percent for domestic bonds—and also sold at a
2 to 10 percent discount,[22] thereby holding out the promise of a capital
gain. And fourth was the questionable policy of some New York issuing
houses which disregarded Hjalmar Schacht's and Gilbert Parker's repeated and very explicit warnings.[23] As a Morgan partner testified be-

20. Harold G. Moulton and Constantine E. McGuire, *Germany's Capacity
to Pay*, pp. 72–73.
21. Reparation 17, L-105 (National Archives, SDF, Record Group 59, Notter).
22. Robert R. Kuczynski, *Bankers' Profits from German Loans*, pp. 164–167.
23. Ibid., pp. 7–31 and Appendix E.

fore the United States Senate, "It is a tempting thing for certain of the European governments to find a horde of American bankers sitting on their doorsteps offering them money. It is rather demoralizing for municipalities and corporations in the same countries to have money pressed upon them. That sort of competition tends to insecurity and unsound practice." [24] In other words, availability of surplus capital, the investors' expectation of sure and easy profits, and questionable business practices were responsible for the extraordinary influx of American capital into Germany.

According to a 1932 study of the Brookings Institution, 135 German dollar loans were publicly offered in the United States between 1924 and 1930. (After July 1930 no German loan was publicly offered in America.) The total par value of these 135 loans was $1,430,525,000. But part of these bonds were sold abroad. The total par value of the bonds floated in the United States was $1,239,031,500.[25] By 1932, 19 of the 135 loans had been entirely redeemed and 100 had been partially redeemed. Of the original par value, 81 percent, or $1,160,400,400, was still outstanding in 1932. The par value of the amount still outstanding located in the United States was $994,330,900. For good order's sake, short-term loans of American banks, totaling $650 million in 1932, also have to be mentioned.[26] They resulted from routine commercial transactions and often entailed revolving credits.

The final question we have to face pertains to the actual connection between the unpaid American loans and reparations payments. It should be viewed in the general framework of Germany's economy, which during the period 1924–1929 had a $1.5 billion foreign trade deficit, an additional outflow of about $2 billion in reparations, and nevertheless wound up with a balance-of-payments surplus of approximately $750 million. The unprecedented influx of more than $4 billion in foreign capital was responsible for rapid economic recovery and the boom years of 1927 and 1928. Moreover, since the strengthening of the economy had as a side effect a substantial increase in tax receipts, the foreign credits also facilitated the payment of reparations. On the other hand, a simple comparison of the magnitudes of American loans and German reparations—$1.6 billion versus $9 billion—will set the record straight and leave the analyst with the conclusion that widespread public disgust with the war debt and reparation problem had provided fertile

24. *Hearings before the Committee on Finance,* 72nd Congress, 1st Sess., pursuant to S. Res. 19, Part 1, p. 25.
25. Kuczynski, *Bankers'* . . . , pp. 4–5.
26. Ibid., p. 31.

TABLE 2. Loans according to borrowers 1924–30

Borrowers	Num-ber of Loans	Total issue	Floated in the United States	Approximate amount outstanding June 1, 1932 Total	Floated in the U.S.
German Republic	2	$ 208,250,000	$ 208,250,000	$ 169,134,900	$169,134,900
States	11	135,000,000	115,650,000	92,784,500	75,796,500
Provinces and municipalities	20	109,400,000	103,425,000	88,132,000	82,915,000
Public utility corporations	41	303,700,000	276,883,000	264,327,000	222,155,000
Industrial corporations	28	301,725,000	214,418,500	227,856,500	171,529,000
Public credit institutions	19	253,350,000	213,435,000	210,547,500	177,082,000
Private commer-cial corpora-tions	11	106,600,000	94,070,000	96,017,000	84,632,000
Religious organizations	3	13,500,000	12,900,000	11,601,000	11,086,500
Total	135	$1,430,525,000	$1,239,031,500	$1,160,400,400	$994,330,900

Source: Kuczynski, *Bankers' Profits from German Loans*, pp. 164–167.

opportunity for seeking scapegoats. It is also apparent that public leaders, as well as historians, directed their attention exclusively to the years after the enactment of the Dawes plan and disregarded the fact that two-thirds of reparations payments were made before a single American loan was extended to Germany. Moreover, public utterances failed to give recognition to the important detail that under the explicit provisions of the Dawes plan the transfer problem was an Allied responsibility. In other words, had there been no foreign loans, Germany would have been able to discharge its responsibilities by depositing reparations payments in German marks with the Allied Reparations Commission. It is of course possible to relate the $800 million of actual cash transfer of reparations after 1924 to the American loans, but even during those years the greatest part of reparations, $1.75 billion, consisted of payments in kind.

As to the putative role of the American taxpayer in reparations fulfillment, it is suggested that there was none. Naturally, the validity of this opinion rests on a definition of "taxpayer" as the American equivalent of the Soviet term "toiler," evoking an image of hard-working citizens who must exert themselves in order to make ends meet. Technically, of course, all American investors who ventured their funds abroad, because they expected high profitability, were taxpayers; however, to refer to them in this context merely introduces the element of political propaganda. In summary, it appears that the policy makers in

World War II had done their homework on lend-lease but not on the reparations issue. Why this discrepancy?

Contemporary studies of decision making which stress the importance of sociopsychological forces suggest that whenever the "logic of the situation" is compelling, there is little room for the influence of personality factors.[27] The question of financial support for Nazi Germany's enemies provides a good example. Actually it was not important whether Roosevelt and his asociates were aware of Lord Liverpool's advice, "In case of war, if you can give at all, give and do not lend." Most of them had observed America's economic policies during the twenties as well as the consequences. Moreover, in 1940–1941 there was indeed no choice: France had fallen; England—financially weak— was fighting with its back against the wall; and the defeats of the Russian armies made Washington expect the worst. Most important of all, there were few who did not consider it America's war. As far as lend-lease was concerned, the "logic of the situation" was indeed compelling.

By contrast, emotional elements came promptly to the fore as soon as reparations appeared on the agenda, obfuscating the fundamental differences of the issue in 1945 and in 1919. For the American people the First World War had been an idealistic venture and, as such, a failure. The nation's mood has been lucidly described by Robert E. Osgood:

> In the years after the war a great many Americans were embittered by the consequences of intervention and thoroughly convinced that intervention had been a terrible mistake. In retrospect, righteousness, honor, and the cause of world peace and democracy seemed inadequate motives for the grim sacrifices of war. The American mission, divorced from a conception of fundamental national self-interest, seemed to have been futile at best, false at worst; and the nation's scholars, journalists, and politicians set to work fixing the blame for intervention upon this group or that individual, as though to purge the nation of its guilt by indicating the selfishness, hypocrisy, or gullibility of a few.[28]

As the public viewed the matter, all that had been harvested was Europe's ingratitude.[29] After the war the Allied nations had squandered their money on armaments while defaulting on their debts. Germany

---

27. Sidney Verba, "Assumptions of Rationality and Non-Rationality in Models of the International System," p. 222.
28. Osgood, *Ideals* . . . , p. 261.   29. Ibid., p. 331.

had not paid reparations, but instead had used the funds of kind-hearted and gullible Americans to rebuild its industries for the next war. Under no circumstances should these tragic mistakes be repeated. It was a set of simple black-and-white images, with all the right-minded duly assembled on this side of the ocean.

More balanced evaluations were of course available: it had been cogently shown that America's participation in the First World War was in the national interest; the question of war debts could be and had been presented in a broader framework which also took the respective human sacrifices into account; the United States' share of responsibility in the excessive reparations claim as well as the unfortunate effects of the Fordney-McCumber Tariff had been well documented; Germany's record in paying reparations had been much better than generally conceded; and the questionable role of America's financial community in the issuing of German loans had been publicly exposed by the United States Senate Finance Committee.

Each of these pieces of evidence—if accepted—would have caused cognitive dissonance, and consequently, in accordance with a well-known pattern, each was rejected.[30] History texts had done little to provide a more objective analysis, and the decision makers, in their roles as politicians, echoed what the masses wanted to hear. Roosevelt's reference at Yalta to "$10 billion" allegedly lent to Germany was symptomatic of a politician's specious style. It actually pertained to the United States Government's credits extended to Germany's enemies and not to the speculative loans totaling $1.3 billion which later had been poured into Germany with the aim of participating in Germany's economic recovery. However, as far as the perceptions of the American people and of their president were concerned, the two issues had merged.

Should one then conclude that the American reparations policy was exclusively based on emotional elements? Certainly not. Only in this case the "logic of the situation" operated in conjunction with rather than against, the psychological factors. The United States Treasury had stated at an early date that the goals of extensive deindustrialization and of reparations from current production were not compatible. It ought to be one or the other. And since the Soviet leaders had to rebuild their devastated country, an American loan—as will be shown—was being considered. At Yalta this was still a viable policy alternative

30. Judson Mills, E. Aronson, and Hal Tobinson, "Selectivity in Exposure to Information," p. 250.

and Stettinius accordingly promised Molotov that he would study the proposal of a loan.[31]

Six months later at Potsdam, the lines had hardened. Truman was now in charge. As a senator viewing the German-Soviet war, he had suggested that the United States should exhaust the two dictators by alternatingly giving aid to the losing side.[32] The reparations problem—as will be shown—was papered over, and the slogan "The American taxpayer paid once, he is not going to pay again" became the rationale for American economic policies in Germany.[33] It was stated more and more emphatically as the wartime pattern changed and traditional anti-Soviet stereotypes began to suppress the American anti-German bias.

31. Edward Stettinius, *Roosevelt and the Russians,* pp. 119–120.
32. *New York Times,* 24 June 1941, p. 7.
33. "People pay more attention to *what* has happened than to *why* it has happened. Thus learning is superficial, overgeneralized, and based on post hoc ergo propter hoc reasoning. As a result the lessons learned will be applied to a wide variety of situations without a careful effort to determine whether the cases are similar on crucial dimensions." Robert Jervis, *Perception and Misperception in International Politics,* p. 228.

CHAPTER FIVE

THE SOVIET REPARATIONS CLAIM

According to the Yalta records President Roosevelt refrained from questioning the intrinsic merits of the Soviet reparations claim and confined himself to stressing that the United States would not again finance German reparations. Actually, there is no evidence that Soviet statements emphasizing the modesty of their claim were ever challenged, and one wonders whether the reticence of the United States in this regard was not prompted by the evaluations of experts intimating a much larger German capacity to pay.[1] Two years later, when Stalin mentioned to the American secretary of state, General Marshall, in the presence of "Chip" Bohlen that at Yalta "all Americans including President Roosevelt, Stettinius and Hopkins had said the Soviet claim was very small" and cited Bohlen as a witness, there was no American reply.[2] And in 1973 when the present writer wrote to Ambassador Bohlen in an effort to clarify this point, his answer was inconclusive.

The large body of cold war literature which deals extensively with the reparations problem also contains no factual evaluation of the Soviet claim but only unsupported comments such as "very great,"[3] "preposterous,"[4] "exorbitant,"[5] "outrageous,"[6] and "extravagant."[7] Because of the obfuscating influence of such judgments on the public mind and the significance of the issue for this study, it will be useful to take a look at the precedent set after the First World War. In doing so, the final, drastically reduced Allied claim rather than the original, highly inflated figure will be used. Furthermore, it is necessary to com-

1. U.S. Office of Strategic Services, Research and Analysis Report 2350, 30 December 1944.
2. U.S. Department of State, *Foreign Relations of the United States . . . Council of Foreign Ministers; Germany and Austria, 1947,* 2: 343.
3. Herbert Feis, *Churchill, Roosevelt, Stalin,* p. 534.
4. William D. Leahy, *I Was There,* p. 423.
5. E. F. Penrose, *Economic Planning for the Peace,* p. 282.
6. Bruce Kuklick, "The Division of Germany and American Policy on Reparations," p. 281.
7. Robert Cecil, "Potsdam and Its Legends," p. 460.

pare the claim with the war damages actually suffered by the Soviet Union. In other words, one must ask if $10 billion—as related to precedent and to actual losses—was a reasonable sum or not?

Once we face the question, the complexities of an adequate answer come to the fore. How should war damages be defined? Should the concept encompass all military expenditures in time of war, in addition to reconstruction costs and subsequent war-connected expenditures such as pensions? Or would it be appropriate to set an arbitrary limit? Second, suppose a city was destroyed in the course of hostilities, should the damages be calculated as a proportionate share of the national wealth on the eve of the war? In other words, should prewar prices be used, or reconstruction costs? Moreover, since the latter will extend over a period of years when inflation is probable, what base year ought to be chosen? And finally, since all losses will have to be calculated initially in Soviet rubles, American dollars, French francs, etc., what conversion rates should be used to arrive at a common denominator?

As far as the definition of "war damages" is concerned, it is helpful to examine the Treaty of Versailles. Its drafters, who faced a similar problem, acknowledged that Germany would not be able to make reparations for all wartime damages, an admission even more appropriate after the Second World War. Accordingly, Article 232 stipulated that "Germany will make compensation for *all damages due to the civilian population* [8] of the Allied and Associated Powers and to their property during the period of belligerency . . . as defined in Annex I thereto." However, as mentioned before,[9] this language was less restrictive than it might seem because Annex I actually authorized claims "for the amount of the separation and similar allowances granted during the war by Allied Governments to the families of mobilized persons and for the amount of pensions and compensations in respect to the injury or death of combatants payable by the governments now and thereafter."[10] In other words, according to the precedent of Versailles, "war damages" encompassed damages to property as well as war-connected pensions and allowances.

As to prices of private property and relevant exchange rates, those prevailing respectively in 1914 and 1938 will be applied. There are two reasons for this. First, no dependable estimates of Soviet reconstruction costs at postwar prices appear to be available, whereas we do have a scholarly analysis of damages at Soviet amortized investment values.

8. Italics added.   9. Page 52.
10. Keynes, *Economic Consequences* . . . , pp. 153–154.

TABLE 3. Original claims (in billions of dollars)

Powers	Damages to property	Damages to individuals	Total
Great Britain & Dominions	4.2	7.6	11.8
Italy	2.3	6.1	8.4
Belgium	3.0	1.2	4.2
Powers not represented	2.2	4.3	6.5
Powers other than France	11.7	19.2	30.9
France	14.0	11.7	25.7
Totals	25.7	30.9	56.6

Source: Extracted from Etienne Weill-Raynal, *Les Reparations Allemandes et la France*, p. 323.
The original data of Tables 3–5 are in gold marks. They have been converted into dollars on the basis of one dollar to four gold marks.

And second, it is simpler to focus on the details of national wealth at a fairly specific date than to try an analysis of reconstruction expenditures which are bound to be distributed over many postwar years during which prices and exchange rates tended to fluctuate. As to the costs other than property damage, the respective estimates in available source material have been used; they pertain to discounted posthostilities costs.

The most detailed data on World War I reparations will be found in Etienne Weill-Raynal's *Les Reparations Allemandes et la France,* a standard work of over 2,300 pages. According to this source, as shown in Table 3, the miscellaneous claims submitted to the Reparations Commission totaled $56.6 billion. It is worthy of note that the decision of the Reparations Commission, reducing these claims to the official reparations bill for $33 billion, was in no way based on any concern for Germany's capacity to pay. It was rather the result of several financial adjustments and application of British-proposed coefficients of conversion which, according to Weill-Raynal's detailed analysis,[11] produced the amounts shown in Table 4.

The final reduction was achieved through a secretly negotiated compromise between the Allied representatives,[12] for which Weill-Raynal

TABLE 4. British proposal (in billions of dollars)

	Property damages	Damages to individuals	Totals
France	9.6	8.2	17.8
Other powers	7.7	12.7	20.4
Totals	17.3	20.9	38.2

11. *Les Reparations Allemandes et la France*, p. 333.
12. Ibid., p. 334.

TABLE 5. Final claims (in billions of dollars)

	Property damages	Damages to individuals	Totals
France	8.1	7.2	15.3
Other powers	6.6	11.1	17.7
Totals	14.7	18.3	33.0

gives the estimated breakdown as shown in Table 5.[13] It is important to remember that all the figures which have so far been mentioned represent, on one hand, estimated *reconstruction* costs and, on the other, discounted pensions and allowances at postwar conversion rates. While it will be possible to draw on comparable World War II data for the second category, it is necessary to establish 1914 values for the damaged or destroyed personal property. Fortunately, there are some scattered official data available which can be pieced together. They reflect a coefficient of 2.2 in the case of French shipping losses and a coefficient of 4 for other damages to property. On the assumption that these coefficients provide a guide for approximate price relations in the other Allied countries, we obtain the estimate of damages to property at prewar values as shown in Table 6.

As is well known, Keynes strongly objected to what he considered highly exaggerated Allied claims.[14] This appraisal was shared by René Pupin, cited as an independent authority by both Keynes and Etienne Mantoux, one of Keynes's severest critics. Pupin estimated French damages to property to be between $3 billion to $4 billion at 1914 prices.[15] Dubois, the rapporteur of the Budget Commission of the French Chamber of Deputies estimated $3.7 billion,[16] and Loucheur, the French minister of industry and reconstruction, $4.3 billion.[17] Weill-Raynal himself, furthermore, provided us with a critical appraisal of British

TABLE 6. Damages to property (estimate)
(in billions of dollars)

France	6.9
Great Britain	1.8
Belgium	1.8
Italy	1.3
Others	1.4
Totals	13.2

13. Ibid., p. 333.
14. Weill-Raynal, *Les Reparations* . . . , passim.
15. Etienne Mantoux, *The Carthaginian Peace*, p. 104.
16. Ibid., p. 105.   17. Ibid.

losses whose 1914 values he estimated to be no higher than $970 million. If one adds this figure to Pupin's conservative estimate and adjusts the claims of the other powers accordingly, one arrives at a grand total of about $6.7 billion, which lets us conclude that damage to property was somewhere between $7 billion and $10 billion at 1914 prices.

The Allied reparations bill of $33 billion, on the other hand, is well known and recorded as such in most history texts. While announcement of that sum was probably meant to provide a sop to Allied public opinion, it had the opposite effect in Germany, where the long-range consequences were most unfortunate. The Allied reparations ultimatum of May 5, 1921, demanded bonds and guarantees in support of the nominal amount; but Keynes was quick to recognize, as indicated above,[18] that the solid part of the settlement was the provision for payment envisaging an annual transfer of $750 million. Germany's official representative at the reparations negotiations, Staatssekretär Carl Bergmann, reached a similar conclusion when he pointed out that "contrary to the terms of the treaty of Versailles, interest was not to be paid on the entire indebtedness, for what was decisive was not the nominal figure of the debt but the annual payment." [19] On this basis, Bergmann calculated a *"present value of 12.5 billion dollars."* [20]

Summarizing, the following figures are of importance for a comparison with the Soviet reparations claim. On one side of the ledger there is an estimated amount at 1914 prices of $7 billion to $10 billion representing damage to property, in addition to Allied claims for $18.3 billion in compensation for pensions, allowances, and similar expenditures (discounted 1921 values.) On the other side of the ledger, there is an official demand for reparations for a nominal sum of $33 billion, consisting of a core of $12.5 billion, plus an amount of $20.5 billion, which, in the opinion of competent observers as early as 1921, was likely to be canceled.

We now come to the Soviet reparations claim after the Second World War. In addition to the official statements by Messrs. Maisky, Vishinsky, and Molotov, we can draw on a 1943 article by the Soviet economist E. S. Varga, "Reparations by Hitler's Germany and Its Accomplices"; [21] on a 1947 paper from the pen of Professor Isakhov Moiseevich Faingar, "Germany and Reparations"; [22] on a book, *The Soviet Economy during the Second World War,* by Nikolai Voznesensky,

18. Page 53.   19. *History of Reparations,* p. 77.
20. Italics added.
21. Voina i Rabochi Klass, no. 10, 15 October 1943.
22. "Stenograph of a Public Lecture," 24 April 1947.

who headed Gosplan during the war; and, finally, on a scholarly analysis prepared in 1944 by the Research and Analysis Branch of the United States Office of Strategic Services, "Russian War Damage and Possible Reparations Claims." It would seem that the latter was among Stettinius's briefing papers at the Yalta conference.[23]

The point of departure for Dr. Varga was the sum of $7 billion,[24] which he mentioned as the estimated World War I damage to property in occupied France and Belgium. While recognizing that this amount was probably exaggerated and that some of the areas of Russia occupied by the Germans in World War II were less affluent, he indicated that the latter were about thirty to forty times as large and arrived at an estimated damage of $100 billion. This sum did not include such losses as those caused by the bombardment of England, shipping losses, or the costs of the German occupation, which, according to his estimate, would add another $50 billion or $100 billion. Varga, however, refused "to add together mechanically the losses of the Allied countries, as was done after the last war, and then to distribute the reparations in direct proportions to the losses." He rather suggested that damages to property had to be made good first, and that only after this had been accomplished should payments for personal damage be made. Moreover, payments received should not be distributed between the individual countries in proportion to the absolute amount of damage, but "in the first place these countries should receive reparations in which the damage done constitutes the largest proportion of their national wealth." Naturally, this was the formula that would entitle the Soviet Union to priority treatment. Turning to Germany's failure to live up to its financial commitment after the First World War, Varga expressed the opinion that this was essentially the result of the transfer problem. Payments in kind were the only possible solution, he wrote, and the most desirable for the Soviet Union, which had a "planned economy in which disproportion cannot arise between production and consumption . . . and in which economic crises are accordingly impossible." The article finally referred to the expected sources of reparations, namely Germany's foreign assets, its national wealth, and its postwar income. As shown, Varga's fundamental approach was reflected in the Soviet position on reparations at Yalta; it also was maintained after the end of the war.

23. Edward Stettinius, *Roosevelt and the Russians,* pp. 120–121.
24. Varga's figures are in gold rubles. They have been converted on the basis of one 1914 dollar to two gold rubles.

Professor Faingar's paper was read for the first time in Moscow on April 24, 1947, and it was hardly a coincidence that this was also the closing date of the Council of Foreign Ministers' Conference where, for the first time, Molotov presented the Soviet reparations claim with the support of concrete data. Collected during the course of about three years by tardy Soviet bureaucrats, the data added up to a total of $128 billion for damages to physical property and $357 billion for "damages to the Soviet State." [25] The purpose of Professor Faingar's lecture was presumably to strengthen the Soviet official position by presenting a politico-economic analysis in some depth. He asserted that, although Germany had surrendered unconditionally, the Soviet Union was not guided by a desire for revenge or by an aim to enslave the German people. It was therefore necessary to distinguish between the Soviet position on reparations and the type of contributions exacted from the vanquished in former wars. The essential feature of such past contributions was their punitive intent and the desire of the victors to enrich themselves regardless of the effects on the economies of their former enemies. By contrast, the Soviet policy was based on the just and fair concept that the aggressors had to contribute to the reconstruction of the victor's destroyed economy but only within the framework of their own continued viability. It followed that the reparations would compensate for only a small part of the damage the aggressors had caused. Citing a speech by Vishinsky, Faingar remarked that this principle of basic fairness had already been enunciated before. It prescribed that "economic demands had to take the obligations, as well as the actual economic condition, of a defeated country into account." Accordingly, the level of reparations imposed upon Germany after the Second World War represented only one-third of World War I demands. The original Allied claims at Boulogne and Spa in 1920 had been for $60 billion and the final amount established at the second London Conference in May 1921 was 132 billion gold marks, which were the equivalent of $35 billion at that time and corresponded to approximately $55 billion in 1947. This comparison was even more significant, he said, if one considered the economic and technical advances made by Germany since the First World War. Professor Faingar concluded by delivering an ideologically inspired critique of the Anglo-American representatives "who wanted to use reparations . . . in order to accomplish the com-

25. An "Extraordinary State Commission for Ascertaining and Investigating the Crimes of the German Fascist Invaders and Their Accomplices" began its work in 1943. *Daily Digest of World Broadcasts,* Part 2 (19 October 1943).

plete economic subjugation of the defeated countries by the big capitalist monopolies" and "insisted on payment in dollars and Pound Sterling"
rather than accepting reparations in kind.

There are a few bits of additional information on reparations in the
chapter entitled "Expenditures and Losses in the National Economy"
in Nikolai Voznesensky's *The Soviet Economy during the Second
World War.* The principal categories of material damage listed here [26]
are the same as those cited by Molotov in March 1947. In addition
Voznesensky indicated that the population of the German-occupied
areas of the Soviet Union amounted to 45 percent of the total population of the USSR, their gross industrial output accounted for 35 percent, their cultivated areas for 47 percent, and their railways equaled
55 percent of the country's total mileage. (Voznesensky's figure of
65,000 km of railroad tracks destroyed is a useful indicator of the
relative magnitudes involved.) Because of the unequal wealth of the
devastated provinces in World War I and of the Soviet Union in World
War II, a comparison on a square mileage basis would hardly be appropriate. However, the official French figure of 2,404 km of railroad
tracks destroyed [27] can be properly juxtaposed with Voznesensky's
datum. The total of damage to property, as well as of other damage is
—as is to be expected—identical with that cited by Molotov, and one
also notes that the head of Gosplan estimated physical damage at prewar prices.[28] The exchange rate used throughout is 5.294 rubles to the
dollar. According to the same source, Soviet property losses amounted
to two-thirds of the prewar national wealth of the territories of the
Soviet Union that underwent occupation.

We now come to the analysis of Soviet war damage prepared in 1944
by the Research and Analysis Branch of the Office of Strategic Services.[29] As far as its list of general categories is concerned, it follows
the pattern established at Versailles of separating damage to property,
war pensions, and allowances as well as other damage to civilians.
General war costs were calculated with the comment that they also
had been seriously considered for inclusion in the reparations bill after
the last war but finally had been dropped as incompatible with the

26. Partly or totally destroyed: 31,850 factories; 1,876 state farms; 2,890
machine and tractor stations; 98,000 collective farms; 216,700 stores; 4,100 railway stations; 36,000 post offices; 6,000 hospitals; 33,000 polyclinics; 82,000
elementary and secondary schools; 605 scientific research institutions; 427
museums; 43,000 public libraries.
27. Keynes, *Revision of the Treaty,* p. 115.
28. *The Economy of the USSR during World War II,* p. 153.
29. U.S. Office of Strategic Services, Research and Analysis Report 1899.

Fourteen Points. The American analysts furthermore separated the damage to property within the pre-1939 Russian borders from that in areas annexed by Russia in 1939 and 1940, while anticipating that the Russian reparations bill would not follow this example.

The OSS study indicated that Soviet statistics on the total amount of investment for almost all types of property were available for one year or another. Whenever necessary these statistics were brought up to June 1941 by extrapolation, even though incomplete information often had to be used. For instance, in the case of household articles and clothing, the total investment as of June 1941 was estimated on the basis of statistics on yearly consumer acquisitions and on the average length of life of these items. In a similar fashion estimates were made of the June 1941 territorial distribution of investment between invaded and never-occupied areas. Whenever prewar data on regional distribution were not available, appropriate indices were used to allocate the investment regionally; for instance, in the case of housing, population figures provided the basis for the regional distribution. As to the estimates of the amount of damage, they were based to a great extent on published reports of the Soviet Extraordinary Commission. The researchers acknowledged that it was difficult to obtain a uniform evaluation of the different types of property, because the original Soviet figures used different types of rubles such as "1927–1928 rubles," "1935 rubles," and "current rubles." Accordingly, the various categories of investment had to be revalued in terms of "calculated 1937 rubles." Since no official Soviet price index numbers had been published for several years, the analysts made an independent estimate of relevant price changes. Essentially, their index of prices was obtained by dividing the calculated value of industrial output in current rubles by the official Soviet index of changes in the physical volume of industrial production.[30]

The estimated values of invested capital were presented net of depreciation. The report, however, stressed that since a great part of Russian housing was very old, reproduction costs undoubtedly would be much higher than the depreciated value. As to current output seized by the Germans, only an estimated value of agricultural and industrial

---

30. Necessarily, the resulting figures reflect the changes in the price level of fabricated and processed goods only. The OSS report therefore cautioned that "for lack of any reliable information on the changes in the price levels of agricultural commodities, the figures on investment in cattle and grainstocks were used in 1937 rubles by use of the overall index . . . quite possibly the values expressed in 1937 rubles represent an understatement."

raw material output produced during the German occupation was given, on the assumption that most of it had either been consumed by the occupying army or exported to the Axis countries. The analysts indicated that information on this category of damage was very incomplete and that the respective figure of 5 billion 1937 rubles expressed only a general magnitude of the item.

The OSS report also included a detailed calculation of war pensions and allowances based on the Soviet war-pension law of 1940 as amended, as well as on an OSS estimate of Russian war casualties. (This estimate, prepared in March 1944, mentioned 6.2 million of "battle and non-battle dead and disabled," whereas the final Soviet figures were, of course, much larger.) The last two categories considered were personal damage for labor deportations and the general cost of the war, both of which are included in Table 7.

It will have been noted that total damage to property, as estimated

TABLE 7. Possible elements in Russia's postwar reparations claims estimated in rubles and dollars (billions)

	1937 rubles	In dollars at official ruble-dollar exchange rate (5 rubles to 1 dollar)	In dollars in terms of whole-sale industrial price parity in 1937 (8 rubles to 1 dollar)
A. Property losses within pre-1939 borders including German requisitions	143.6	28.7	18.0
B. Property losses in incorporated areas	35.0	7.0	4.4
C. War pensions and allowances	96.6	19.3	12.1
D. Totals: A-C	275.2	55.0	34.5
E. Personal damage to civilians (labor deportations)	4.9 [a]	1.0 [a]	.6 [a]
F. War costs	353.3 [b]	70.7	70.7 [c]

a. Not including damage due to labor deportation from annexed areas, which might amount to another two billion rubles.

b. This represents the magnitude of defense expenditures in terms of current rather than 1937 rubles.

c. For defense expenditures the general industrial price parity is believed to be a less accurate indicator of the actual value of the war costs in dollar terms than is the official rate of exchange.

by the Office of Strategic Services, namely 178.6 billion rubles, represents only 26 percent of the official Soviet datum. Voznesensky wrote "that the property losses amount to two-thirds of the national wealth of the USSR," [31] whereas the OSS estimate indicated about one fourth.[32] There is no point in trying to evaluate any further these two competing estimates, but it ought to be recognized that OSS analysts themselves indicated that "the estimates of damage to property in the invaded areas, for the most part, are based on scattered current information on the destruction in various liberated localities." [33] It also should be remembered that the above estimates took into account only damage sustained up to July 1944, although the increase in Soviet property losses after that date was probably not significant.

We can return herewith to our initial question, Was the Soviet reparations claim excessive? Undoubtedly the reader surmises by now that it was moderate by any reasonable standards. Even if one dismisses the global category, "material damage to the national economy of the Soviet Union," as not pertinent and the official Soviet figures for "damages to property" as probably exaggerated, the conservative OSS estimate of $35.7 billion [34] would still let us conclude that the requested compensation corresponded to no more than 30 percent of actual physical damage.

By contrast, the Allied reparations demand of $33 billion after World War I would have to be seen as indicative of French-British greed, were it not for the fact that in 1921, when "the vast emotions of an outraged and quivering world" had just begun to calm down, the responsible statesmen still felt obliged to maintain the *appearance* of a large reparations bill. By 1929 this was no longer considered necessary and political and economic realities were sufficiently strong to produce a reduced and final reparations bill of $10.8 billion [35] in the form of the Young Plan. One will recognize that this sum corresponded to and satisfied objective estimates of physical war damages. Consequently, even if one takes the relatively moderate Young Plan as a precedent-setting norm and uses as a basis the OSS estimate of physical damage, the Soviet Union still would have been entitled to present a much larger reparations bill—namely about $35 billion.

31. Voznesensky, *Economy* . . . , p. 133.
32. R&A Report 1899, p. 10.   33. Ibid., p. 7.
34. In the opinion of the present writer the alternate estimate of $22.4 billion should be disregarded since it fails to take the reduced value of the 1947 dollar into account.
35. Weill-Raynal as cited in Richard Castillon, *Les Reparations Allemandes*, p. 66.

For those who are not prepared to accept Professor Faingar's explanation of Soviet magnanimity, the question arises, Why was the larger bill not presented? The answer includes ideological, economic, and political considerations.

First, one must recall that the Bolsheviks denounced the Versailles settlement in the twenties as unjust, vindictive, and imperialistic. A resolution of the Fourth Congress of the Third International "On the Versailles Peace Treaty" described Germany as "the new colony of the imperialist robbers," suggesting that "it was being converted into a plaything in the hands of England and France." [36] Lenin himself referred to Versailles as "a thousand times more predatory than Brest Litovsk." [37] It would therefore seem that ideological consistency alone imposed on the victorious Soviet Union a certain degree of moderation, at least in financial matters. Second, the socioeconomic problems caused by German reparations in the twenties undoubtedly were on the minds of the older generation of Soviet economists. Although, according to Professor Varga, the transfer problem did not exist for the Soviet Union, they were probably aware of Keynes's caveat: "At a given time the economic structure of a country in relation to the economic structure of its neighbors permitted a certain level of exports, and arbitrarily to effect a material alteration of this level by deliberate devices is extremely difficult." [38] Third, there was the anticipated Western opposition. And finally, as one will recall, at the time of Yalta an undivided Germany was still a good possibility. Of course, as far as the Kremlin was concerned, it was desirable that it should be a Germany under the governing influence of the Soviet Union, that is, a Germany which ought not to be antagonized unnecessarily. Accordingly, since Silesia and East Prussia were taken away from this Germany, wise statesmanship could only recommend financial moderation.

36. E. H. Carr, *The Bolshevik Revolution,* 3: 449.
37. Lenin, *Sochineniya,* Third Edition, 24: 545.
38. "The German Transfer Problem," in *Readings in the Theory of International Trade,* ed. Howard S. Ellis and Lloyd A. Metzler, p. 167.

CHAPTER SIX

LEND-LEASE AND THE PROSPECT
OF A LOAN

The contentious issue of German reparations was a critical element in the deterioration of American-Soviet relations at the end of the war. The uncertainties of lend-lease and of an American loan added to the tensions. As to lend-lease, the liberal handling of the program for Russia by President Roosevelt, as well as its sudden termination by President Truman, has come under varied forms of criticism depending on the political proclivities of the respective writers. Actually in both cases military considerations had provided a valid rationale for the actions taken.

There is probably no better or briefer way to illustrate Western dependence on the fighting qualities of the Soviet army than to cite from the terms of the Anglo-American pledge to invade France in the spring of 1944. "It must not be possible for Germany," it said, "to transfer [from the Eastern front] more than 15 first quality divisions during the first two months of operations." [1] This commitment to open a second front was made in October 1943—almost two years after the United States had entered the war—moreover, it was the last in a series of similar promises, each of which had remained unfulfilled. Without question, there had been good reasons for the delays, and when the landings actually took place, the tide of battle on the beaches demonstrated that if the invasion had been undertaken earlier and had been less carefully prepared, it might well have failed. On the other hand, the Soviet government, concerned with its own military predicament, had pleaded for active military assistance by its allies from the beginning of the war. Stalin, in his first letter to Churchill after the German attack, had asked not only for an immediate British front in northern France but also for

1. John R. Deane, *The Strange Alliance*, p. 19.

one in Norway, with the British providing naval and air support and Russia sending army, naval, and air force units to cooperate with a Norwegian division to be shipped from England.[2] Obviously, the request had to be turned down, but new requests were forthcoming, with the one of September 15, 1941, demonstrating how desperate the Soviet military situation really was. "It seems to me," Stalin had cabled, "that Great Britain could without risk land in Archangelsk 25 to 30 divisions or transport them across Iran to the Southern regions of the USSR. In this way, there would be established a military cooperation between the Soviet and British troops on the territory of the Soviet Union. A similar situation existed during the last war in France. The arrangement would constitute a great help." Churchill could only marvel at this proposal. "It is almost incredible," he later wrote, "that the head of the Russian government with all the advice of their military experts could have committed himself to such absurdities." [3] Possibly the prime minister had overlooked one point, however: Stalin's suspicion that the prospect of Communists and Nazis hacking away at each other was by no means displeasing to some circles in England and in the United States. This also could have been a reason for Stalin's rude reply to Churchill's suggestion that two of his top military leaders, Generals Wavell and Page, be sent to Moscow: "They will be able to tell you exactly how we stand, what is possible and what we think is wise." If the two generals were empowered to sign an agreement about mutual military assistance, the Soviet Premier's reply read, they would be welcome. Otherwise "it would be very difficult for me to find the time for the conversations." [4]

As soon as the United States entered the war, the pressure for a second front was applied with equal emphasis in Washington and London. The military situation of the Soviet Union during 1941 and 1942 had continued to deteriorate, and Molotov, during his first visit to Washington in the spring of 1942, minced no words regarding the possibility of a military collapse if the Western allies did not come to Russia's aid by invading Europe. Roosevelt's cautious reply, that "full understanding was reached with regard to the urgent tasks of creating a second front in Europe in 1942," might have been interpreted as a promise by the anxious leader in the Kremlin, especially since it was followed by a plan for a small-scale bridgehead on the Continent in the

2. Winston Churchill, *The Grand Alliance* (paperback), vol. 3 of *The Second World War,* p. 324.
3. Ibid., pp. 390–391.   4. Ibid., pp. 445–446.

fall of 1942, to be further exploited in the spring of 1943.[5] As is well known, this project was soon shelved in favor of the invasion of North Africa, with Churchill accepting the unpleasant task of explaining the change to Stalin in person. The fall of 1943 was now mentioned as the date for the invasion; but when the Allies decided to follow up their African successes by invading Sicily and the Italian mainland, Operation Overlord was again postponed, this time until May 1944. In other words, the desired military assistance was not forthcoming when the Soviet armies needed it most, and it was therefore in America's self-interest to furnish without hesitation all the military supplies which the Soviet Union required in order to continue the fight. Lend-lease was clearly seen in this light in Washington, and General John R. Deane, head of the American Military Mission, also made the point quite succinctly when he wrote, "Unfortunately in the early part of the war the United States was in a position where it had to meet all Russian demands to keep Russia in the war." [6] The same officer, on the other hand, had considerable doubts as to the wisdom of continued lend-lease without the customary restrictive provisions once the military situation on the Russian front had greatly improved [7]—a reservation also expressed by others. Professor George C. Herring, for instance, in a paper entitled "Lend-lease to Russia and the Origins of the Cold War 1944–1945," [8] is quite critical of President Roosevelt's "generosity" in assisting the Russians. "None of these reservations [for other allies] applied to Russia," he writes. "Soviet requests were accepted at face value, no supporting evidence was required. These requests compiled in annual programs called protocols were represented in binding commitments and limited only by the availability of supplies and shipping. Roosevelt vigorously resisted any efforts to modify his unconditional aid program." Herring explains this accommodating attitude by the president's belief that "it would help to break down the ingrained Soviet suspicion of the West, that it would convince the Russian leaders of American good will, and that it would provide a firm foundation for the Soviet-American cooperation upon which he came to base his hopes for a lasting peace." [9] While evidence indeed exists that Roosevelt on occasion rationalized his benevolent policy toward Russia in these terms, a very realistic underlying consideration operated in favor of unrestricted support for the man in the Kremlin: the possibility of a

5. Deane, *Strange Alliance*, p. 16.   6. Ibid., p. 297.
7. Ibid., p. 90.
8. *Journal of American History* 56 (June 1969): 93–113.
9. Ibid., pp. 94–95.

separate German-Russian peace. The suspicion of such an eventuality arose as soon as the Soviet military situation had improved and it seemed substantiated by Russia's establishment of a "Free Germany Committee" in the summer of 1943. Composed of German Communists and a group of high-ranking German officers which included a grandson of Bismarck, the creation of the committee had to be seen as a preparatory move toward the establishment of a pro-Russian German government as soon as the opportunity presented itself. Moreover, rumors of a possible separate peace between Russia and Germany abounded at the time, and it was feared that once the enemy had been pushed beyond the so-called Curzon Line in Poland, the Soviet Union might make a separate peace with Germany in order to let the German army bleed the Western powers as long as possible.[10] No wonder, then, that one of the first questions the president asked Ambassador Standley upon the latter's return from Moscow was, "Do you think, Bill, he will make a separate peace?" [11] While the admiral's reply that the Soviet armies would continue to push on toward Berlin sounded reassuring, even a less cautious president than Franklin Roosevelt could not have permitted himself to take any chances. If the Soviets, repeating their performance of August 1939, were to change sides again, at least the chief executive of the United States would have done everything in his power to prevent a course of events that for all practical purposes would have precluded a victorious end of the war. The example of French-British dilatory tactics in the summer of 1939 was not going to be followed.

Because it is always difficult to appreciate fully the import of a perceived danger once the crisis has passed, it will be useful to look at the historical record; it was one of the reasons why Western decision makers had to consider a separate peace within the realm of possibility. Russia and the newly created German Reich had been allies for ten years in the last part of the nineteenth century; after its defeat in World War I Germany had again turned to Russia at Rapallo and challenged French and British supremacy. This diplomatic move was followed by a secret understanding permitting the clandestine training of the Reichswehr on Russian soil. Even after Hitler had come to power

10. Albert Z. Carr. *Truman, Stalin and Peace,* pp. 21, 24. See also Admiral William D. Leahy Diary 1941–1946, entry 31 July 1942 (U.S. Library of Congress).

11. William H. Standley, *Admiral Ambassador to Russia,* p. 498. The suspicions were mutual; just six weeks after the Teheran Conference *Pravda* published a report which suggested that the British were negotiating a separate peace with Germany behind Russia's back. See John L. Snell, *The Wartime Origins of the East-West Dilemma over Germany,* p. 51.

Soviet-German commercial cooperation continued for some time. The Molotov-Ribbentrop agreement not only could be considered a logical phase in this chain of events, but it also demonstrated that moral compunctions were not necessarily a factor in the dictators' diplomacy. In addition to the consideration of the historical past, the psychological handicap of Western leaders, who again and again had had to go back on their promises to open a second front, must be considered. And finally there were the conservative appraisals by the United States Joint Chiefs of Staff, who traditionally overestimated the resilience of the enemy and thus were prone to support a generous lend-lease policy.

While there were indeed sound reasons for the most liberal supply of the Soviet armies as long as the war in Europe was in progress,[12] the situation changed with Germany's surrender. Now a new president who had a different attitude toward the Russian ally was in office—a fact that undoubtedly sped up an inevitable development. As long as the war continued, President Roosevelt as commander-in-chief could feel secure in going to the limits of congressional authorization, often overriding advisers who suggested a more careful screening of Soviet orders.[13] After the capitulation at Rheims when a return to normality was in the offing, it had to be expected that the congressional power of the purse string would be quickly asserted, and that civil servants traditionally wary of the legislators would be careful not to cause any raised eyebrows on Capitol Hill.[14] Moreover, as far as Congress was concerned, it reflected a public opinion which had accepted lend-lease because of the inescapable logic of the situation. Truman obviously did not need any advice regarding congressional sentiments, but he heavily depended on the views of his ambassador in Moscow, who had ample reasons to complain about Soviet violations of the Yalta agreements.[15] Harriman suggested that American-Soviet relations would be on a much sounder basis if the United States was firm and the Soviets were made to understand that lack of cooperation would adversely affect their interests.[16] (The ambassador's concurrent recognition of a common Russian trait to interpret generosity as weakness is surprising only because it came so late.) [17] In other words, advice from abroad as well

12. "At the height of the Anglo-American effort on the Continent the Western Allies engaged only 33 percent of the total German forces." Diane Shaver Clemens, *Yalta*, p. 75.
13. George C. Herring, Jr., "Lend-lease to Russia . . . ," pp. 95–97.
14. Ibid., p. 108.
15. U.S. Department of State, *Foreign Relations of the United States . . . Europe, 1945*, 5: 822.
16. Ibid.   17. Ibid.

as legislative considerations at home suggested the prompt curtailment of lend-lease in accordance with the governing statute. That this was accomplished in an unnecessarily abrupt and even rude fashion was at least in part the result of the lack of coordination in Washington's conduct of foreign affairs.[18] Whether the remaining share of responsibility should be charged to the inexperience of a new president or his basic dislike of the Soviet system will remain debatable. As far as the Soviets were concerned, they never forgot the Missouri senator's hostile remarks about their government,[19] and presumably preferred the second interpretation.

American public opinion in general advocated ending lend-lease. When questioned on this point in December 1945, 49.4 percent of a national sample indicated that the program should have been stopped the way it was; 18.4 percent agreed that the program should have been stopped, but not so suddenly and not without consulting the recipient countries; only 19 percent felt that the program should have been extended up to a year to help put countries receiving lend-lease back on their feet; and 13.25 percent of those questioned expressed no opinion.[20]

General Deane, when summarizing the basic reasons for lend-lease, wrote that "it is necessary to be honest with ourselves and to admit that our most compelling motive in sending supplies to Russia was to save our skin." [21] The Soviets, of course, had no illusions on this point and consequently "there never was gratitude among their leaders and there never will be." [22] On the other hand, there is evidence that the Russian government did not fully grasp the significance of legislative restrictions tying lend-lease shipments to the direct prosecution of the war.[23] Otherwise the Kremlin would hardly have caused the break-off of the protracted American-Soviet negotiations, which—as will be shown below —were aimed at establishing a modus vivendi once lend-lease supplies had to be ended. In other words, there was enough blame to give everyone his share. The resulting friction, although overdrawn by revisionist writers, could well have been avoided. Truman's termination of lend-lease was in accordance with congressional wishes and required by law. The way it was accomplished simply reflected the eroding influence of victory on the American-Soviet brotherhood of arms.

18. Herring, pp. 106–108.
19. When the present writer visited the war museum in Minsk in 1965, he saw a clipping from the *New York Times* of 24 June 1941 exhibited under glass. It mentioned Senator Truman's anti-Soviet remark cited on page 60.
20. Cantril and Struck, *Public Opinion 1935–1945*, p. 415.
21. Deane, *Strange Alliance*, p. 143.   22. Ibid.
23. *Foreign Relations . . . Europe, 1945*, 5: 1019–1021.

While the termination of lend-lease at the end of hostilities actually confirmed the basic rationale for the program's existence, the failure to grant the Soviet Union a loan for reconstruction had more important implications. The statutory limit for lend-lease had made it self-evident that any continuation of economic aid for the Soviet Union after the war would require a new instrument and new legislation. This aspect, as well as the hope for continued friendly American-Soviet relations and the recognition that the Soviet Union had suffered in human and material terms infinitely more than any of its allies, operated for some time in favor of a new program. This goal was more or less actively pursued in four not always like-minded quarters: the American business community, the American Embassy in Moscow, the United States Treasury, and the Soviet Foreign Office.

Donald M. Nelson, the chairman of the War Production Board, was apparently the first to mention the desirability of American-Soviet economic cooperation once lend-lease had come to an end. With the president's concurrence, he brought up the subject when talking to Molotov and Stalin on a visit to Moscow in the fall of 1943. Since he occupied an official position at that time, Nelson was careful to emphasize that he was speaking only as an American businessman and not in his official capacity. He suggested that in his opinion the establishment of sound industrial and commercial relations after the war would be supported by the business community of his country and the American public at large.[24] Stalin's reaction and first question were predictable: "Do you think American business would extend long-term credits to Russia?" When Nelson replied in the affirmative, Stalin produced a tentative shopping list which encompassed steam and hydroelectric equipment, 10,000 locomotives, 50,000 flat cars and 30,000 km of rail.[25] The conversation then turned to the terms of credit, with both men agreeing in very general terms on five lean years to be followed by a gradually increasing scale of payments.[26] No specifics regarding this crucial aspect were mentioned. The American Embassy in its customary follow-up confined itself to mentioning the extreme cordiality of the meeting and to stressing that "the established agencies of the United States Government channeled through the State Department should take the initiative and direct these matters." [27] Stalin's conversation with Nelson was followed by a similar meeting with Eric Johnson, president of the United States Chamber of Commerce, in the summer

24. Carr, *Truman* . . . , p. 19.   25. Ibid.
26. Ibid., p. 20.   27. Ibid., p. 21.

of 1944, and by some brief conversations of Molotov and Mikoyan with Nelson, who then was on his way to China. The last action of the American business community regarding a loan was a memorandum by Nelson to President Truman at the time of the Potsdam conference in which he suggested active support of American-Soviet trade relations and complained about the State Department's lack of interest.[28] The Nelson and Johnson *pourparlers* in Moscow reflected a pattern of American-Soviet trade conversations which also could be observed during the subsequent thirty years: an enticing list of Soviet potential purchases and a concurrent neglect of the crucial element of the contemplated trade—the Soviet products the United States would have to buy in order to get paid! Usually this discrepancy was hidden by clever Soviet representatives who never tired of emphasizing the insatiable demands of a huge and unexplored Soviet market, as well as the proved credit worthiness of their government.

The prospect of a loan for the Soviet Union did not come up when Roosevelt talked to Stalin at Teheran, but it was mentioned at the time of the conference in the president's conversations with Hopkins and Harriman. Subsequently the topic also emerged in Moscow, where American officials were duly concerned about the legal limitations on the categories of lend-lease shipments, tying them to the effective prosecution of the war. Under conservative interpretation Soviet orders for dual-purpose equipment such as industrial and agricultural plants as well as equipment for public services—all useful both in war and in the reconstruction of devastated areas—could actually be viewed as not covered by the program. Moreover, there was continued uncertainty as to the duration of the war, persisting even in its closing days, when American military estimates still envisaged the possibility of a Bavarian "redoubt" and protracted guerilla warfare by a well-advertised but nonexistent German "Werwolf" organization. Since plans for production and shipment of lend-lease supplies had to be related to a very uncertain deadline, there was ample reason for American administrators of the program, and for Soviet administrators as well, to welcome the existence of a postwar dual-purpose program that could ease, if not eliminate, the legal problems of transition. As seen in this light, the relevant American-Soviet negotiations which continued throughout 1944 appear to have focused more on the need for an epilogue to lend-lease than

28. Thomas G. Paterson, "The Abortive American Loan to Russia and the Origins of the Cold War," p. 82.

for a long-range reconstruction program. Thus, when Harriman returned from Teheran, he told Molotov that the president regretted not having had the time to discuss with Stalin the question of United States participation in the reconstruction of Russia and that he was authorized to pursue the subject further.[29] He also pointed out that the legal limitations on lend-lease made it necessary to devise other methods of handling Soviet requests which could not be justified as needed for the direct prosecution of the war. This opening was followed by a number of conferences with Molotov and Mikoyan and an embassy telegram to Washington suggesting an "expeditious" study with regard to the financing of projects that could not be properly included in the lend-lease program.[30] Harriman stressed that it was "impossible to draw a clear cut line between war and post-war capital requirements." Consequently lend-lease ought to be used for reconstruction to the fullest extent possible under the law while in addition a transitional program would be worked out. Replying to this suggestion and "in order to assure an orderly liquidation of these war programs at the conclusion of hostilities,"[31] the State Department proposed that the Russians should agree "to take any equipment in certain categories not delivered at the conclusion of hostilities under a separate contract calling for regular payments on terms of interest and amortization to be laid down." Initially, the powers of section 3-C of the Lend-Lease Act would be used to permit such contracts; subsequently with congressional authorization the Export-Import Bank might be able to finance regular reconstruction activities. As the State Department pointed out, this might require amendments of the Export-Import Bank legislation as well as the repeal of the Johnson Act.[32]

The proposal was promptly taken up by the Soviet government and became the basis for protracted negotiations; the Russians subsequently presented a one-billion-dollar shopping list and persisted for more than a year in haggling for the most advantageous terms. Finally, in March 1945, when the Kremlin's approval of a carefully negotiated 3-C agreement for the period of transition had not been obtained and a large long-term loan had come under discussion,[33] President Roosevelt agreed that the American offer should be withdrawn.[34] As Dean Acheson, who

29. U.S. Department of State, *Foreign Relations of the United States . . . Europe, 1944*, 4: 1033.
30. Ibid., p. 1055.   31. Ibid., p. 1060.
32. Ibid., p. 1061.   33. Ibid., pp. 1139–1147.
34. *Foreign Relations . . . Europe, 1945*, 5: 991.

had been in charge of the negotiations, saw it, "Moscow knew that in the last bitter struggle with a desperate Hitler we could not interrupt the flow of supplies in the East while we had all we could handle in the West." [35] From subsequent Soviet reactions to the termination of lend-lease, however, it would seem that the Soviet government had actually overplayed its hand in this case. When the program came to an end, Stalin as well as Mikoyan feigned surprise, complaining that they had not been cautioned on what would arise at the end of the war if credit arrangements were not made.[36] In order to relieve the impasse President Truman subsequently asked Congress to expand the Export-Import Bank's lending authority, while also including $1 billion for possible negotiations with the Soviet Union.[37] Apparently the congressional committees were informed in executive session that this sum would be used only if events so warranted and appropriate legislation was obtained.[38] Congress complied without raising objections, but because of a Russian refusal to accept the bank's standard interest rate, the credit for $1 billion was not activated.[39]

One year before the end of the war the United States Treasury had also begun to take an active interest in the problems of Russian reconstruction; the starting point had been an intramural memorandum which explored the feasibility of a large credit to the Soviet Union in exchange for needed strategic raw materials. The memorandum, which had been prepared on Morgenthau's request by Harry D. White, listed American domestic reserves of petroleum, manganese, tungsten, zinc, lead, chrome, and mercury and concluded that they would be dissipated by 1954. Since the Soviet Union was richly provided with a wide range of strategic raw materials, and since rapidly expanded resources development could greatly enhance the export surplus of the USSR, it appeared that "a financial agreement whereby the United States would extend a credit of five billion dollars to the Soviet Union for the purpose of industrial and agricultural products over a five year period to be repaid in full over a 30 year period chiefly in form of raw material exports, would be advantageous to the United States as well as helpful to the USSR." The memorandum included a repayment schedule for American credits, while cautioning that "the prewar restricted pattern of trade ought not to be used to define the potentialities of post-war

35. Dean Acheson, *Present at the Creation*, p. 85.
36. *Foreign Relations . . . Europe, 1945*, 5: 1018–1021.
37. Paterson, "The Abortive American Loan . . . ," p. 81.
38. *Foreign Relations . . . Europe, 1945*, 5: 1011.
39. Paterson, "Abortive American Loan . . . ," p. 83.

trade between the United States and the Soviet Union." [40] The memorandum was submitted to the secretary on March 7, 1944; its principal points were included in Morgenthau's draft memorandum of May 16, 1944, which, however, as a handwritten note indicated, was not sent; [41] and they were again incorporated, albeit with significant changes, in the secretary's memorandum for the president of January 10, 1945. [42] In Morgenthau's draft, as well as in the final document, the sum of $5 billion which White had suggested was doubled. Why was this done, especially since the Soviets in the meantime had asked for merely $6 billion? Furthermore, how could a credit of $10 billion be justified in economic terms, since Harry D. White had already used some imagination in order to come up with a repayment schedule that had some aspects of plausibility? As to the first question, Henry Morgenthau's emotional "hang-up" with the contemplated destruction of Germany's industrial power provides the clue. According to his much-discussed plan, Germany's heavy industry was to be dismantled and there would be no reparations from current production. It was to be expected that such a radical solution would not be readily accepted—and least of all by the Soviet Union, which had repeatedly indicated that its reconstruction plans entailed the receipt of German industrial machinery and equipment. As Morgenthau had explained to Roosevelt, however, "there was a good chance of their going on with us providing we offer something in lieu of reparations—after all, the Russians are very intelligent and reasonable men." [43] In other words, a substantial loan might win the Kremlin's concurrence.

But how could such a large loan be amortized, considering the limited number of products the United States could reasonably be expected to purchase from Russia? The draft memorandum of May 16 still left this question unanswered—a possible reason why it was not sent. By January 10, 1945, however, the secretary had found a solution which provides some useful insight as to how wishful thinking tends to corrupt good judgment. In addition to listing the strategic raw materials enumerated by White as sources of repayment, Morgenthau first suggested proceeds from tourist trade—in a country which was so utterly destroyed that it would take ten to fifteen years to rebuild the most es-

40. U.S. Senate, 83rd Congress, 2nd Sess. Report 1627 *Accessibility of Strategic and Critical Materials in Time of War*. Report of Committee on American and Insular Affairs, Appendix 4: 370–377.
41. *Morgenthau Diary: Germany*, 1: 380.
42. *Foreign Relations . . . Malta and Yalta, 1945*, p. 315.
43. John Morton Blum, *Roosevelt and Morgenthau*, p. 593.

sential housing for its own population; second, he listed sales to the United States of nonstrategic goods, which traditionally had consisted of furs, some wood products, and caviar; the third item was a non-existent surplus of Russia's trade with other hard-currency countries; and last came payments in gold, which the Soviet Union always had kept as its war chest, releasing small quantities only in the direst emergencies. This then was Henry Morgenthau's plan for Russia's reconstruction.

A comparison of the Treasury's terms for a loan with the Soviet proposal of January 3, 1945,[44] will reconfirm the secretary's motives. The Soviet aide-memoire, after an opening reference to "the repeated statements of American public figures concerning the desirability of receiving extensive large orders for the post-war and transition period," suggested a $6 billion credit repayable within thirty years at an annual interest rate of 2 1/4 percent. By contrast the Treasury suggested thirty-five years and 2 percent. In other words, the Morgenthau proposal entailed a much larger loan, a longer amortization period, and a lower interest rate. Significantly, at the same time the Treasury proposed reactivating the stalled 3-C agreement by offering the Russians an interest-free credit.

The State Department's reaction was on sound economic grounds.[45] It mentioned that the Soviet Union could afford to take a highly independent position in the negotiations of foreign credits because Russia could attain its prewar level of capital investment by 1948 through reparations and limited use of its gold but without foreign credits. Prewar exports from the USSR to the United States had averaged only $26 million annually; even if this figure could be increased to $100 million, the sum would be fully available for interest and loan repayment only if no allowance was made for current imports from America. The Treasury's dollar values for United States imports of strategic materials not only were "completely out of line," but its proposal also failed to recognize the serious political consequences of the suggested reduction or cessation of American purchases of products such as Canadian nickel and asbestos, Cuban manganese, Chilean copper, and Brazilian mica.[46] The proposed resumption of the 3-C negotiations at more favorable terms for the Soviet Union was also rejected.[47]

The question of a loan was not on the Yalta or the Potsdam agenda. During the Crimean conference it was mentioned, however, by Molotov

44. *Foreign Relations . . . Malta and Yalta, 1945,* pp. 310–312.
45. Ibid., p. 322.
46. *Foreign Relations . . . Europe, 1945,* 5: 974–975.
47. *Foreign Relations . . . Malta and Yalta, 1945,* p. 318.

in a private conversation with Stettinius,[48] who promised that he would study the issue carefully. Prior to this conversation the State Department had notified the Soviet government that it was examining ways and means of providing long-term credits, but that it would be some time before the necessary legislation could be enacted.[49] The fact that the project was subsequently put on ice and dropped entirely after some lame excuses [50] has caused a vivid debate among historians who disagree on the political significance of this policy. Some diplomatic dispatches of the period, suggesting that economic aid to the Soviet Union ought to be offered only in exchange for political gains, have been cited in this connection. George Kennan, for instance, advised that no loan should be made "unless . . . the Soviets give some assurance that their international trading will proceed along lines consistent with our overall approach to international economic collaboration." [51] Looking at the issue soberly, what then was the loan's potential as a diplomatic tool? Above all, the traditional handicap of the American diplomat, who usually is obliged to conduct economic negotiations with one arm tied behind his back, must be considered. All he can promise is to take a negotiated agreement back to Congress in the expectation—often unduly optimistic—that it will be endorsed. In apparent recognition of this perennial predicament, it has been suggested that a properly informed American public and Congress might have supported the use of a loan as a "diplomatic weapon." [52]

A number of important factors have to be brought out in this connection. Lend-lease was approved by Congress and the American public only because of its implications for the nation's security. That the program was never popular was emphasized in Congress,[53] and this unpopularity was reflected in a series of public opinion surveys from January 1941 to December 1945.[54] The majority of those in favor of lend-lease, furthermore, indicated that the United States should be repaid in some ways for the supplies which were sent.[55] Two and a half years after the end of the war, when the Marshall Plan was proposed in the face of threatening economic and social collapse for Western Europe, a national citizens' committee, consisting of three hundred

48. Edward Stettinius, *Roosevelt and the Russians: The Yalta Conference*, pp. 119–120.
49. *Foreign Relations . . . Europe, 1945*, 5: 951.
50. *New York Times*, 2 March 1946.
51. Cited in Paterson, "The Abortive American Loan . . . ," p. 86.
52. Paterson, pp. 80–81.
53. *Congressional Record*, 79th Congress, First Sess., 13 March 1945, p. 2121.
54. Cantril and Struck, *Public Opinion . . .* , pp. 409–415.
55. Ibid., p. 413.

prominent public leaders, had to be organized to enlist the support of the people for the plan. Regional committees were set up, the cooperation of scores of national organizations was secured, and relevant publications were given wide circulation.[56] Extensive advertisements and speeches by leading citizens aided the effort. In other words, a massive public-relations campaign was required to overcome apathy or resistance. Moreover, the thought was expressed that, had the Soviet Union not excluded itself from the program, the Marshall Plan presumably would not have won congressional approval. A public-opinion survey on the desirability of giving Russia the requested $6 billion loan, for instance, showed 60 percent disapproval, 27 percent approval, and 13 percent expressing no opinion.[57] In sum, the suggestion that a large, long-term loan might have been approved by Congress is not supported by the available evidence.

As to the effectiveness of the recommended diplomatic tool, one has to consider the potential economic impact of a loan on Soviet economic reconstruction. According to the estimates of economists at the State Department and in the Office of Strategic Services, it would have reduced the period of reconstruction by only a few years. A factual State Department analysis enumerating the possible political gains of a loan therefore listed among other minor points merely the establishment of "a proper role for the United States" in the Allied Control Commission and in the economies of the East European countries.[58] That the Kremlin would not be so naive as to trade territorial gains and other elements of national security for short-range economic advantages appeared to be self-evident. (As shown below, this attitude was demonstrated when Secretary Byrnes at Potsdam attempted a relevant gambit.) George F. Kennan's advice cited above can therefore be read only as a suggestion that there should be no loan. As he knew better than most observers, a proposal calling for the relinquishment of bilateral state trading practices actually implied the demolition of an economic cornerstone of the Soviet system.

To summarize, even if the improbable had happened and a blanket authority from Congress had been obtained, only very minor political concessions on the part of the Soviet government could have been expected. Very likely, however, if used as a bargaining chip in strictly economic negotiations, short-term credits in the form of raw materials

56. Harry Bayard Price, *The Marshall Plan and Its Meaning,* pp. 55–60.
57. Cantril and Struck, p. 213.
58. *Foreign Relations . . . Europe, 1945,* 5: 960.

might have served some useful purposes. If offered at Potsdam, a few billion dollars in credits directly or through Germany might have been instrumental in providing the Soviets with needed equipment, thus defusing the most explosive aspects of the reparations issue. Although the Russians would not have agreed to treat credits as a substitute for reparations, since the former had to be repaid, a suitable combination might have been worked out. Six months later, on the occasion of Harriman's farewell visit to the Kremlin, Stalin cautiously inquired about the status of the loan and was given an evasive reply.[59] Since this evasion made it fairly clear that neither the loan nor reparations would be forthcoming, a new appraisal of East-West relations seemed warranted. It was presented in the framework of Stalin's election speech of February 9, 1946,[60] an opening shot of the cold war.

59. W. Averell Harriman's letter of 8 October 1974 to the present writer. Herbert Feis mentions the date of the visit, i.e. 23 January 1946. *From Trust to Terror, The Cold War 1945–1950*, p. 73.
60. *New York Times,* 10 February 1946. Using Marxian terminology, Stalin told his listeners that Communist cooperation with capitalist countries had only been temporary. He intimated that a third world war was a possibility, and he emphasized that the Soviet army was wholly capable of defending the country.

CHAPTER SEVEN

REPARATIONS AT POTSDAM AND THEREAFTER

The ambivalent character of American occupation policies has been stressed by many writers, but their principal constant feature—the determination to reject new financial obligations—has attracted less attention. This firm position emanated from several often contradictory sources. On one end of the spectrum was the Morgenthau policy, which aimed at Germany's deindustrialization and demanded a "hands-off" policy so that the Germans might "stew in their own juice." On the opposite end of the scale were the Russia-haters, who rejected any financial support for Germany lest it might be of economic benefit to the Soviet Union. And between the two extremes were the vast numbers of American people who had accepted lend-lease—not from a sense of equity—but as a temporary program dictated by a rationale of self-preservation. The nation's perception that twenty years earlier the United States "had been had" militated equally against new financial involvements. As an American representative at the Control Council's Finance Directorate later wrote, "No cry or slogan was more popular in key policy-making circles than this one. At the negotiating table or before congressional committees, and in a wide variety of forms the principle has been laid down that America will not 'finance' the payment of reparations by Germany to the Soviet Union." [1] Admiral Leahy's praise, cited above, of Truman's "patriotic" stand at Potsdam for refusing to be "bulldozed" into a reparations agreement reflected the predominant sentiments of the American people.

The guidelines for Ambassador Pauley on his Moscow reparations assignment accordingly had included the specific instruction to make sure that a reparations agreement would preclude the need for American

1. Manuel Gottlieb, "The Reparations Problem Again," p. 34.

subsidies and that the "first charge" principle had to be the cornerstone of any settlement.[2] At Potsdam the same attitude was evident when Truman tied the issue to the territorial question of Poland's western boundaries. The nascent East-West conflict thus emerged in a brief exchange which revealed in capsule form the American and Soviet diplomatic positions on a political problem:

> *Truman:* I wanted the administration in the four Zones to be as we
>   have agreed [i.e. without assigning an occupational Zone to
>   Poland]. We cannot agree to reparations if parts of Germany
>   are given away.
> *Stalin:* We are concerned about reparations, but we take the risk.[3]

In the preceding months the American ambassador in Moscow, W. Averell Harriman, had repeatedly suggested that the United States take advantage of Russia's economic weakness and trade economic concessions or financial aid for Soviet cooperation in the political field. It was therefore only natural that Truman tried an analogous approach. Stalin's reaction, on the other hand, only confirmed what American economists had predicted,[4] namely that the Soviet Union, with a few years delay if necessary, would be able to pull itself up by its own bootstraps. Moreover, any review of Soviet history should have made it clear to American diplomats that Soviet leaders never had been willing to trade political concessions with long-range effects for short-term economic benefits. Nevertheless the same gambit was used by the United States throughout the Potsdam conference. The above-cited exchange had taken place on July 21 in the framework of the Fifth Plenary Session at Cecilienhof. Two days later the issue was again taken up by Secretary Byrnes in several meetings with Molotov which reconfirmed the Soviet unwillingness to accept the "first charge" principle in spite of Byrnes's repetitive insistence that the United States would not provide the money for reparations "as we did after the last war."[5] The secretary's tentative feeler that, under these circumstances, each country might take reparations from its own area brought forth a Soviet offer to reduce its original demand to $8.5 billion or even $8 billion, with $2 billion coming from the Ruhr. No further progress was made, as the draft-

2. *Foreign Relations . . . European Advisory Commission, 1945*, 3: 1224.
3. U.S. Department of State, *Foreign Relations of the United States . . . The Conference of Berlin (Potsdam), 1945*, 2: 217.
4. Office of Strategic Services, R&A Report 1899 (National Archives).
5. *Foreign Relations . . . Berlin . . . ,* 2: 274.

ing committee continued its search for an acceptable formula. A Soviet proposal which would have given equal priorities to reparations and exports for payment of essential imports was not accepted by the two Western powers.

On the occasion of the Ninth Plenary Meeting on July 25 Churchill indirectly alluded to the reparations issue by stating that the question of Poland's western boundaries was "at the root of the success of the conference." [6] For all practical purposes the Poles were admitted as the fifth occupational power, he said; if no arrangements could be made for the spreading of food equally over the whole population of Germany, the conference would undoubtedly break down. In such case all the occupying powers would hold on to what was in their respective zones. The same view was expressed by the Soviet foreign minister two days later. There was really no difference between a lack of a reparations agreement, he remarked, and a decision that each country would take reparations from its own zone. The result would be the same. He then referred to the American emphasis on the vast destruction in West Germany, stating that, according to his government's information—as it turned out, correct—only 10 to 15 percent of the Ruhr's productive capacity had been destroyed. There was no American reply.[7]

The impasse which threatened the success of the conference was eventually broken by Byrnes's offer of a package deal involving American de facto acceptance of the Polish western boundaries in exchange for a reparations agreement which precluded the establishment of a definite sum and which assigned the collection of reparations in each zone to the respective occupying power. In addition the two Western governments yielded a percentage of equipment to be dismantled in their zones.[8] The setting up of a percentage and the establishing of the principle of Soviet counterdeliveries occupied the delegates during the remaining days of the conference.

The final agreement emerged at the Eleventh Plenary Session. The meeting provided Stalin with the opportunity to get back at Western critics of Soviet troop behavior by reading a communication from Marshall Georgi K. Zhukov reporting the removal of more than ten thousand loaded railroad cars by American and British troops prior to their withdrawal from the Soviet Zone. Again there was no reply and Stalin dryly remarked that he only wanted to show that "both sides had

6. Ibid., p. 385.   7. Ibid., p. 451.
8. Ibid., pp. 472–473.

sinned." [9] Secretary Byrnes's "deal" [10] provided that 10 percent of industrial equipment "unnecessary for the German peace economy" would be transferred from the Western Zones to the Soviet government and that an additional 15 percent of such equipment would be supplied in exchange for an equivalent value of food, coal, and other commodities. In addition to the Potsdam reparations agreement [11] several of the "Economic Principles" of the Potsdam Protocol [12] also affected the reparations issue. Paragraph 14, for instance, stipulated that Germany was to be treated as a single economic unit and accordingly common policies were to be established with regard to concerns such as industrial production, reparations, and foreign trade. Paragraph 15 established the basis for the dismantlement process and paragraph 19—in lieu of Pauley's clear mathematical formula which the Soviet Union had rejected—stated the critical "first charge" principle in the following terms:

> In working out the economic balance of Germany the necessary means must be provided to pay for imports approved by the Control Council in Germany. The proceeds of exports from current production and stocks shall be available in the first place for payment for such imports.

It is generally recognized that next to the establishment of four zones of occupation the setting up of a zonal reparations plan was the most important step on the road to the division of Germany. In the light of the well-documented fact that at the time of Potsdam a unified Germany was still a three-power goal, one wonders why this step was taken. Pauley's statement to Maisky that it was "regrettable but inescapable" because of Soviet unilateral actions [13] is not convincing, and subsequent comments by analysts that the United States was resolved to protect the German economy as a bulwark against aggressive communism imply the existence of a governing grand design at a time when demonstrably there was none. John Gimbel mentioned in this regard [14] the connection between the zonal reparations plan and President Truman's directive of July 29, 1945, to the army,[15] which also endorsed the "first charge"

9. Ibid., p. 514.
10. It included an additional concession on the part of the Soviet Union in the form of its concurrence to Italy's entry into the United Nations.
11. *Foreign Relations . . . Berlin . . . ,* 2: 1485–1487.
12. Ibid., 1483–1484.
13. *Foreign Relations . . . Berlin . . . ,* 2: 896.
14. *The Origins of the Marshall Plan,* p. 58.
15. *Foreign Relations . . . Berlin . . . ,* 2: 821–823.

principle. But the relation between the two documents was not causal and the underlying reason for the emerging American position was simple and clear: in the administration's judgment Congress and the country had had enough of foreign aid.

Two more questions require an answer. To what extent did the Potsdam agreement settle the reparations issue and why did the Soviet Union finally accept "first charge"? It may be recalled that at Yalta the Big Three had endorsed the three sources for reparations: dismantlement, production, and labor. On a tentative basis Potsdam took care of the first by establishing a research organization in the form of the quadripartite Level of Industry Committee. Its mission was to determine within six months a level of reparations which permitted "the maintenance of a German average living standard not to exceed that of other European countries." (European countries meant all countries excluding the United Kingdom and the Soviet Union.) Reparations through labor did not come up at Potsdam because it was recognized that within the confines of international law each country could utilize the services of its prisoners of war. The protocol did not mention reparations from current production either, and consequently a bitter and fateful controversy arose. When eleven months later Molotov again brought up the $10 billion claim, Secretary Byrnes was incensed. As he later wrote, "Nowhere in the Potsdam Protocol is there any provision for the payment of reparations from current production. All prior discussions were superseded by the formal reparations agreement in Potsdam. The Soviet Union's renewal one year later of its demand for $10 billion of reparations from current production and its continued use of German labor is inexcusable." [16] In other words, as of July 1946 the official United States position was that the Potsdam agreement had replaced the Yalta Protocol and since reparations from production were not mentioned in the former, it had been agreed that there would be none. As one would expect, defenders of this interpretation rarely failed to quote paragraph 19 as conclusive evidence. The Soviet Union, on the other hand, held a different view. As the Kremlin saw it, Potsdam had only been the first implementing step and the question of reparations from production remained open. The defense of the Russian position, however, was clumsy since Molotov merely continued to bring up the $10 billion claim without ever taking advantage of significant and available evidence which would have supported the Soviet position.

16. James F. Byrnes, *Speaking Frankly,* p. 86.

As to Russia's last-minute endorsement of paragraph 19, the American president's threat to depart, even if it meant a failure of the conference, usually has been considered decisive. Undoubtedly, this threat played a major role, but there was another even more important factor which so far has escaped the attention of researchers. As will be shown, the Soviets had been informed that the principle of "first charge" as defined in the text, was not relevant to the reparations issue.

Accordingly, and contrary to the prevailing opinion of analysts, the *priority of commercial exports over reparations was never acknowledged by the Soviet Government.*

The Control Council had six months to come up with a detailed solution, but the Soviets, for their part, were not willing to delay the collection of reparations until a quadripartite research project had been completed. Their seizure of "war booty," as they called it, actually had begun as soon as the Russian army entered Germany. A detailed plan encompassing the collection of foodstuffs, animals, farm machinery, transportation equipment, and miscellaneous household goods had been prepared in Moscow and special "trophy brigades" on division and army levels were made responsible for its faithful fulfillment. The plan not only prescribed the tons of grain and the numbers of cattle, hogs, tractors, mowing machines, automobiles, and trucks which had to be seized, but also specified quantities for items such as bathtubs, water closets, sewing machines, pianos, and silverware.[17] The task of collection was made easier by the fact that during the advance of Soviet troops across East Prussia hardly any Germans were encountered since most of the inhabitants had fled, leaving all their possessions behind.[18] But even in places where the population was present the ruthless implementation of military requisition orders made certain that the plans for the seizure of "war booty" were always fulfilled.

As far as the collection of reparations through the dismantling of capital goods was concerned, the Soviets were equally in a hurry, possibly in the expectation that the establishment of a quadripartite reparations plan would put an end to unilateral removals.[19] During the first postwar years a Special Committee chaired by Malenkov and reporting directly to the Council of Ministers in Moscow acted as the Russian reparations agency.[20] It operated independently from the Soviet army

17. Vassily Yershov, "Confiscation and Plunder by the Army of Occupation," p. 2.   18. Ibid., p. 1.
19. Vladimir Alexandrov, "The Dismantling of German Industry," p. 15.
20. Vladimir Rudolph, "The Administrative Organization of Soviet Control," p. 19.

of occupation, as well as from the Soviet Military Government (SVAG). The initial targets of the Special Committee—coal-mining installations, railway repair shops, power stations, electrical works, locomotive factories, and similar highly developed technical plants—were dismantled with great speed. The work was performed, however, by unskilled labor without overall direction or the benefit of technical instruction essential for the disassembly of complicated machinery.[21] As a result much damage was done in the dismantling process itself. Shortages of crating material and of railway transportation facilities equally impeded the task. Only a part of the dismantled equipment could be shipped to Russia immediately; the remainder had to be left out in the rain and weather, subject to pilfering until loading space became available.[22] The loading itself was done in a disorderly fashion without the preparation of inventories or bills of lading, with the result that the equipment arrived at transfer points in Russia without any indication of the relation of one piece of machinery to another.[23] Moreover, in most cases the blueprints and layout plans of the dismantled plants had been lost because the dismantling crews frequently burned all papers in the factory offices. While subsequent dismantlement was accomplished by the Soviet authorities in a more competent manner, the initial disillusioning experiences drove home the point that it was more economical and faster to extract reparations from a plant which was permitted to operate in its original position. By the time the experts of the occupying powers in Berlin had agreed on an economic ceiling for the envisaged dismantlement process, the Russians had already reached the conclusion that removing existing plants was not the answer to their needs and that there should be a greater emphasis on collecting reparations from current production.

Ambassador Pauley, when discussing reparations in Moscow, had complained about the method of wholesale seizures in the Russian area of occupation, and Secretary Byrnes had raised the subject at Potsdam in a conversation with Molotov. In both cases the American comments had some moralistic overtones which also can be found in other Western appraisals of Soviet reparations policies. It is clear that Soviet practices are not to be condoned; on the other hand, the present writer, who served with one of the American airborne divisions throughout the European campaign, cannot help wondering whether it would not be

21. Vladimir Alexandrov, "The Dismantling . . . ," p. 14.
22. Ibid., p. 15.   23. Ibid., p. 17.

more appropriate to compare this behavior to General Sherman's scorched-earth warfare in the South during the Civil War than to judge it from the vantage point of American experiences in World War II. The American troops who entered Germany in 1944 had left a country physically untouched by the war and were serving in an "army of plenty" where three hot meals a day were the custom and where PX supplies were usually available even at the front lines. By contrast the Russian soldiers came from a country whose occupied areas had been utterly destroyed, which had suffered millions of civilian casualties, and whose army more often than not was compelled to live off the land. Moreover, as every soldier knows, peacetime moral values tend to disintegrate rapidly under combat conditions. Accordingly, the behavior of the Western armies was not above reproach; for example, the removal from the Soviet Zone by American and British units of more than ten thousand loaded railroad cars—a substantial part of East Germany's rolling stock—plus extensive industrial equipment, cannot be explained as economic necessity.[24]

Some other transactions of the Western powers also provoked Soviet denouncements. In accordance with President Truman's coal directive of July 26, 1945,[25] coal exports from West Germany were stepped up during the first years of the occupation. Germany's economic interests were protected since the exported 20.4 percent of production in 1946 and 14.6 percent in 1947 were in conformity with the prevailing peacetime pattern.[26] However, from the end of hostilities throughout most of 1946 coal exports were either billed below the European market price or they were not billed at all but shipped against quantitative receipts. The principal reason for this was, of course, the absence of a usable German currency and the near-impossibility of enforcing payment in scarce American dollars as reflected in a communication from Clay's headquarters: "The British express skepticism over the ability or willingness of our European customers to pay dollars for coal and we share that skepticism unless the two governments will be willing to support our dollar demands with the right to cut off shipments when dollar payments are not forthcoming. . . ."[27] According to some tentative esti-

24. "Report of Marshal Zhukov to Supreme Commander in Chief, J. Stalin. (The writer was unable to find any document which might have supported or challenged the Soviet claim. But Gabriel Kolko, *The Politics of War*, p. 572, accepts the Soviet statement as valid.)
25. *Foreign Relations . . . Berlin . . .* , 2: 1028–1030.
26. Nicholas Balabkins, *Germany under Direct Controls*, p. 123.
27. CINCEUR signed Clay to AGWAR for WDSCA Ref. No. CC-9199 (May 1947) (OMGUS records 355/1/5.)

mates of this writer,[28] the 23 million tons which were exported during these thirty months should have yielded about $340 million as compared to approximately $145 million initially collected by the Military Government.[29] It seems that the outstanding claims resulting from quantitative receipts were eventually settled—some of them in connection with the Marshall Plan—but at the time of the acute reparations controversy the Soviet Union was in an excellent position to reject Western criticism and to quote Stalin's "We all have sinned!"

As mentioned above, the administrative organ set up by the Control Council to work on reparations was the quadripartite Level of Industry Committee, which functioned as a subordinate part of the Economic Directorate. The first American delegate on the committee was Dr. Calvin Hoover from Duke University, with Dr. Benjamin U. Ratchford as alternate. Members of the committee conducted the major part of the negotiations, and only when an agreement could not be reached were matters referred to the Economic Directorate and from there to the Co-ordinating Committee composed of the four military governors.

In essence the committee was an economic planning group which, under the terms of reference established at Potsdam, was given the responsibility of determining production and consumption ceilings for a German economy to become effective at an undetermined date. This date was, however, far away. As a practical example, the committee argued about whether the German steel production should be limited to five, seven, or nine million tons annually at a time when actual steel production was about one million tons. According to the best available estimates, at least four years would elapse before the ceiling could be reached.[30] In the same vein, while a future annual level of 3 billion RM of German exports was being discussed, actual exports for 1946 approximated 600 million RM. In other words, the committee's extensive research actually represented a highly theoretical exercise. Its principal pragmatic aspect was the assumption that it would establish an upper limit on the number of plants and equipment selected for reparations. And even this objective soon had to be discarded.

By the end of March 1946, after seven months of intensive efforts, the work of the Level of Industry Committee, with the active assistance of the Economic Directorate and the Coordinating Committee, came to

28. Source: Deutsche Kohlenbergbau Leitung, Zahlen zur Kohlenwirtschaft Nov. 1951; 1936 Statistisches Reichsamt, *Statistisches Jahrbuch fuer das Deutsche Reich* (1937) pp. 145, 253.
29. Backer, *Priming . . .* , pp. 124, 152.
30. John Gimbel, *The American Occupation of Germany*, p. 58.

an end. The final product of its labor, the "Plan of the Allied Control Council for Reparations and the Level of Post-War German Economy," usually referred to as the "First Level of Industry Plan," constituted a compromise between four independent draft plans submitted by the representatives of the four Allied governments. Generally the levels of industry proposed by the USSR were the lowest, and extensive bargaining was required to arrive at a compromise. The plan reduced the original American figure of 7.8 million tons of steel to 5.8 million; instead of 100,000 passenger cars only 80,000 were authorized; a capacity of 11 million kilowatts of electricity was reduced to 9 million kilowatts; the annual production of copper was reduced from 160,000 tons to 140,000, of lead from 130,000 tons to 120,000 tons.[31]

Dr. Ratchford later wrote that General Clay and General Draper had been too anxious to reach decisions, thereby letting the Soviets outwait and outwit us.[32] While this was probably a valid comment, the American military governor had good reasons to be accommodating. By the spring of 1946 he undoubtedly had begun to recognize the theoretical aspects of the Level of Industry Plan. During the many months when the economic experts of the four powers were deliberating, Clay had attempted in vain to establish unified administrative agencies and to reach agreement on the drafting of a quadripartite export-import plan. The former had been blocked by the French and the latter by the Russians, who claimed that a joint export-import program could be prepared only after the question of reparations had been settled. Within the American Military Government there was a growing suspicion that this was only a delaying tactic. If this was actually the case, a joint Level of Industry Plan would soon become meaningless. On the other hand, assuming that a four-power agreement on German foreign trade could be reached, it would take several years of continued economic progress until the limitations established by the plan would become effective. In the meantime political changes would probably occur affecting the theoretical assumptions on which the plan was based. Under these circumstances prolonged arguments about figures which soon would become obsolete served no purpose.

As indicated, the plan's sole practical significance was the establishment of a ceiling for the dismantling of plants and equipment, but—as it soon turned out—even this was essentially a paper activity. On the basis of the plan, 1,546 plants were earmarked as surplus and available

31. B. U. Ratchford and W. D. Ross, *Berlin Reparations Assignment*, p. 145.
32. Ibid., p. 78.

for reparations. This included 336 war plants, such as airplane factories and plants for the production of high explosives, war chemicals, shells, and cartridge cases, which would have been dismantled under the Potsdam provisions even without a quadripartite Level of Industry Plan. In other words, the starting figure for deindustrialization, excluding the war plants, was 1,210 plants. As of May 1946 only 24 of these plants had been allocated as "advance reparations" in the American Zone and their dismantling had actually begun.

Almost immediately after the signing of the First Level of Industry Plan, General Clay increased the pressure for the acceptance and the implementation of a quadripartite export-import program. It was clear to him that his mission to put the American Zone of occupation quickly on a self-supporting basis was doomed to failure unless a fundamental change in the existing situation could be brought about. If the treatment of Germany as an economic unit, as prescribed by Potsdam, could not be accomplished, it would particularly affect the American Zone, which had no raw materials, and would create a continuing financial liability for the United States for many years. During the first twelve months of the occupation the Military Government had been able to master the prevailing chaotic conditions. As will be discussed below, some of the underbrush had been cleared, but the increase in productivity had been small, with monetary "overhang" acting as a major depressant. Among the German people memories of the World War I inflation were very much alive and no one had any doubt that a currency reform would eventually have to be enacted. In the meantime a suppressed inflation and an unsettled reparations issue provided negative incentives, causing workers, farmers, and business people alike to save their energies for the day when a sound national accounting basis had again been established.

The Soviet Military Government, on the other hand, by voiding all claims and liabilities of financial institutions, as well as the Nazi public debt, had created the necessary financial incentives for the active cooperation of the German people.[33] Moreover, the ruthless methods of Soviet administrators experienced in handling a recalcitrant population made sure that prescribed production goals in industry and on farms were achieved. In terms of comparative economic revival Soviet Zone coal output in 1946 reached 98 percent of the 1936 level while output in the Anglo-American Zones was only 53 percent—a telling differ-

33. Manuel Gottlieb, *The German Peace Settlement and the Berlin Crisis,* p. 58.

ence.[34] In other words, whereas the American side urgently needed economic unification, the Soviet Military Government could wait while proceeding with the economic development and the exploitation of its zone.

Lucius Clay clearly was not the man to tolerate a "mission not accomplished" on his military record. He therefore was determined to force a top-level decision by bringing the conflict into the open. If economic unification could not be obtained, he concluded that a merger of the British and American Zones might provide an acceptable alternative. Accordingly, during the meetings of the Control Council he continued to emphasize that the Level of Industry Plan was based on a balanced export-import program. If there were no such program, he said, then the reparations plan had no validity.[35] Finally, on May 4, 1946, when several attempts in the Control Council had failed to activate the administering of Germany as an economic unit, he ordered a halt to all further dismantling in the United States Zone.

A few weeks later, in a summary report to Washington on the German situation, Clay suggested among other things the economic unification of the American and British Zones.[36] In other words, thirty-seven days after its promulgation, the quadripartite Level of Industry Plan lost whatever practical significance it had had. After Clay's dramatic move his announced policy was somewhat modified when, as of June 28, 1946, all war plants were made available for destruction or dismantling.[37] The total so classified in the United States Zone was 98 plants, of which 69 had been completely or partly dismantled. This very slow implementation of the reparations program was also evidenced by an American statement a year later at the Moscow Conference of Foreign Ministers indicating that in the American Zone no more than 80 war plants had been dismantled and that the total number of plants allocated for reparations was 174 as of that date.[38]

The Soviet government responded to the American challenge quite promptly. At the diplomatic level Molotov reopened the reparations issue at the Council of Foreign Ministers meeting in Paris by again presenting the original Soviet claim for $10 billion. Moreover, the difficulties encountered with dismantlement in the Soviet Zone gave him the

34. Ibid., p. 80.
35. Lucius Clay, *Decision in Germany,* pp. 73–78.
36. Ibid.
37. "A Year of Potsdam, The German Economy Since the Surrender" (National Archives, OMGUS Records.)
38. *U.S. Department of State Bulletin* 16, no. 404 (30 March 1947): 563–564.

opportunity of an about-face in the form of a propaganda blast against alleged current Western plans for Germany's deindustrialization. On the economic front the Soviets reacted by expropriating two hundred of the largest industrial works in their zone—the property of monopoly capitalists and Nazis, as they explained. They were transformed into Soviet corporations, better known as SAG, which from then on produced mostly for the Soviet Union or for export on Soviet account.[39] By October 1946 the establishment of these corporations, in which the Soviet government held 51 percent of the stock, had been completed. Subsequently the Soviet Council of Ministers decided to return to a German administration 30 enterprises which were of importance mainly to the German economy. The remaining 170, organized into 9 Soviet-owned corporations, operated in conjunction with 400 small German firms for the fulfillment of reparations orders.[40] Since a number of the expropriated firms had been originally earmarked for dismantlement, the new policy reflected the recognition that reparations from current production would be more efficient and that the output of the Soviet Zone could be taken more quickly and more cheaply if the factories were left in their original places.[41]

On the Western side, as a result of the bizonal merger, a revaluation of the reparations program was also made eventually. The economic calculations which had formed the basis of the quadripartite plan assumed the existence of a unified Germany. Since this assumption was not valid any longer, a new basis had to be established. The resulting Revised Plan for Level of Industry in the US/UK Zones of Germany, which was published in August 1947, drastically changed original production levels. In contrast to the old plan limiting total industrial capacity to 70–75 percent of German production in 1936, the revised plan aimed at approximating the level of industry which had prevailed in Germany in 1936, a year not characterized by either boom or depression. The effect of the revised plan on the contemplated extent of reparations was considerable, and 687 plants were removed from the list of 1,210 nonwar plants earmarked for reparations, thus reducing the total to 523 nonwar plants. Furthermore, as a result of a rapidly changing political climate, and in accordance with a tripartite agreement, 159 plants were dropped from the reparations program in April 1949. Subsequently, under the pressure of the newly formed Adenauer govern-

39. Peter Nettl, "German Reparations in the Soviet Empire," p. 304.
40. Rudolph, "Administrative . . . ," p. 57.
41. Nettl, "German Reparations . . . ," p. 305.

ment, an additional 17 plants were eliminated from the critical list, thereby reducing the final grand total to 347 plants, plus 336 factories designated as war plants.

A brief summary of reparations totals on the two sides of the Iron Curtain seems appropriate here. As to the value of all plants and equipment removed from the three Western Zones, estimates have been made ranging from $270 million to $625 million.[42] Whereas the actual effects of the dismantling process on the West German economy are difficult to appraise, the relative impact can be judged by comparing the high German estimate of 2.5 billion DM or $625 million with West Germany's investment figure of 19.3 billion DM for the first year after reparations had come to an end. The total officially reported value of reparations from the Soviet Zone,[43] on the other hand, is $4.292 billion. A scholarly, non-German study confirmed this amount as it estimated $1.3 billion from the dismantlement of capital goods, an equal amount from stocks and current production and the balance from other sources.[44]

42. Clay, *Decision* . . . , p. 325. E. C. Harmssen, *Am Abend der Demontage*, p. 176.
43. As quoted in Jens Hacker, *Sovietunion und DDR zum Potsdamer Abkommen*, p. 118.
44. Peter Nettl, *The Eastern Zone and Soviet Policy in Germany*, p. 237.

CHAPTER EIGHT

RECONSTRUCTING THE GERMAN ECONOMY: A SUMMARY [1]

A number of historians have castigated President Roosevelt's neglect of postwar planning and his single-minded concentration on the attainment of victory. One early critic of the "policy of no policy," Philip Mosely, drafted a telegram for Ambassador Winant in August 1944 which suggested the prompt dispatch of American representatives to Russia in order to work out a reparations policy that would satisfy a part of the expected Soviet demands without involving an undue burden for the United States. Mosely correctly predicted "that it would be almost impossible to achieve such an agreement after the close of hostilities" [2] and it seems conceivable that earlier negotiations —without endangering the alliance—might have led to a workable occupation statute. The president's priorities, on the other hand, were prompted by his awareness that the American army was hastily trained and inexperienced, that the staying power of the American people in a prolonged war was questionable, and that a defection of the principal ally could not be ruled out. In other words, as far as the commander-in-chief was concerned, it was the better part of wisdom to take care of first things first.

As one would expect, there was a greater sense of urgency at the lower levels of government, especially at SHAEF, where planning officers envisaged that they would be ultimately responsible for the effective administration of occupied Germany. One of the first products of their labor, the *Handbook for Military Government in Germany,* reflected the pragmatic approach of men who had no illusions about

---

1. A more detailed treatment of this topic by the present writer was published in 1971 by Duke University Press under the title *Priming the German Economy: American Occupational Policies 1945–1948.*
2. Philip Mosley, "The Occupation of Germany," p. 595.

the complexity of a task which soon would be thrust upon them. They knew that the state of the German economy would be chaotic and they were aware that the army would not have the personnel qualified to handle the resulting responsibilities. Accordingly, the *Handbook* listed as the first concern of the Military Government that "the machines worked and worked effectively," concluding that "it may not be possible to dismiss every Nazi from every position of responsibility at the very outset. The main and immediate task of Military Government is to get things running, to pick up the pieces and to restore as quickly as possible the efficient functioning of German civil government." Moreover, steps would have to be taken, the *Handbook* said, "to import needed commodities and stores, to convert industrial plants from war to consumer goods, to subsidize essential economic activities where necessary and to reconstruct German foreign trade with priority for the needs of the United Nations." [3]

All this was anathema to the planners at the Treasury, who, under Henry Morgenthau's direction, proposed that Germany should be partitioned, that its heavy industry should be removed or destroyed, and that in its place an agricultural economy should be developed. The ensuing clash of ideas began within the framework of an ad hoc committee of the cabinet chaired by Harry Hopkins. The committee found the Departments of State and War aligned against the Treasury, with the president and Hopkins tending to favor the position of the latter. [4] No agreement was reached and the scene of action moved to Quebec, where Roosevelt and Churchill initialed a memorandum—the pastoral letter [5]—which incorporated most of the Morgenthau concepts. In a quick reaction the outflanked opposition resorted to a time-honored device, a leak to the press, which brought the conflict into the open, and, under the pressure of public opinion, Roosevelt was obliged to repudiate his signature.

The responsibility for developing an occupational policy thus reverted to the War Department, which in the course of the following months, in cooperation with the Departments of State and Treasury, drafted the controversial JCS# 1067. Signed by President Truman in May 1945 and released to the press in October of the same year, it became the object of often immoderate criticism in the early postwar

---

3. Backer, *Priming . . .* , p. 8.
4. Henry L. Stimson, *On Active Service in Peace and War*, pp. 567ff.
5. A term used by John J. McCloy when discussing the Morgenthau plan with the present writer.

years. Because of the opposing views of its authors, the directive was a compromise with contradictory elements still in evidence. Its punitive provisions and even more its generally negative tone reflected the influence of Henry Morgenthau. "The principal Allied objective," it said, "is to prevent Germany from becoming a threat to the peace of the world." The Germans should therefore not escape responsibility for what they brought upon themselves. The elimination of nazism and militarism in all their forms, the immediate apprehension of war criminals for punishment, the industrial disarmament and demilitarization of Germany with continuing control over Germany's capacity to make war were essential steps to accomplish the basic purposes of the occupation. Since most of these provisions corresponded to the often-declared war aims of the Allied Powers, they did not arouse much opposition. The roots of the public controversy were in the directive's economic section where Morgenthau had been able to insert instructions that "the commander in chief should take no steps which would lead toward the economic rehabilitation of Germany or which were designed to maintain or strengthen the German economy." Furthermore, "no action was to be taken that would tend to support basic living standards in Germany on a higher level than that existing in any of the neighboring United Nations." [6]

Lewis Douglas, General Clay's first financial advisor, when examining these provisions in the light of a chaotic German economy, concluded that JCS# 1067 "had been designed by economic idiots" and rashly resigned from his position. Another American official, E. F. Penrose, who served as John Winant's economic counselor, was equally severe. In his judgment the directive was "one of the most discreditable state documents ever written," [7] a view shared by many writers who also found support in the autobiographies of Lucius Clay [8] and Robert Murphy; [9] both men—for reasons of their own—have mentioned JCS# 1067 as a major impediment to their mission.

Later researchers, however, have examined the occupation directive in a more balanced frame of mind. [10] They recognized the fundamental significance and effectiveness of the War Department's escape clause,

6. Paul V. Hammond, "Directives for the Occupation of Germany, the Washington Controversy."
7. E. F. Penrose, *Economic Planning for the Peace*, p. 268.
8. Lucius Clay, *Decision* . . . , pp. 17–19.
9. Robert Murphy, *Diplomat among Warriors*, p. 283.
10. John Gimbel, *The American Occupation of Germany*, pp. 8, 9, 30; Hammond, "Directives . . . ," p. 390.

which directed the Military Government to "insure the production and maintenance of goods and services required to prevent starvation or such disease and unrest as would endanger the occupying forces." The Treasury had been aware of the ultimate purpose of this provision,[11] but its attempt to emasculate it by inserting "epidemic" disease and "serious" unrest had failed; the Military Government thus was able to disregard the economic restrictions of JCS# 1067 whenever necessary.

A second factor rendering the negative economic sections of JCS# 1067 inapplicable was the Potsdam agreement itself, since it not only stipulated that Germany was to be treated as an economic unit but ordered that "steps were to be taken promptly to effect essential repairs of transport, to enlarge coal production, to maximize agricultural output and to effect emergency repair of housing and essential utilities." Potsdam also expressly stated that the program of reparations should leave enough resources to enable the German people to subsist without external assistance.

Although Clay's legal advisor ruled in August 1945 that JCS# 1067 had been superseded by the Potsdam agreement,[12] the fact that the directive's negative economic provisions thus had become inoperative was never explained to the general public. Accordingly, it is often overlooked that JCS# 1067 was de facto and de jure the exclusive controlling instrument of the American Military Government only from May 14 to August 2, 1945.[13] In a similar vein Clay's telegram to Washington in December 1945—". . . JCS# 1067 as modified by Potsdam has proved workable. I don't know how we could have set up our Military Government without it"[14]—has not received the attention it deserved.

The selection of an army engineer for the military governor's position was no coincidence. Roosevelt's first choice—so it seems—had been John J. McCloy. One day in the early spring of 1945, when visiting the White House, the latter had been greeted jovially by the president with the words, "Heil, Reichskommissar for Germany." Taken aback, McCloy had pointed out that he was not the right person for a job which in his judgment required a military man trained and experienced in disaster control. He recommended Lucius Clay, whom Roosevelt did not know, but who had distinguished himself as Justice Byrnes's deputy

11. Hammond, ibid., p. 372.
12. Memorandum, Charles Fahy, Legal Advisor, Hq. U.S. Group Control Council (Germany) to Assistant Deputy for Public Services, 9 August 1945.
13. Backer, *Priming . . .* , p. 27.
14. Memorandum, Milburn to all divisions. (OMGUS records, shipment 16.)

on the War Production Board as well as in the speedy clearance of the captured harbor of Cherbourg.[15] Clay's mission in Germany, as it soon turned out, indeed contained a number of responsibilities for which his training in the United States Corps of Engineers had prepared him well. Most of the heavily destroyed German cities were without water, gas, and electricity. Moreover, the war had wrought havoc with Germany's transportation system. Railroad bridges, marshaling yards, railroad stations, and tunnels had been priority targets for Allied bombers, and in the closing months of the war the scorched-earth tactics of the Nazi High Command had aimed to destroy whatever the bombers had left intact.[16] In addition, the north German harbors were filled with sunken ships and the Rhine was closed to navigation because of destroyed locks and bridges. These and other essentially tangible and physical problems such as the repatriation of millions of displaced persons and the resettlement of equally large numbers of refugees from the East could still be considered within the responsibilities of an army engineer. The organization of large-scale food imports, on the other hand, as well as the control of inflation, the revitalization of an extinct export industry, and the reestablishment of a German administration and government obviously exceeded the customary experiences of any military man.

By July 1945 the Military Government had succeeded in having three-fourths of the railroad tracks in the American Zone in operation, although railroad facilities were limited by single-track bridges and had to be used primarily for military traffic, as well as for the return of millions of displaced persons to their homelands.[17] A year later the Rhine was opened to navigation throughout its entire length and considerable progress had been made in repairing the ports.[18] In a similar fashion the revival of the German government-operated communications system was expedited by the work of a small group of American professionals, with the result that three months after the surrender post offices in the American and British zones were functioning normally.[19] The food situation, however, presented an infinitely more difficult problem.

Early surveys of available food supplies had revealed that only 950 calories per day could be distributed to the average nonself-supplier. Since this allowance also encompassed priority categories such as heavy laborers entitled to larger rations, only 720 calories were available for

15. As told to the present writer by John J. McCloy.
16. Clay, *Decision* . . . , pp. 188–190.
17. Ibid.   18. Ibid.
19. Ibid.

the so-called "normal consumer." This was less than half the amount which public health advisors of the Military Government considered an essential minimum for the maintenance of a working population. Even pessimistic forecasts by agricultural experts had not foreseen such a disastrous emergency.

The experts had been aware of Germany's dependence on food imports, but they had not foreseen the great exhaustion of the country's national economy after five years of war. Nor could they have anticipated the emergency conditions created by the separation of the eastern provinces and the influx of seven million refugees from the East. During the years 1933–1937 the area east of the Oder-Neisse line, although it contained only 14 percent of the population, actually produced 25 percent of Germany's food output. Approximately one million tons of breadgrains, a little less than one million tons of potatoes, and 400,000 tons of sugar annually came from the regions which at the war's end became the Soviet Zone of Germany and the area east of the Oder-Neisse rivers annexed by Poland. In addition annual imports from abroad in the American and British Zones had averaged 700,000 tons of breadgrains, 1.2 million tons of food grains, 1.5 million tons of oil seed and large quantities of foods such as fruit, vegetables, rice, chocolate, and coffee.[20] In other words, the loss of the breadbasket provinces of East Germany in addition to the increase of the West German population by more than 20 percent created a food crisis of such magnitude that the Western Allies were hard pressed to cope with it.

It is indicative of the American realistic approach to the negative policies emanating from the highest Washington quarters that SHAEF had prepared for the contingency of feeding the Germans and had brought along 600,000 tons of grain in order to "prevent disease and unrest." While the SHAEF grain reserve was without doubt of decisive importance in helping the German people over the first year of occupation, the actual ration level maintained was an essential minimum acceptable only because of the emergency and because most German homes still had some hidden food reserves. The crucial question for the Military Government therefore was, Where do we go from here?

No problems of policy had to be considered, but two bottlenecks of cardinal significance—a world food crisis and the question of funding —were responsible for the fact that Germans often received less food than they needed during the first years of the occupation. When it be-

20. Hoover Report, "Food and Agriculture U.S.–U.K. Zone of Germany," February 1947, p. 9.

came clear that economic aid for the occupied areas would be required on a large scale and over many years, a special program, Government Aid and Relief in Occupied Areas (GARIOA), was set up and included in the War Department's budget. At the end of an expensive war Congress was in no spending mood, but as previously in the case of lend-lease the "logic of the situation" was compelling. For those in Congress who expressed some doubt, the War Department had a ready answer: "If you don't feed, you'll have disease and unrest; so you have to send more troops—but troops we don't have!" [21] And when a congressman, still unconvinced, inquired what would happen if the requested appropriations were not forthcoming, Howard Peterson, the assistant secretary of war, replied that "the first thing would be to reduce the German food ration to 900 calories per day and the second, to take our troops out." Whereupon the questioner unhappily remarked: "Then somebody else might move in." [22]

In conclusion then, Congress was obliged to provide the funds for keeping the German population alive. On the other hand, in the summer of 1946, the American people were not ready to go beyond this point. When William Draper, Clay's economic advisor, suggested adoption of the sensible business practice for companies in temporary distress—the provision of funds to crank up the German export industry —the proposal was rejected out of hand.[23] As subsequent developments demonstrated, had Draper's advice been followed, in conjunction with an early currency reform, the German recovery would have been expedited by about twenty-four months; moreover, after one or two fallow years, the German economy would have been able to provide the contested reparations from current production, thus removing the roadblock which eventually led to the country's partition. However, with the memory of Hitler's misdeeds still very much alive, the American Congress was in no mood to go any further, and the specious thesis, "The American taxpayer did it once—he is not going to do it again," was used as a comfortable alibi. When Congress inquired about the likely duration of the unpopular feeding program, General Eisenhower replied: "When we can get out will depend upon when we reach the point where we can treat the country as an economic unit and the local government in Germany as one which is responsible . . . and against

21. 80th Congress, 1st sess., House. Hearings on *First Deficiency Appropriations Bill 1947,* p. 693.
22. Ibid., p. 744.   23. Clay, *Decision* . . . , p. 196.

the type of thing they had under Hitler." [24] Half a year later—in view of the Bizonal Merger—the War Department was more specific and submitted to an impatient and critical Congress an estimate of gradually increasing exports and a small export surplus by 1950.[25]

This estimate summed up a fundamental aspect of General Clay's mission: the American Zone was to be made self-supporting and the responsibilities were to be turned over as quickly as possible to a German democratic government. Because of the prevailing climate, however, this plan had to be carried out the hard way; beyond foodstuffs no supplies from abroad would be forthcoming and Germany would have to be pulled up by its own bootstraps. Accordingly German imports were divided into two groups: category A, or imports, encompassing food, fertilizers, and petroleum paid from appropriated funds, and category B, or industrial raw materials, which had to be funded by proceeds from German exports. If one considers these constraints and the state of the German economy, it is not surprising that it took the Military Government more than two years to generate $200 million worth of exports and that the dramatic take-off point came only in the summer of 1948 with the unduly delayed currency reform.

A great deal has been written about the rapid acceleration of Germany's economic recovery and the years of stagnation which preceded it. In this regard it is significant that two aspects of a spectacular transformation have hardly come into focus: on one hand, the deceptive appearance of bombed-out German cities, which led to unduly pessimistic conclusions about the resilience of the German economy, and, on the other, the role of negative production incentives which were replaced by positive ones only by June 1948.

A shocked Walter Millis, when arriving in Berlin in 1945, compared the appearance of the city with the face of the moon. And another American observer referred to city blocks which "looked like unfinished airports . . . and endless rows of empty, burnt-out structural shells . . . which reached into the sky like twisted fingers of a leprous hand. . . ." [26] While these descriptions were valid, they failed to indicate that some components of an advanced industrial economy were still

24. 79th Congress, 2nd sess., House. Hearings on *Military Establishment Appropriations Bill for 1947*, p. 1125.
25. 80th Congress, 1st sess., House. Hearings on *First Deficiency Appropriations Bill 1947*, p. 703.
26. Hubert Meurer, "U.S. Military Government in Germany," p. 2.

intact below the surface appearance.[27] It was the strategic bombing survey, conducted by the United States Air Force during the closing days of the war, which brought out the astonishing fact that, in spite of constant bombing, German industry was able to operate at nearly full peacetime capacity until December 1944 and that only the destruction of the German transportation system in January 1945 was able to paralyze Germany's industry.[28] The survey also revealed that the German economy did not appear to have suffered from shortages of machine tools, general machinery, or even plant facilities except temporarily in a few isolated cases.[29] As to the effect of bomb damage on the civilian economy, no evidence was found that shortages of civilian goods ever reached a point where German authorities were forced to transfer resources from war production in order to prevent disintegration on the home front.[30] And the Air Force was obliged to conclude that the strain imposed on the economy through an air war might slow down or temporarily halt the process of expansion without causing an actual diminution of production in the vital industries.[31]

With regard to the debilitating effects on German productivity of negative incentives such as inflation and inadequate food rations, students of Russian history could have reminded military administrators of an "economic miracle" that had taken place twenty-five years earlier in Soviet Russia. In 1921, when the civil war and "war communism" had come to an end, the number of workers employed in Russia's industries was less than half of the prewar figure; the average productivity per worker had fallen to about 30 percent and the total industrial output of Russia to 14.5 percent. The Moscow worker's monthly wage in 1920 was sufficient to keep him alive for only eleven to thirteen days and the meager bread ration of one eighth of a pound for workers was issued only on alternate days. In October 1920 the purchasing power of the ruble was not more than 1 percent of what it had been in October 1917.[32]

The promulgation of the New Economic Policy in 1921 entailing a return to the market for broad sectors of the economy and two successive devaluations of the currency resulted in an industrial recovery to

27. The present writer gratefully acknowledges Professor Alexander Ehrlich's emphasis of this important point.
28. The U.S. Strategic Bombing Survey, "The Effects of Strategic Bombing on the German War Economy," p. 63.   29. Ibid., p. 8.
30. Ibid., p. 13.   31. Ibid., p. 11.
32. Maurice Dobb, *Soviet Economic Development since 1917*, pp. 98–160.

a level of about 25 percent of prewar production by 1922 and of about a third by 1923. Two years later industrial and agricultural production had reached the prewar level.[33] In other words, the key to a drastic increase of productivity in the Russian as well as in the German case had to be the reestablishment of positive incentives in lieu of the negative ones which had pushed farmers, workers, and entrepreneurs to the side lines, transforming them into disspirited observers of the economic scene.

In Germany the nefarious impact of inflation had become noticeable promptly with the collapse of the Third Reich; moreover, the still vivid, traumatic experiences of an earlier German generation had expedited the process, although the two inflations were not fully alike. In 1923 the German mark had been traded against other currencies on international and German markets, and although the dollar eventually was quoted at 4.2 trillion marks, it was always possible to establish an international price for the mark. In 1945, after the collapse of the Third Reich, on the other hand, there were no quotations for the Reichsmark on the international market and all trading of Reichmarks against foreign currencies had ceased.

Since the days of the runaway German inflation of 1925 most governments had mastered the techniques of monetary controls, and Dr. Hjalmar Schacht had perfected the art to a very fine degree. Although there had been a tenfold increase of currency in circulation since 1930 and an estimated concurrent growth of the public debt from 15 to 700 billion RM,[34] prices and wages in Nazi Germany had remained stable. This feat had been accomplished, on one hand, by rigid controls, and, on the other, by the rationing of all essentials at an adequate level, a policy that could be fully implemented as long as Germany held most of Europe in bondage. The draconic enforcement of economic laws by the Gestapo also played an important role. In short, there was little inclination to acquire additional supplies illegally, especially since the risks incurred by anyone involved in black-market transactions were extraordinarily high. When the American Military Government took over in Germany, it found an elaborate and carefully composed set of regulations which governed food collection, rationing, and pricing. Furthermore, in the words of one astute observer, the Allied administrators inherited "the deeply rooted discipline of the German masses and their

33. Ibid.
34. Colm-Dodge-Goldsmith Report, p. i.

fear of authority into which twelve years of Nazi terror had bludgeoned them." [35]

In the next three years, however, two interrelated developments brought about a gradual erosion of the wartime economic pattern and thereby produced a progressive economic paralysis. On the one hand, the American and British Military Governments were unable to maintain or implement the ration levels of the Nazi economy, and, on the other, as the Germans became acquainted with the ways and means of their democratic conquerors, their fear of authority gradually lessened until it came close to the vanishing point. Generated by steadily decreasing inhibitions and growing temptations, a new economic pattern developed. The German market became divided into two sectors, one in which entirely insufficient quantities of rationed goods were sold at official prices against the payment of Reichsmarks, and the other in which most products were available, provided that items of equal scarcity could be offered in exchange. In the second sector, the Reichsmark had been eliminated as a currency, although it was often used as a means of camouflage in order to give barter deals the appearance of legal transactions.

After World War I it had taken considerable time for the German people to grasp the significance of a runaway inflation so that the German middle class was wiped out for all practical purposes. By contrast, in 1945 the earlier lesson was well remembered and blue- and white-collar workers, merchants, and manufacturers knew precisely what to do in order to limit the dreaded impact of an obviously unavoidable currency reform. The general rule was to sell as little as possible against payment in the threatened currency and to seek protection in the acquisition of *Sachwerte,* i.e., real property. As far as the farmers were concerned, it meant to deliver at the official prices to the governmental authorities the minimum quantities they could get away with, while bartering the remainder against needed industrial supplies.[36] In the case of laborers and employees it meant working only the hours which were necessary to acquire funds to pay for rationed food, rent, and utilities at controlled prices. Additional time was used to forage on the black market, while care had to be taken to avoid undue exertion with the resulting caloric loss, which was difficult to replace. As far as dealers and manufacturers were concerned, the recipe was to resort to barter whenever possible and to hoard all commodities for the day when a

35. Gustav Stolper, *German Realities,* p. 96.
36. Backer, *Priming . . . ,* pp. 95–98.

new currency would be introduced. This then was the socioeconomic background of the effort of the Military Government to crank up the German export industry in order to make the country self-supporting.

There are few assignments for which a government agency would seem poorer equipped than the promotion of foreign trade. The necessary diligence, flexibility, ingenuity, and innovative zeal, so amply available in the business community, rarely is found in bureaucratic circles. Clay and his senior advisors were quite aware of this as they continued to stress that the job of revitalizing Germany's foreign trade should be returned to the hands of business as quickly as possible. For the first years of the occupation, however, the transition could not be made. Well into 1946 Germany had no regular mail service with other countries. Security considerations prevented contractual communications even as late as 1947. The same applied, of course, to contracts by telephone. When the occupying army's restrictions on business travel were lifted, no foreign currency was available to pay for trips abroad, and when foreign buyers tried to enter Germany, the absence of housing and feeding facilities precluded the granting of entry permits. Legislative restrictions such as the Trading with the Enemy Act complemented these obstacles. Understandably, during the first eighteen months of the occupation, the primary efforts of responsible officials had to be directed toward the removal of these impediments.

The key problem was the absence of a currency. Domestically the Reichsmark had lost most of its usefulness as a medium of exchange and was not quoted any longer on the international money markets. It seems odd and even ironic that, because of these conditions, an agency of the United States Government was obliged to assume the role of a Soviet-type ministry of foreign trade during the first postwar years, with complete operational responsibility for all aspects of exports and imports, including the arbitrary determination of export prices. In a Communist-controlled economy, market forces have little or no effect on prevailing price patterns, and the establishment of the cost factor becomes an object of governmental decisions. In a similar fashion, prior to the currency reform, OMGUS was obliged to determine its export prices unilaterally, as there was no definite relation between controlled domestic Reichsmark prices and those obtainable in foreign exchange on the world markets.

As indicated, in view of the tight controls and because of adequate supplies, German prices during the war had remained relatively stable; actually during the long period from 1936 to 1944 the index of German wholesale prices rose by only 13 percent and the cost-of-living index increased by 14 percent.[37] After the German surrender Allied policies aimed at the maintenance of existing price levels.[38] However, since the two main factors of wartime price stability, i.e., adequate supplies and draconian controls, no longer existed, a gradual thaw of the frozen prices set in, with the result that prices for consumer goods during the period May 1945 to July 1947 rose by 97 percent while the price increase for industrial raw materials was held to 22 percent.[39]

The isolation of German prices from the influence of world markets over a period of years had been brought about not only by price policies but also by extensive governmental subsidies and a very complex system of foreign-exchange controls. Accordingly, OMGUS was faced with the problem of establishing sale prices in foreign currency abroad and of deciding on the Reichsmark prices to be paid to the German exporter. After scrutinizing the former pattern of German export prices at a time when the objectives of German export policy under the Third Reich no longer applied, OMGUS decided that all future Reichsmark payments to German exporters would be based on the controlled internal price. In other words, since German exporters would continue to be paid in Reichsmarks, the actual sale price abroad was immaterial to them.

The second part of the problem, namely, the establishment of an international exchange medium and the determination of export prices in foreign currency, was far more difficult to solve. As one would expect, barter proposals were made, but there were reasons which precluded this route. Imports had to be confined initially to essentials in order to keep the German people alive, and most of the items offered in exchange for German industrial products were low on the priority list. Moreover, the economic tradition of the United States militated against any form of bilateral barter. The eventually chosen method, billing in readily convertible dollars, was an emergency solution; and it was severely and continuously challenged by European governments until the currency reform in the summer of 1948 disposed of the problem. The highly complex and difficult task of determining dollar export prices by governmental fiat has already been discussed by the writer in considerable detail.[40] Two additional obstacles impeded an early re-

---

37. Burton H. Klein, *Germany's Economic Preparations for War*, p. 154.
38. OMGUS, *Trade and Commerce*, March 1946, p. 12.
39. Ibid., August–September 1947, pp. 7–8.
40. Backer, *Priming . . .* , pp. 90–156.

vival of German exports: German industrialists were not interested in sales and European buyers were reluctant to buy German goods. As to the former, the expected currency reform made it advisable to hold on to *Sachwerte* and to reject additional Reichsmark holdings. As to the latter, the memory of the Nazi occupation was still very much alive. In other words, the small Export-Import Section [41] in Berlin with a staff of about fifty, in addition to solving problems of logistics and pricing, was given the responsibility of convincing Germans to sell and other countries to buy. It is less surprising that under these conditions export proceeds were small than that any transactions could be completed at all.

At the time of Potsdam it had been expected that a centralized German administration would be quickly organized and that Germany's economic unity would be restored. Twelve months later only the rudiments of a German administration had been established in the American Zone and—as will be shown below—French and Russian resistance had blocked the pooling of economic resources. Inasmuch as Congress could not be expected to finance the trade deficit indefinitely, an economic unification of the British and American zones presented at least a partial and interim solution of the economic problem. The British Zone had the industrial potential to make the area self-supporting eventually, but it was weak in agricultural production. Moreover, the financial situation of the occupying power made it highly questionable whether the dollar subsidies required for an interim period of several years actually could be made available. The American Zone, on the other hand, had more agriculture but much less industry, and the prospect of a deficit in the balance of trade for many years to come. The economic merger of the two zones could hardly be regarded as a panacea. It will be shown that General Clay was more apprehensive of the fateful and far-reaching consequences of a bizonal solution than the political leaders of his country. One can therefore conclude that his recommendation to merge was prompted by the need to move off dead center and to bring an impossible assignment to an end.

As a preparatory move toward Bizonia and in recognition that the established export procedure under OMGUS was highly unsatisfactory, Clay ordered the delegation of certain procedural authorities to the Military Government offices in the *Länder*. Accordingly, even before the bizonal merger, and the establishment of a Joint Export-Import

41. It was headed by Roy J. Bullock from Johns Hopkins University.

Agency (US/UK), the Export-Import Section of OMGUS was dissolved and part of its staff transferred to the field. The results of the decentralization were beneficial because branch offices were authorized to license most export transactions without any further reference to higher headquarters. Furthermore, since nontransactional mail between German exporters and foreign buyers had been approved somewhat earlier, direct contacts between German and foreign firms again had become possible. Although the new procedures still had onerous bureaucratic aspects, they probably were the best that could be adopted under the prevailing conditions and represented an important step toward the elimination of the countless obstacles obstructing German export trade.

When General Clay surveyed the economic and political scene in his area of responsibility at the end of 1946, he could conclude that the army had fulfilled the essentials of its mission. The German transportation and communication system had been restored; millions of displaced persons had been returned to their homelands; a system of food subsidies through imports had been organized; in the individual states democratically elected governments were in control; and responsibility for denazification had been turned over to German authorities. The 1946 balance of trade for the American Zone was much less impressive, with $28 million of exports against imports of almost $300 million for food, fertilizer, and seed. Even so, the underbrush had been cleared and with the bizonal unification in the offing, the road to a full recovery seemed open. The remaining problems, such as a currency reform, the establishment of centralized German agencies, and the economic unification of Germany, would have to be negotiated at the governmental level—essentially a diplomatic task. As Clay saw it, the time had come for the State Department to take over, but in spite of his emphatic plea the proposal was not accepted.[42] For three more years the army was to remain in charge.

42. Clay, *Decision* . . . , p. 83.

CHAPTER NINE

A CONVENIENT LEGEND

The United States should press vigorously and persistently for the unification of Germany. A split of Germany would gravely endanger both the stability and prosperity of Europe and the country that sponsored it would incur the permanent enmity of the entire German national community. If there ever should be such a split, it must be clear to the whole world that it was in spite of United States policy and not because of it.[1]

Among the four members of the Allied Control Council in Berlin, Marshal Georgi K. Zhukov was the only one able to cope from the very first days of the occupation with the most insidious aspect of the Reichsmark overhang—economic paralysis. Whereas in the three Western zones only the bank balances of leading National Socialists and Nazi institutions were frozen, the Soviets promptly ordered all banks closed and all deposits blocked. Subsequently municipal savings banks and agricultural credit cooperatives were reopened, but only payments of RM 300 were permitted to depositors whose total account did not exceed RM 3,000; depositors with more than that amount were considered undeserving capitalists and received no funds.[2] In the second year of the occupation a partial unblocking was authorized by the Soviet Military Government for individuals who were unable to work and who had no other means of support; they were permitted to draw RM 400 even if their accounts exceeded RM 3,000. All financial claims and liabilities of financial institutions were voided, along with the Reich's debt, which served as their main backing.[3] The private banking system

1. Report of the Secretary's Policy Committee on Germany, 15 September 1946, p. 17 (National Archives, State Department Files, Records Group 43, Records of Council of Foreign Ministers).
2. Hans A. Adler, "The Postwar Reorganization," p. 333.
3. Manuel Gottlieb, *The German Peace Settlement and the Berlin Crisis*, p. 58.

was replaced by five big state banks, which took over the available assets of the former without any consideration of existing liabilities.[4] As a result of these ruthless measures, the economy in the Soviet Zone was drained of nearly four-fifths of its monetary assets;[5] and while this action was compensated in part by the issuance of Moscow-printed occupation currency, the purchasing power of the German people was nevertheless drastically reduced, inflationary pressures eased, and work incentives reestablished. Naturally no similar action could be taken in the Western zones where the democratic principles governing military policies required the enactment of a comprehensive currency reform in order to create eventually the necessary incentives for production.

The need for an early elimination of the monetary overhang was equally obvious to officials in the West. However, as a former member of the American Finance Division's delegation to the Control Council wrote, on the French side there was a predisposition to oppose all measures which tended to centralization.[6] Moreover, an early reform would have impeded French exploitation of German resources and production for their purposes. As far as the British were concerned, orthodox Treasury views prevailed; they not only included the explicit desire to protect the existing banking system but also entailed a recognition of the Reich's debt as well as provisions for its service.[7] It is also understandable that in view of the ambivalent nature of American postwar policies General Clay was in no particular hurry to tackle the difficult and controversial currency issue. It was one thing to utilize the "disease and unrest" clause when disregarding prescribed restrictions on production, but quite another to initiate a thorough and salubrious overhaul of the German economy.

Nevertheless, by March 1946 the decision was reached to invite a group of economic experts to study the problem and arrive at appropriate recommendations. The resulting "Plan for the Liquidation of War Finance and the Financial Rehabilitation of Germany" was the work of Gerhard Colm, Joseph M. Dodge, and Raymond W. Goldsmith; prepared with the assistance of a small staff, it was submitted to General Clay on May 20, 1946. In the eight intervening weeks, the American economists talked to British, Soviet, and French members of the quadripartite Finance Directorate, made trips through all four zones, met with

4. Adler, "Postwar Reorganization," p. 333.
5. Gottlieb, *German Peace Settlement* . . . , p. 58.
6. Manuel Gottlieb, "Failure of Quadripartite Monetary Reform 1945–47," p. 399.
7. Ibid., p. 402.

German tax officials, bankers, industrialists, and academic experts, and presented an outline of their recommendations to a special meeting of the *Länderrat* in Stuttgart.

Their recommendations proceeded from the premise that Germany faced the danger of the repudiation of the Reichsmark by its own people and of disintegration into a number of localized barter economies. The principal cause was of course a tenfold increase of currency in circulation since 1935, a fivefold increase in bank deposits, and a twenty-sevenfold growth of the Reich's debt, excluding war damages and other claims. Although a prompt currency reform would not be able to remove all the obstacles which stood in the way of a rapid increase in industrial and agricultural production, it would at least "draw away a confusing veil of money" and reintroduce a firm accounting basis for the recovery of the German economy.

The report also discussed an alternative approach, namely, to postpone reform until a higher level of production was reached.

While recognizing that there was some advantage in such a postponement, Colm and his associates concluded, however, that the risk of a continued erosion of confidence in the Reichsmark, accompanied by further deterioration of worker and business morale, would outweigh all other considerations. As the report correctly predicted, the real danger was not a sudden collapse of the economy but a creeping paralysis. The reform was needed not only to support price controls, which were so far quite effective, but also to protect production and to prevent economic chaos. Wages could be held only as long as the Reichsmark would buy at least a minimum of food and other necessities. If a substantive amount of production was going to be diverted from regular channels of supply, the whole body economic would be endangered. Inflation controls become illusory, the report said, when services are no longer rendered and goods no longer sold for official prices. The very imminent danger in Germany was not that inflation controls would break down but that they would become meaningless. An increasing part of total output was going into the black market, where prices often were fifty to several hundred times greater than official prices. Accordingly purchases could hardly be made out of current earned income but only out of money hoarded or from the sale of property or from black-market profits. The general knowledge that a worker could collect a day's wage by selling just one cigarette in the black market was bound to affect his willingness to work. The expanding barter trade was quantitatively more important than cash sales at black-market prices. Barter was bound to become a threat to the economy when workers stayed away from their jobs in order to obtain food by trading with farmers. This was happening on a large and growing scale. In many parts of the Western zones, the primary motive for working was not the need to meet living expenses but simply the desire to obtain a ration card. As a result there was a labor scarcity in spite of the fact that productive employment was at a low level. In a similar way businessmen's incentive to sell was greatly affected by abundant funds and the lack of confidence in the currency: "To sell as little as possible has become today's art of business." The German people believed that the situation simply could not continue as it was, and this fact alone was bound to prevent an economic recovery.

In accordance with these conclusions, the reports recommended converting the old currency by issuing one Deutschmark for every ten Reichsmarks. This rate would apply not only to notes, but to all bank deposits, private debts, and mortgage and other money obligations, including those of local governments. The Reich debt was to be invalidated, but since this would bankrupt all banks, insurance companies, and charitable organizations, they were to receive sufficient amounts of a new German governmental debt in order to be able to meet their reduced obligations. Prices, wages, salaries, and taxes were to remain unchanged; they would be paid in the same amounts in Deutschmarks as they would have been paid in Reichsmarks. In other words, all existing balances of money would be reduced to one-tenth of their original purchasing power. Furthermore, a 50 percent mortgage would be imposed on all physical assets, including real estate, plants, and stocks, in order to reduce the disparity in sacrifice imposed on holders of monetary claims and owners of real assets. The final recommended step was a progressive capital levy on individuals' net worth in order to extract greater contributions from the more affluent Germans in accordance with their respective financial capabilities. The three economists envisaged a levy ranging from 10 to 90 percent, to be paid in installments over a period of ten years. The proceeds of the mortgage and of a capital levy would be vested in a War Losses Equalization Fund, to be administered by a German bank for the whole of Germany. As to the value of the new currency, a rate of approximately twenty-five cents for the new Deutschmark was suggested, "in order to enable Germany to compete in the world markets without giving her an undue advantage over the competitors." The first part of the plan was to be implemented in the fall of 1946, with the mortgaging of all real assets to be accomplished a year later and the capital levy two years later. By 1949 the currency reform was to be completed.

The Colm-Dodge-Goldsmith report was promptly forwarded to Washington, where it was scrutinized by the Departments of War, State, and Treasury. Simultaneously copies were sent to the Allied members of the Finance Directorate in Berlin.[8] As it soon turned out, the plan's principal virtue—its comprehensiveness—negatively affected its political fortunes. Colm and his associates had recommended that a monetary reform be combined with the issuance of new notes. While the psychological advantages of this recommendation with regard to the German public were persuasive, the proposal entailed a delay of about a year, during which time the new currency had to be printed. Moreover, it caused an American-Soviet dispute regarding the location of a suitable printing plant, which will be discussed below. In a similar vein, the plan's provisions to couple a monetary reform with fundamental measures of property taxation and burden equalization (*Lastenausgleich*) tended to delay a quadripartite agreement.

In 1948, when the monetary reform in West Germany was finally enacted, a decision was also made to separate the equalization measures from the reform and to leave the relevant legislation to German authorities.[9] A similarly simplified reform in 1946 not only would have facilitated Clay's task to put his zone on a more self-supporting basis but it would also have had a positive effect on the reestablishment of Germany's economic unity. However, the scrutiny of the complex equalization program retarded Washington's concurrence as well as four-power negotiations. Moreover, by the fall of 1946 a bizonal solution began to move into the foreground with the result that the American interest in a quadripartite reform gradually waned. A provision of the bizonal fusion agreement of December 1946 indicated that financial reform should be effected at an early date and Generals Clay and Robertson were instructed to proceed with the printing of a bizonal currency so that in the event of a failure of the impending Council of Foreign Ministers meeting in Moscow a financial reform on a bizonal basis "could be introduced with a minimum of delay."[10] More will have to be said about this later.

As the C-D-G report had predicted, the postponement of the mone-

8. Clay, *Decision* . . . , p. 210. Major General Draper to K. I. Koval, Deputy for Economics to Soviet Commander in Chief, 17 June 1946 (OMGUS records, 148-3/3).   9. Clay, *Decision* . . . , p. 214.
10. U.S. Department of State, *Germany 1947–1949*, p. 452, as quoted in Gottlieb, "Failure . . ."

tary reform was accompanied by a continued economic paralysis in the West, with the embarrassing result that industrial output lagged considerably behind that of the Soviet Zone in spite of the much greater production potential.[11] One of the roots of the problem could be traced to agriculture, where collection agencies seemed unable to apply effective sanctions and farmers increasingly evaded delivery quotas. In contrast to their Soviet colleagues, American officials simply had no experience in the art of collecting foodstuffs in a hungry land. By the middle of 1947 General Clay consequently had to conclude that more than twice as much food had been imported as in the preceding year, without improving the ration. The amount of food collected by the German authorities, he discovered, was negligible.[12] The obvious cause of this development was a blossoming barter market which provided the otherwise unavailable supplies for the farmers. According to a German agricultural journal, definite exchange rates for barter transactions had actually developed: sixty nails, for instance, bought one pound of lard; one sack of twine was traded for twelve pounds of bacon; 100 kilograms of fertilizer for 200 kilograms of potatoes, and so on.[13]

On the industrial side a similar situation prevailed: mine workers soon learned that a week's work in the mines yielded just enough wages to buy a package of cigarettes and that it was better to work only two or three days. The rest of the week was more profitably spent by traveling to the countryside for extra food or by engaging in other black-market activities. It was therefore no wonder that all trains were overcrowded as people spent more time in searching for means of survival than in working. In the Third Reich barter or compensation trading, as it was called, had been forbidden by a War Economic Ordinance of March 25, 1942.[14] This ruling was enforced without too much difficulty because there were adequate supplies. By contrast, the relevant policies of the American Military Government were contradictory and German enforcement measures inadequate. Some efforts were made to distinguish between "legal" and "illegal" barter, the latter pertaining to trade in rationed food. In general, though, the views of Clay's advisors regarding the impact of barter on the economy varied, with some taking the position that there was no point in legislating in this area. An

11. Gottlieb, *German Peace Settlement* . . . , p. 80.
12. Bipartite Board Minutes, BIB/M (47), 5, 13, 14, (48), 1, 3, 4, 6, as quoted in Gottlieb, ibid., p. 81.
13. Rheinische Landwirtschaftsverband, *Landwirtschaftliche Zeitung* 115, no. 1 (1948): 13.
14. *Reichsgesetzblatt*, Part 1 (26 March 1942).

attempted suppression of compensation trading was bound to affect production, it was argued, whereas legalization of barter would affect monetary controls.[15] One document even theorized that barter actually contributed to price stability and tended to neutralize much of the inflationary pressures.[16] In view of this legal twilight it was hardly surprising that the extent of barter transactions, as well as enforcement policies, varied from region to region. Moreover, there were at least two United States Army–sponsored installations where barter transactions took place in an organized fashion, with the American part of the bargains consisting of food supplies. According to an estimate of the Dusseldorf chamber of commerce, about half of all business transactions in 1947 took place outside regular business channels.[17] In the black market cigarettes took over the role of money because they fulfilled some of the prerequisites of a currency, such as durability, divisibility into small "denominations," transportability, and wide acceptance in Germany as well as abroad. The principal suppliers were of course the occupying forces, who had access to the post exchanges; their limited weekly rations, however, did not suffice, and when demand began to exceed supply, a veritable flood of cigarette shipments was organized through the mail with the help of willing exporters. At a market price of RM 1,500 for a carton of cigarettes [18] and a reconversion rate of one dollar for ten marks, small fortunes could be and were made in a hurry. During the initial phases of the occupation, administrative supervision was inadequate. Initially, troops were simply admonished to stay away from the black market; later currency-control books were introduced to prevent each soldier from converting back into dollars more marks than he had originally received as pay. However, enforcement was lax, and when in the summer of 1946 dollar instruments in the form of military scrip finally replaced the Allied marks, the American armed forces held $380 million worth of foreign currencies in excess of appropriated dollars. Of these $250 million were in marks, $75 million in yen, and the remainder in Austrian schillings and other currencies.[19] In other words, the resulting dollar deficit did not relate only to Germany but to all the areas where American troops had been deployed, and the sums of the individual holdings corresponded approximately to the size of the respective oc-

15. Backer, *Priming* . . . , p. 98.   16. Ibid.
17. Ibid.
18. Russell Hill, *The Struggle for Germany*, p. 37.
19. 80th Congress, 1st Sess., Senate. Hearings on *Occupation Currency Transactions*, p. 3.

cupation forces. Although the problem demonstrated a considerable degree of administrative mismanagement, it was fundamentally a minor one. The various areas involved would remain occupied, and there were numerous opportunities for the army's finance offices to utilize the excess foreign currencies and thus to set their dollar balances straight. However, in the case of the Allied occupation of Germany there were a number of special circumstances which not only supplied material for a sensational story but actually generated the fabrication of one of the minor devil's theories of history. When the details of the embarrassing dollar shortage became known, public attention was attracted to the fact that the Soviet government had issued identical occupation currency, that the only difference between the notes was a small dash preceding the serial number, and that this printing had been made possible by a United States Treasury–authorized delivery of duplicate printing sets to the Russians. Soviet troops, not paid during combat, had received their back pay in occupation currency, which, moreover, was not exchangeable into rubles. This circumstance, as well as the alleged sympathies of key Treasury officials for the USSR, added some more dramatic twists. By the winter of 1946—the time when the story broke —the bizonal solution was about to become a reality. Since it required a separate currency, the myth of a Communist conspiracy was a convenient device to demonstrate that the split of Germany was going to occur in spite of and not because of American policies. Moreover, Roosevelt's friendly policies toward the Soviet Union had come under sufficient public criticism to provide receptive audiences for a story which tied the printing plates in Moscow to the excess foreign currencies in the coffers of the United States Army.

The supposed link was widely accepted, with the result that an aroused public opinion prompted an early investigation by a Republican-dominated United States Senate. In June 1947, after two days of listening to sworn testimonies and examining stacks of official documents, the Senate Committees on Appropriations, Armed Services, and Banking and Currency were able to dispose of the intriguing myth. Nevertheless the legend of the Communist plot will be found in history texts even today.

At the opening session of the joint committees on June 17 the chairman, Senator Styles Bridges from New Hampshire, announced the principal purposes of the hearings, namely, the examination of the methods employed by the federal government in the field of occupation currency, an investigation of the circumstances which surrounded the turning over of the engraving plates to Russia, and a scrutiny of the reasons why there had been no agreement with the Soviet government limiting the amount of German marks to be issued. The senator then set the tone for the hearings by referring to the American tax-payers, "who recently were refused a tax reduction and who undoubtedly would be extremely interested in whether a large sum of their tax dollars were used to furnish a free ride to the Russians via printing press money of our own devising." [20]

The hearings soon brought out the fact that the decision to print military occupation currencies similar to the local ones was based on unsatisfactory experiences in North Africa, where gold seal dollars had been used.[21] On one hand, one of the witnesses said, there was the need to keep dollars from the enemy and the risk that a large number of men and amounts of money might fall into enemy hands in the course of major military operations. On the other, there was the danger that the use of dollars would foster a lack of confidence in the local currency and eventually even cause a breakdown in the economic life of the occupied country. As to the excess holdings of foreign currency, it was pointed out that at their maximum in the fall of 1946 they had totaled $380 million. In the meantime about 60 percent of the holdings had been liquidated by paying the wages of prisoners of war and of foreign United States Army auxiliaries in Germany; this had resulted in a reduction of total foreign currency holdings to the equivalent of $160 million, which included RM 100 million and 60 million yen. Plans for the liquidation of the remaining balance had been approved and would be implemented within eighteen months.[22]

As Howard E. Petersen, the assistant secretary of war, explained, the American armed forces, through the operation of their finance offices overseas, necessarily had been engaged in large-scale foreign exchange operations which involved the handling of over $11 billion. Under combat and redeployment conditions, currency controls had been entirely adequate, although, as he admitted, they had proved unsatisfactory once hostilities had come to an end. Subsequently, in the summer of 1946, the issuance of military payment certificates in Japan and Germany had resolved the problem.[23] With regard to the turning over of engraving plates to the Soviet government, Petersen said that both the United States and British Governments had desired that the Soviet Union and the Allied Expeditionary Force should use the same

20. Ibid., p. 2.
22. Ibid., pp. 8, 9, 12, 110.
21. Ibid., p. 115.
23. Ibid., p. 3.

Allied military currency as part of the plan to treat Germany as an economic whole; and he added that "to agree to the Russians using a different currency would have constituted an agreement in advance to what unfortunately happened—the division of Germany into four airtight compartments." With regard to the actual decision to turn over the plates, Petersen indicated that it was made in April 1944 and he suggested that representatives of the State and Treasury Departments who were responsible for this action would have to explain how it had come about.[24]

Actually it was a former War Department official, General John H. Hilldring, who provided important information in this regard. Having been personally involved in the issue, he reminded the committee of the atmosphere which existed at the time the decision was made. Eisenhower was still in England and preparing for an invasion. At that time the Soviet forces had broken loose from Stalingrad, had entered the eastern parts of Poland, and had cleared Odessa. "It would have been an exceedingly difficult thing in the light of these conditions," he said, "for any responsible official of this government to have decided then that we would have two Germanys and not one by saying to the Russians: you cannot have these plates, you must print your own kind of invasion currency in the part of Germany that you occupy."[25] Hilldring might have added that the United States had had to go back repeatedly on its promise to establish a second front, that the commitment to invade in the spring of 1944 was contingent on a Soviet promise to continue to engage the German army to an extent which would "make it impossible to transfer [from the Eastern front] more than 15 first quality divisions during the first two months"[26] and that even under these conditions the outcome of the landings—as Omaha Beach later demonstrated—was by no means a sure thing. Against this background a refusal of the Soviet request had to be weighed.

In reply to a question by a senator, Hilldring testified that the Soviet government had been adamant in its rejection of the Treasury's proposal to supply the notes instead of the plates; the Soviet ambassador had made it very clear that the Russians would print their own occupation currency rather than accept notes.[27] Under these circumstances, Hilldring said, "the first decision that the American government could not agree with its partners to get along in the solution of the problems

24. Ibid., p. 17.
26. Deane, *Strange Alliance*, p. 19.
25. Ibid., pp. 118–119.
27. *Currency Transactions*, p. 119.

of Germany would have been made by the United States." [28] He remarked that it seemed not unreasonable for a chief of state to say, "I want to have under my own control the means necessary for my armies to achieve the military objective of a campaign." A determined effort had nevertheless been made to convince the Soviets that the better way to do the job was to let the American government print the money and transport it, but it remained unsuccessful.

Hilldring and other witnesses made it clear that the actual decision to surrender the plates had been primarily the responsibility of the Departments of State and of the Treasury. Relevant testimony and documents submitted on this occasion provided an illuminating picture of bureaucratic buck passing. It appears that preliminary discussions with representatives of the Soviet government regarding the use of a common occupation currency were held in January 1944. On January 29 the American Embassy in Moscow had informed Washington in this regard that the British government attached great importance to the Russian government's participation in such an arrangement.[29] In its reply of February 8 the State Department pointed out that the printing of the currency would start on February 14, and that the production of sufficient currency to take care of Soviet requirements "if desired" was being contemplated. "The Department was very anxious to ascertain whether the Soviet government expected to use this currency, and in the negative, what type of currency would be used." [30] In spite of this deadline, the American Embassy was able to advise the department only on February 15 that a Soviet note had asked for proposals about the contemplated exchange rate while indicating a desire to collaborate in the issuance of military currency in Germany; "in preparing the currency," the Soviet note said, "it would be more correct to print a part of it in the Soviet Union in order that a constant supply of currency may be guaranteed to the Red Army." Accordingly, "it will be necessary to furnish the Commissariat for Finance with plates of all denominations, a list of serial numbers . . . ," and so on.[31] Obviously cognizant that it had a hot potato on its hands, the State Department forwarded a paraphrased copy of the Moscow telegram to General Hilldring with the suggestion that it be brought to the attention of the Treasury.[32] "The Department would however like to be consulted before any decision is taken respecting the exchange

28. Ibid.
30. Ibid., p. 147.
32. Ibid., p. 149.

29. Ibid., pp. 146–147.
31. Ibid., p. 148.

rate for military currency and its relationship to the Reichsmark," the letter of transmission said. With traditional bureaucratic caution no reference was made to the key issue of the telegram—the question of the plates.

Hilldring promptly called a meeting of an ad hoc Committee on Monetary and Financial Planning in the course of which the representative of the Treasury merely remarked that his Department had "never before allowed use of its plates by others." [33] As it turned out, the principal resistance to the surrender of the plates originated with Alvin W. Hall, who as director of the Bureau of Engraving and Printing was not only relatively low on the administrative totem pole but a permanent civil service employee sufficiently immune to political pressures. In his first communication on the subject addressed on March 3 to Under Secretary D. W. Bell, Hall mentioned the inviolable custom of bank-note manufacturers to retain in their possession all plates; and since part of the printing had to be done by a private contractor, the Forbes Company in Boston, he added that in his judgment "under no circumstances would the contractor agree to the manufacture of duplicate plates to be printed by any agency outside of his plant." He doubted that the Treasury could force him to do so.[34] The memorandum was sufficiently emphatic to produce in the under secretary and secretary an equally negative reaction,[35] although the State Department's concurrence was considered desirable.[36] A drafted negative reply to the American ambassador in Moscow was not sent but a Morgenthau-Gromyko meeting arranged instead. Incredible as it may sound for a country at war, the secretary on this occasion rested the case of his government entirely on the refusal of a private company, which "insisted that it could not go on with the contract." [37] In lieu of the plates an ample supply of the actual currency was offered. The meeting was followed by several inconclusive conversations with the Soviet ambassador [38] and an instruction to Hall to come up with another memorandum outlining once more his objections. This paper [39] was taken by Harry Dexter White, one of Morgenthau's closest advisors, to another meeting with Gromyko, who must have had difficulty not showing derision at the suggestion that a private contractor in a country at war could obstruct an important decision of his government. Gromyko's

33. Ibid., p. 228.
35. Ibid., p. 179.
37. Ibid.
39. Ibid., pp. 180–181.

34. Ibid., pp. 175–177.
36. Ibid., pp. 179–180.
38. Ibid., p. 182.

question whether the American government was ready to propose that the Soviet government print German marks of its own design brought forth the evasive reply that "such was not necessarily the view of our government but merely an expression of the possibility. . . ." [40] The resistance of the Forbes Company to the release of the plates, however, enabled the Treasury to buck the issue to Admiral Leahy at the Combined Chiefs of Staff; he was informed that in view of the expected refusal of the contractor to cooperate, sufficient quantities of military currency could not be made available for the impending invasion.[41] Copies of this communication were sent to the State Department and the American Embassy in Moscow.

The Combined Chiefs of Staff were apparently in no hurry to pull the Treasury's chestnuts out of the fire, and by April 8, when the Kremlin's final reply reached the Moscow Embassy, no decision on the part of the military had been reached. The Soviet note was quite specific: if there were no plates, the Soviet government would proceed with the independent preparation of military marks for Germany.[42] In the meantime Morgenthau's letter of March 22 to Admiral Leahy had been passed back and forth between the Combined Civil Affairs Committee and the Combined Chiefs of Staff [43] with the result that by April 12 a reply to the Treasury was ready, indicating that the question of availability and nonavailability of plates for the Russians "was not one that should be settled on military grounds." It was entirely a political decision, but "whatever decision was taken must be made in such a way as not to affect our military relations with the Soviet Union." [44] Expressed more plainly the reply meant: it is your decision, but beware —if it affects our military operations, you will be responsible.

The following day at a meeting of the Combined Civil Affairs Committee, General Macready could announce that the proposed letter from Admiral Leahy to the secretary of the treasury had been cleared by the Combined Chiefs of Staff. And he added—probably with relief— that "the action took the matter out of the hands of the military and returned it to the State Department, the Foreign Office and the two Treasuries where it rightfully belonged, since the considerations were political and technical." [45] The crucial paragraph of the letter—it was actually signed by General Marshall—read as follows:

40. Ibid., pp. 183–184.
41. Ibid., pp. 182–183.
42. Ibid., p. 151.
43. Ibid., p. 184.
44. Ibid., pp. 184–185.
45. Ibid., p. 46.

It is the opinion of the Combined Chiefs of Staff that present commitment of furnishing Allied military marks to the Supreme Commander Allied Expeditionary Force, should be met. It is understood that under present schedules these commitments will be fulfilled by May 1, 1944. If the United States Treasury and the State Department, in conjunction with the Foreign Office and the British Treasury decide to furnish duplicate plates to the Soviet Government, it appears that this action could be taken any time after May 1, 1944 without interference with General Eisenhower's requirements for Allied military marks currency.[46]

The following day Secretary Morgenthau, after obtaining the State Department's concurrence, informed the Soviet ambassador that the United States would supply the requested plates.[47] As common sense would have suggested all along, the threatened resistance by the Boston contractor failed to materialize as soon as the seizure of his plant under the War Powers Act was taken into consideration. In other words, as the record indicates, the decision to surrender the plates was reached because *there was no agency of the United States Government which on the eve of a hazardous invasion would have been willing to shoulder the responsibility for a refusal.* Moreover, as compared to a lend-lease program for Russia entailing expenditures of about $11 billion, the economic risk of the duplicate plates—under any circumstances—was a minor one.

With regard to the suggested link between the Moscow-printed currency and the excess foreign currency holdings of the United States Army, General Hilldring's testimony was clear and explicit. According to the experiences of the American army in other countries, he said, the long position in mark currency would have occurred even if the Soviets had been unable to print their own Allied military marks with plates supplied by the United States government. Had this been the case, the Russian government would have printed a supplementary currency of Soviet design, and the United States, under its policy of treating Germany as an economic unit, would have been obliged to recognize such notes as legal tender in Germany.[48] Hilldring also remarked that in his opinion "the shipment of the plates had no material connection with the conversion of the marks in the hands of our troops nor to the long holding of our army. . . ." [49] When challenged on this

46. Ibid., p. 45.
48. Ibid., p. 128.

47. Ibid., pp. 152–153.
49. Ibid., p. 121.

point by the chairman, he explained that "contact between American and Soviet troops was confined to relatively small areas, whereas the excess marks came from all parts of the American Zone." The committee had briefly discussed the possibility of issuing subpoenas to Harry Dexter White and former Secretary Morgenthau,[50] but in view of the ample evidence already on hand, this action was apparently considered unnecessary. After only two days of hearings, the committee therefore adjourned.

Returning to the monetary negotiations in Berlin, the reader will recall that by December 1946 the possibility of a separate currency for the British and American Zones had come under consideration. During the preceding three months considerable headway had been made in the relevant quadripartite meetings of the Finance Directorate. As Manuel Gottlieb, one of the participants, wrote, "Within a few months an amazing body of agreement was registered utilizing the main elements of the C-D-G plan and modifying it briefly with respect to the mode and ratio of liquidating the monetary overhang . . . but then a snag was struck." [51] The Americans proposed that the printing facilities in Berlin should be used, whereas the Soviets suggested that the new notes be printed simultaneously in Leipzig. Both installations should be under identical quadripartite supervision. No agreement could be reached and the issue was unsuccessfully taken up at the Moscow Council of Foreign Ministers Conference. After its failure, quadripartite discussions of the reform were resumed in Berlin and since the French and British had accepted the Soviet proposal, Clay came forth with a compromise plan. It entailed an interim solution whereby the German state printing plant would be placed in an enclave under the Allied Kommandatura, which would proceed with the printing of a new currency without prejudice to the settlement of the question whether the German currency would be ultimately printed in two places.[52] The Russians objected, whereas the French and British indicated their willingness to accept either the American or the Soviet plan.[53] At this point the negotiations came to a temporary halt—possibly because a decision to print the new currency in the United States had been reached by the Department of State in the meantime.[54] On February 11, 1948, the Soviets, at last aware of what was at stake, relinquished their objections. An "eyes only" message from Clay to Draper casts a revealing light on

50. Ibid., p. 102.   51. Gottlieb, "Failure . . . ," p. 409.
52. *Foreign Relations . . . Council of Foreign Ministers, 1947,* 2: 879.
53. Ibid., p. 881.   54. Clay, *Decision . . . ,* p. 211.

the American resolve nevertheless to move ahead toward partition: "Yesterday Soviets agreed to printing of new currency in Berlin under quadripartite control and that establishment of central finance administration was not a condition to currency reform. We had to accept this proposal or else be forced into position before German people of making the next step toward partition without specific cause. Technical details, however, must be fully agreed within sixty days. Actually, if these details are not agreed, we will lose no time as we will proceed concurrently with Bizonal plans. . . ." [55] In other words, as the British representative at the Finance Directorate, S. P. Chambers, correctly concluded, "It would be wrong to assume that a technicality of this kind was all that separated the representatives of the four occupying powers. Behind this disagreement on the technicality lay fundamental differences in objectives." [56]

55. Jean Edward Smith, ed., The Papers of General Lucius D. Clay, Document 331, p. 561.
56. S. P. Chambers, "Post-War German Finances," p. 373.

Chapter Ten

The Division of Germany:
A Second-Level Analysis

It will be recalled that the Big Three had toyed with the idea of partitioning Germany even as late as Yalta and that the subject was dropped only after the victorious Allied armies executed a quadripartite division of the Reich. The reader may also recall that the Department of State opposed partition all along and cautioned that reunification unavoidably would become an emotional and explosive issue for nationalistic elements in a divided Germany. The Soviet government probably reached similar conclusions in the end, because on May 8, 1945, Stalin took the limelight and announced in a "Proclamation to the People" that the Soviet Union had no intention of dismembering or destroying Germany. Since most of East Germany was firmly in Russian hands and Roosevelt's comment about an early American withdrawal from Europe was still fresh in Stalin's mind, it would be surprising indeed had he not also thought of Lenin's reference to the German proletariat as "the most faithful and reliable ally of the Russian and world-wide proletarian revolution." Twenty-five years earlier the German workers had disappointed the Soviet leaders, but with history—according to the doctrine—on the Marxist side, the time might now be at hand to fulfill the expectations of the master.

A few months later, at Potsdam, the United States and Great Britain followed suit, although their endorsement of German unity was given with less fanfare and with primary emphasis on its economic ramifications. In other words, at least as far as rhetoric was concerned, German unity had become a tripartite goal. For the fourth partner in the occupation, on the other hand, this policy objective was unacceptable. Russia and the United States could rely on their respective strength by which they had defeated Germany to cope—in one way or another—with any resurgence of German power. Great Britain was willing to depend on Anglo-Saxon support from across the ocean, but France was not. Defeated twice and nearly defeated another time, it knew that as the neighbor of an undivided German Reich its role as an independent first-rate power would have come to an end. Furthermore, as one of the early protagonists of collective security and as a witness to its collapse, France could have no illusions about the concept's revival.

For more than a hundred years French foreign policy in Europe had been guided by two fundamental objectives: to establish the Rhine and the Alps as national borders and to prevent the emergence of a single predominant power on the Continent.[1] Clemenceau had remarked in 1919 that "the move towards the Rhine was the tradition of our ancestors. It was the tradition to create a frontier—a true frontier marking the French territory." And twenty-five years later, although speaking for a defeated country, de Gaulle had expressed an identical view: "The Rhine is French security and I think the security of the whole world. But France is the principal interested party. It wishes to be established from one end to the other of its natural frontier." As to the second aim of its foreign policy, France had actively contributed to the European balance of power by a system of alliances and counteralliances. Prior to 1914 a treaty with imperial Russia had served the purpose of keeping an expansionist Germany in line, and in 1919 France had utilized the breakup of the Austrian-Hungarian empire to form a *cordon sanitaire* of small states; it not only was meant to contain Soviet communism but also to prevent Germany from moving east. The occupation of the Rhineland, the envisaged permanent separation of the Saar, and a heavy reparations demand were additional means of preventing a resurgence of German power. French policy objectives as of 1944 were almost identical: a long occupation of the defeated country, the separation of the Rhineland and the Saar, the internalization of the Ruhr, heavy reparations, and a defensive treaty with the Soviet Union. It must be emphasized that these were not only the aims of the French Provisional Government and of the governments which followed prior to 1947, but they also carried the endorsement of all the political parties in France.[2]

Accordingly, as soon as his country was liberated, de Gaulle rushed to Moscow to negotiate a Treaty of Mutual Assistance in which the two nations agreed to "take all necessary measures in order to eliminate any new menace coming from Germany and to take the initiative

1. Roy C. Macridis, "French Foreign Policy," p. 67.
2. F. Roy Willis, *The French in Germany, 1945–1949*, pp. 36–41.

to make any new effort of aggression on its part impossible." Besides safeguarding the future security of France, the treaty also clearly served the purpose of putting the United States and Great Britain on notice that France was going to follow an independent foreign policy. It was guided by "an almost panicky fear"[3] of setting up a central German government which in de Gaulle's words "would inevitably fall into Russian hands. . . . France in no event would be a match for a revived Germany within the Russian orbit."[4]

A few days after the closing of the Potsdam conference the French foreign office consequently sent six letters to the ambassadors of the United States, Great Britain, and the Soviet Union which expressed its reservations with regard to the tripartite protocol.[5] Neither economic unity, nor a centralized German administration in Berlin, nor the readmissions of unified political parties were acceptable terms in the eyes of a government which was resolved to see Germany dismembered. A similar view was given to Truman in August 1945 by de Gaulle, who added the disquieting comment that Prussia had always been the motivating force of German imperialism and that under the influence of a powerful Slavic bloc it would be even more dangerous than in the past.[6] The same objections to the Potsdam Protocol were presented by the French delegation to the Council of Foreign Ministers in a memorandum of September 14, 1945, which also informed the Allies that France's representative at the Control Council in Berlin was being instructed not to authorize any measures contrary to the reservations expressed by his government.[7] France was the weakest member in the quadripartite administration of Germany, but its occupational policy was thus clearly prescribed: to present extensive economic and territorial demands, to be continuously difficult, and to make concessions only as the last resort. It was at the Military Government level that most of the struggle took place, and it was Lucius Clay who had to try to solve the resulting problems.

The long-range policy objectives of France had been lucidly stated and its short-range moves at the Control Council in Berlin provided the necessary obstructionist support. In a more general way the long-range policies of the Soviets and the Anglo-Americans were equally

3. *Foreign Relations . . . European Advisory Commission . . . 1945,* 3: 878.
4. Ibid., p. 879.
5. Ministère des Affaires Etrangères, *Documents français relatifs à l'Allemagne,* pp. 7–11.
6. *Foreign Relations . . . Europe, 1945,* 4: 709.
7. *Documents français,* pp. 17–19.

transparent. Their aim was to reconstruct a unified Germany as closely as possible in accordance with their respective social order. While the unifying term "democratic" was used at the conference table for convenience sake, the Kremlin, of course, wanted an antibourgeois and the United States an anti-Communist German society. The short-range policies of the two principal protagonists, on the other hand, were less firm than those of France, and on both sides a "wait-and-see" attitude seemed to prevail. There was, however, one extraneous factor which soon acquired crucial significance: the United States, because of its constitutional constraints, was in a hurry to cut the expenses of the military occupation. When de Gaulle visited the White House in August 1945 and discussed Europe's problems, as well as France's territorial demands, the American president, in addition to engaging in well-meaning generalities, had only one substantive comment to make: "The United States has no intention of financing German reparations as it had done after the last war." [8] Truman undoubtedly expressed the public view similar to the one which came to the fore in the course of the GARIOA hearings.[9] It was a point which an experienced public servant like Clay had very much on his mind and which more than any written directive guided his actions. Germany had to be made self-supporting in order to satisfy Congress and—it was hoped—to permit an American withdrawal.

The minutes of the Control Council reflected the resulting clash of interests. A formal American proposal on September 22, 1945, to establish a central German transportation administration was rejected by the French representative, General Koeltz, who briefly explained that "the French government has made its reservations through diplomatic channels." [10] To make certain that there could be no doubt about the French motives, General Koenig followed suit by explaining to the Control Council on October 1 that France was unable to concur with the establishment of centralized German agencies as long as the question of the future of Rhineland-Westphalia had not been settled.[11] Accordingly, Clay's renewed attempts on October 16 and November 23 to reopen the issue were equally unsuccessful.[12] On October 9, when the creation of a central Finance Agency was under discussion, France sent only an observer [13] and on December 17 it objected to an Ameri-

8. *Foreign Relations . . . Europe . . . 1945*, 4: 710.
9. See page 108.
10. Lucius Clay, *Decision . . .* , p. 110.
11. *Documents français*, p. 16.   12. Clay, *Decision . . .* , p. 110.
13. Gimbel, *American Occupation . . .* , p. 24.

can-British proposal to open all zonal boundaries to the passage of Germans.[14] Even a proposal to permit the federation of trade unions throughout Germany was rejected by General Koeltz with the explanation that "the objects of the administration in Germany will be the decentralization of political structure and the developing of local responsibilities. Thus trade unions are political structures and will be decentralized." [15] Whereas the French policy regarding decentralization was firm and consistent, the Soviets seemed more vascillating. On September 11 the Russian representative at the responsible quadripartite committee declared that his government did not consider the time ripe for setting up a central German administration for food and agriculture.[16] But on October 16 General Sokolovsky stated that "the Soviet delegation had always been of the opinion that German central agencies for transportation and communication should be created. It is about time, in my opinion, to start establishing these central German agencies." [17] On the other hand, when Clay reverted to the subject on November 24, after having obtained from Washington authority to proceed without France, the Russian representative declared that he was unable to negotiate such a separate agreement since the Potsdam decisions called for central organs for all four zones.[18] And it appears that even the British government occasionally was reluctant to support the American desire for speedy centralized action because, when on December 21, 1945, the United States suggested the prompt establishment of a quadripartite export-import bureau, the British representative replied that "the American plan was too far advanced for dealing with present day realities." [19]

Lucius Clay was not a man to take no for an answer, and having exhausted all suitable means at the Control Council level for the time being, he turned to Washington with a request to put pressure on the French government through diplomatic channels. His suggestion coincided with an identical one submitted to the president by Byron Price, who on Truman's request had visited Germany to survey "the general subject of relations between the American Forces of occupation and the German people." [20] When Clay, accompanied by Robert Murphy,

14. Clay, *Decision* . . . , p. 112.   15. Ibid., p. 110.
16. *Foreign Relations . . . European Advisory Commission . . . 1945*, 3: 868–869.
17. Clay, *Decision* . . . , p. 110.
18. *Foreign Relations . . . European Advisory Commission . . . 1945*, 3: 911.
19. Backer, *Priming* . . . , p. 109.
20. Memorandum, Byron Price to the president (OMGUS records 177-3/3).

his political advisor, visited Washington early in November, he used the occasion to emphasize—in contrast to the State Department's views— the primary French responsibility for the impasse in Berlin. His comment that Soviet representatives believed that the United States and Great Britain tacitly supported the French position was correct as far as the Russians at the Control Council in Berlin were concerned.[21] At the higher level of the Soviet Foreign Office, however, the recognition of United States concern over the uncertain stability of the French government was bound to lead to a more sophisticated analysis. As it turned out upon his return from Washington Clay had the opportunity to find some substance in the State Department's suspicion of the Kremlin when the Soviet representative reversed himself regarding the establishment of a centralized German transport administration.

In the closing months of 1945 the War Department, in accordance with recommendations by Clay and Byron Price, repeatedly approached the State Department with the request that "the full force and prestige of American diplomatic power be used to break French resistance."[22] The replies were somewhat dilatory, and Dean Acheson explained that it was necessary to wait for the outcome of quadripartite conversations regarding French proposals for the future of the Rhineland and the Ruhr.[23] John Gimbel's comment that "the State Department delayed, procrastinated, and resisted each time the army asked for diplomatic pressure and/or economic and political sanctions against France"[24] is supported by adequate evidence. However, as a glance at the political scene in France will show, there were very good and overriding reasons for the State Department's unwillingness to take drastic action.

In the first postwar elections in France five million Frenchmen had cast their votes for the French Communist party (PCF), thereby giving the Communists 161 seats in the parliament. As the largest party, the PCF actually might have been able to take over the government by legal means.[25] However, for the time being at least, Stalin had decided to cooperate with de Gaulle, and as usual the French Communist party obeyed. Even when de Gaulle ordered the dissolution of the armed

21. Memorandum, J. H. Hilldring to assistant secretary of war, 7 November 1945, with attached "Resume of Meeting at the State Department, 3 November 1945" (National Archives, ASW 370.8 Germany, Control Council).
22. *Foreign Relations . . . European Advisory Commission . . . 1945*, 3: 908–909.
23. Ibid., pp. 919–920.
24. John Gimbel, "U.S. Postwar German Policy," p. 253.
25. David Caute, *Communism and the French Intellectuals*, p. 161.

resistance units in which the Communists had played a leading role, Maurice Thorez, head of the PCF, endorsed the order. The PCF had five seats in de Gaulle's government, although it was denied the Ministries of the Interior and of Foreign Affairs. When de Gaulle resigned in January 1946, the American Embassy in Paris followed the ensuing crisis with great concern. It is not difficult to envisage the State Department's reactions to Ambassador Caffery's report of January 22, indicating the likelihood of a Communist-Socialist coalition with Thorez as president.[26] When eventually a tripartite cabinet under the moderate Socialist Felix Gouin emerged, a subsequent exchange of cables shows that Washington was most anxious to avoid rocking its weak foundations. Secretary Byrnes's instructions of February 1, 1946, to the Embassy on the subject of establishing central German agencies ended with the suggestion that when talking to Foreign Minister Bidault, Ambassador Caffery "might discreetly inject the thought that any steps which the French government may publicly take at this time in the way of cooperating with American aims should help to create a more favorable atmosphere for the impending economic and financial talks in Washington."[27] And when Caffery commented four weeks later on his fruitless conversations with Bidault, he assured the department that he would continue his efforts to bring about an evolution in French thinking but cautioned that a resignation by Bidault might cause a governmental crisis "on which the Communists would certainly capitalize." As he saw it, "it would be definitely unwise at this juncture to press this matter further."[28] To this the State Department replied that "the French should not be pressed to a point where there is real danger of Bidault's resignation and of a split in the coalition government which would have wide political ramifications in France."[29] To sum up, the American diplomatic effort in support of centralized German agencies collapsed in the face of a potential Communist take-over in Paris. That the Communist members of the French Cabinet had kept their bosses in Moscow duly informed of the American diplomatic moves can be considered a safe assumption.

There remained one more avenue of working toward unification. It entailed generating German support at the grass-roots level, and Clay

26. U.S. Department of State, *Foreign Relations of the United States . . . The British Commonwealth; Western and Central Europe, 1946*, 5: 403–404.
27. Ibid., p. 498.   28. Ibid., pp. 509–511.
29. Ibid., p. 511.

pursued this goal vigorously. The first German state administrations had been appointed by the Military Government; they were replaced by elected officials in June 1946. Eight months earlier Clay had set up a German agency, the *Länderrat,* with the mission to coordinate the former national administrative services which were beyond the responsibility of the individual states. The new council was located in Stuttgart and composed of the chief German officers of each of the three *Länder* (states) in the American Zone. Undoubtedly the failure to establish central agencies for all of Germany was the primary incentive for early action at the zonal level.[30] However, a number of additional factors also played a role. Some administrative responsibilities—for instance, the resettlement of vast numbers of refugees or the allocation and distribution of imported food—could be handled more efficiently through German than through American channels; it was desirable to have Germans with administrative training and experience available once the hoped-for centralized agencies became activated; the Länderrat of the American Zone could be expected to serve eventually as a model for a similar four-zonal organization; there was the practical consideration that American personnel expenditures ought to be cut quickly and drastically in order to please the legislators back home. (The goal to reduce the initial number of Americans in the Military Government from twelve thousand to five thousand was reached by December 1946. It is indicative of the respective national policies that the British still had a staff of twelve thousand in 1947, and the French Military Government, with a much smaller Zone to administer, had a staff of 8,000.) [31] And finally there was the hope that an active German participation on a zonal governmental level would have a spillover effect into the other parts of Germany, thereby creating indigenous pressures toward unification.

The *Länderrat* had no excutive authority, although it established a directorate for transportation on American orders and actively implemented the food and agricultural policies of the American Military Government. It participated extensively in the drafting of a zonal denazification law and engaged in a great number of economic and political planning activities, including those which pertained to the organization and powers of future central agencies for all of Germany. As Gimbel pointed out, a review of the early Länderrat activities shows the American interest in using the German council as a stepping stone to broader

30. Gimbel, *American Occupation* . . . , p. 36.
31. Clay, *Decision* . . . , p. 66.

economic unity.[32] It also demonstrated that the need for economic unification for budgetary reasons was foremost on the military governor's
mind and that political considerations actually played a secondary role.
Only toward the end of 1946 did the hoped-for spillover effect from the
work of the *Länderrat* produce some noticeable—although minor—results on the German political scene. They will be discussed below.

Blocked on the Control Council and at diplomatic levels and making
only slow progress with the establishment of a German administration,
General Clay must have waited with impatience for the quadripartite
Level-of-Industry Committee to complete its assignments. The Russian
representatives on the Control Council had repeatedly stated that they
could not proceed with a combined export-import plan for all of Germany until the reparations issue had been settled. And while there was
an uneasy feeling that this might be merely a delaying tactic, the Soviets
had to be given the benefit of the doubt. Accordingly, once the "Plan
of the Allied Control Council for Reparations and the Level of the Post-
war German Economy" [33] had been completed by the committee, Clay
promptly resumed his pressure for the amalgamation of quadripartite
export-import activities. As he feared, however, the response was negative, and on April 5, 1946, the Soviet representative at the Economic
Directorate declared that "the principle of zonal foreign trade had to be
substituted for the collective responsibility of all the Powers." [34] Three
days later the military governor issued a final warning, which was followed four weeks later by his order to discontinue further dismantling
of reparations plants in the American Zone. The general's dramatic
move subsequently became the subject of various interpretations, usually expressed in politico-ideological terms reflecting the proclivities of
the respective critics. Considering Clay's professional background, however, the present writer would suggest a more prosaic and simpler
explanation. Clay had been given the mission to put the German
economy on a self-supporting basis. Contrary to occupational policy
statements from the highest American level, the War Department had
just been compelled to submit to Congress an appropriation request for
financial aid to the German economy. Accordingly, it was only proper
for the military governor to stop all outflow until income was secured.
Moreover, if the basic premise of Clay's mission was erroneous, it was

32. Gimbel, *American Occupation* . . . , p. 44. According to Reinhold Maier,
however, initial British reactions to these efforts were rather negative. *Ein Grundstein wird gelegt*, pp. 172, 216, 312.
    33. B. U. Ratchford and W. D. Ross, *Berlin Reparations Assignment*, passim.
    34. Statement by K. I. Koval at ACA, 5 April 1946 (OMGUS records 5-1/1).

appropriate to bring this fact into the open as quickly as possible. It is, therefore, no coincidence that shortly after the dismantling halt had been announced, Clay submitted a comprehensive review of the German problem to the heads of the departments in Washington.[35] As was to be expected, it dealt primarily with economic and financial problems. Clay pointed out that if a common economic policy could not be fully implemented in all the zones of Germany and if the present boundaries were to be changed, the concept of Potsdam would be meaningless. Economic unity could be obtained only through free trade within the country and through a common foreign trade policy to serve the nation as a whole. A unified financial policy and drastic fiscal reforms were equally essential. The territorial questions of the future of the Rhineland, the Ruhr, and the Saar should be promptly decided. The loss of the Saar would not require a serious revision of the level-of-industry plan, but the loss of the Rhineland and of the Ruhr would necessitate complete revision. As to the principal problem of the military administration, the general suggested that economic chaos would "particularly affect the U.S. Zone which had no raw materials and would create a continuing financial liability for the United States for many years." On the other hand, the military governor saw no reasons why the reparations plan should not be implemented promptly if economic unity were obtained. But he was apprehensive of developing pressures to revise the reparations plan in favor of production of reparations. In this regard he actually repeated the Morgenthau thesis that "this [i.e., reparations from current production] ignores the real danger which Germany would still present if restored to full industrial strength." He suggested the early establishment of a provisional German government with the *Länderrat* serving as an initial model, and he proposed the creation of a Ruhr Control Authority for the coal and steel industry in the area. Clay predicted strong French resistance (which was unavoidable since all the French parties wanted Germany dismembered), and he suggested that his proposals might be acceptable to the Russians (who were interested in a unified Germany although preferably under their tutelage). In case, however, no quadripartite agreement could be reached, Clay proposed the economic merger of the British and American Zones, which would become self-sufficient within a few years, thus providing relief in accordance with congressional wishes.

Clay had discussed the substance of the report early in the spring with

35. Clay, *Decision* . . . , pp. 73–75.

Secretary Byrnes, who apparently decided to hold the bizonal solution in abeyance until Allied reaction to his proposal for a twenty-five year demilitarization treaty for Germany had been tested. The plan, which was a sincere effort on the part of the United States to maintain the wartime alliance,[36] would have established after the peace treaty a quadripartite inspection force on German soil; if these technically skilled inspectors reported a treaty violation, a majority of the four Allies could have decided on intervention with military force. The proposal was well received by Britain and France, although the latter made it clear that the treaty would not be a substitute for German territorial concessions in the West. As to Russia, it first reacted favorably; but later, possibly because the treaty legitimized American interventions in Europe and precluded a Soviet veto, its tactics became dilatory. An open rejection was avoided.

When discussing the treaty in the Council of Foreign Ministers at Paris, the Soviet foreign minister used the occasion to denounce General Clay's reparations stop as "unlawful"; moreover—prompting an emphatic denial by Secretary Byrnes [37]—he declared that the reparations issue was still unsolved. He continued his counterattack the following day by trying to exploit German fears about their future. "It would be a mistake to contemplate Germany's annihilation as a state," Molotov remarked, "or to plan its agrarianization and the destruction of its principal industries." The aim of the Soviet government was not to destroy Germany, he said, "but to transform it into a democratic and peace-loving state which besides its agriculture will have its own industry and foreign trade. A policy directed toward the creation of a pastoral state and the elimination of its principal industries, would only result in making Germany an incubator for dangerous sentiments of revenge."

Lucius Clay had used the reparations issue as a club to oblige the four occupying powers to settle the question of Germany's economic unification. The acrimonious American-Soviet debate in Paris made it clear that for the foreseeable future no progress would be made and that an alternate solution would have to be sought. The eventual political risks of a bizonal merger were self-evident, but nevertheless the dollar shortage of Great Britain and the attitude of congressional appropriations committees in Washington both pointed in that direction. Accordingly,

36. This point was stressed by Ambassador James W. Riddleberger, one of the drafters of the proposed treaty (interview, 23 January 1975). To meet Soviet objections, the United States subsequently suggested making it a forty-year treaty.
37. James F. Byrnes, *Speaking Frankly,* pp. 179–180.

when Secretary Byrnes on July 11 invited his colleagues to merge their zones and Great Britain soon accepted,[38] the move was still seen as a financial stopgap measure with the aim of moving the situation off dead center. No long-term political decisions had yet been reached.[39]

The American answer to Molotov's provocative speech came in Stuttgart a few weeks later, in the form of Secretary Byrnes's policy statement, which Clay had repeatedly and urgently requested. It actually reconfirmed the terms of the Potsdam agreements whereby Germany was to be demilitarized and compelled to pay reparations. Germany's war potential was to be reduced by the elimination of its war industries, and its economic power had to be curtailed by the reduction and the removal of industrial plants not needed for its peacetime economy. The aim was to enable Germany to maintain average European living standards without assistance from other countries. Addressing himself to the Soviet Union, the secretary remarked that in many important respects the Control Council was neither governing Germany nor allowing Germany to govern itself. The United States regarded a common financial policy as essential for the successful rehabilitation of Germany and considered it quite certain that a runaway inflation accompanied by economic paralysis would develop unless the German house could be put in order through such a common financial policy. With regard to territorial issues, Byrnes indicated that "the American government would support the French claim to the Saar" and that it was also prepared to recognize the annexation of some territory in East Germany by Poland.[40]

While German listeners could derive little comfort from the above, they were undoubtedly pleased to hear that the United States considered the Ruhr and the Rhineland indisputably German. It therefore would not support any encroachment on this territory nor any division of Germany not genuinely desired by the people concerned. Byrnes summed up his speech by declaring that the United States could not relieve Germany from the hardship inflicted upon it by the war which the National Socialist regime had started, but that it would attempt to give the German people "an opportunity to work their way out of these hardships so long as they respected human freedom and clung to the path of peace." Contrary to a popular belief, the speech contained no change in substance

38. *Foreign Relations . . . Council of Foreign Ministers, 1946,* 2: 897–898.
39. See among other documents a memorandum of 5 December 1946, prepared jointly by United States and United Kingdom military governors, "Soviet Proposals for Economic Unity" (OMGUS, 177–313, Council of Foreign Ministers File, National Archives).
40. Byrnes, *Speaking Frankly,* pp. 188–191.

when compared with previous American policy statements, but there was a very considerable difference in the tone; furthermore, while the priming of the Germany economy in the American Zone had been underway for more than a year, it now was recognized as a major policy aim of the United States.

There was one short paragraph in the speech, however, which, although frequently overlooked, was of historical significance. "Security forces will probably have to remain in Germany for a long period," Byrnes declared. "I want no misunderstanding. We will not shirk our duty. We are not withdrawing. We are staying here and will furnish our proportionate share of the security forces." For the first time, the world was thus put on notice of a radical shift in the political views of the United States. Whereas at Yalta Roosevelt, in accordance with prevailing sentiments back home, had suggested that American forces might remain in Europe for two years, and whereas the public—based on the past record of the United States—had arrived at similar conclusions, Byrnes's declaration heralded an entirely new foreign-policy approach. The barrier of the Atlantic thus seemed removed and the fate of the United States officially tied to that of Western Europe.

From Clay's vantage point, the secretary's speech had the great merit that it cleared the air and eliminated numerous misapprehensions. Washington's rhetoric was now in line with the grass-root activities of the Military Government; the American position as to territorial changes had been clearly defined; and friend and foe were given notice that the United States would not withdraw. With regard to the military governor's primary concern, the attainment of economic self-sufficiency, Byrnes had also declared that "Germany must be given a chance to export goods in order to import to make it self-sustaining. European recovery will be slow . . . if Germany . . . is turned into a poorhouse." This complemented the envisaged economic merger of the British and American Zones.

Clay himself had suggested this fusion out of economic necessity but he had no doubts about its political consequences and long-range perils. Called to New York in November by Byrnes, he handed the secretary an up-to-date analysis of the German problem, listing four issues which could not be solved at his level: the disarmament treaty, the peace treaty, the question of Germany's boundaries, and the conditions which had to be fulfilled for the economic unification of Germany.[41] The first

41. Jean Edward Smith, ed., *The Papers of General Lucius D. Clay,* Document 167, pp. 279–284.

two items were considered intergovernmental problems. "It would be presumptious for Military Government," Clay wrote, "to comment or to offer suggestions." As to the question of boundaries, he merely summarized earlier comments on the respective economic consequences of ceding the Ruhr and the Saar. It was the impasse in Berlin in obtaining political and economic unity which occupied the greatest part of this remarkable memorandum. As Clay pointed out, the stalemate resulted on one hand from French opposition to any unification proposals until boundary claims had been settled, and on the other hand from Soviet resistance to a common utilization of German resources and to a common acceptance of responsibility for deficits.

With regard to France Clay concluded that only full agreement by the three other powers and a firm presentation of their agreed views would succeed in obtaining French cooperation. In addition, the Saar would probably have to be ceded to France. As to Soviet opposition, Clay acknowledged that "it rested primarily on its need and desire for current production as reparations." Fully aware of the crucial significance of the issue, Clay then mentioned some promising reparations studies by his economic experts [42] and, after listing the pros and cons of a compromise, he offered the following statesmanlike appraisal:

> It is impossible to evaluate specifically the advantages and disadvantages until there is an agreed plan for the German economy in which the cost of reparations from current production is determined in dollars and cents. . . .
>
> The question is, therefore, whether or not such a proposal deserves full consideration. . . . If in fact, German unification is impossible unless this question is resolved, a *failure* to investigate it fully means the partition of Germany. . . . Obviously this establishes the frontier of Western democracy along the Elbe. [Clay's emphasis.]
>
> Certainly no consideration should be given to a plan for economic unification in which production for reparations is authorized without complete understanding that political unification would be undertaken simultaneously, and that production for reparations would cease if political unification proved impossible along democratic lines. . . .
>
> We have much at stake in gaining the opportunity to fight for

42. Memorandum, Don Humphrey to Draper, 2 November 1946 (OMGUS 177–313, Council of Foreign Ministers File, National Archives).

democratic ideals in Eastern Germany and in Eastern Europe. This opportunity would result from the true unification of Germany under quadripartite control.

Therefore, it does appear worthwhile to investigate fully this possible solution to the internal German problem. How much we are willing to pay to achieve our objectives is unknown, but *it is possible that the investigation may indicate that the cost in dollars and cents is not too high, particularly when measured in terms of European stability and the possible contributions of such stability to world peace.* [Emphasis added.] [43]

Inasmuch as the decision to continue or discontinue cooperation with the Soviet Union in Germany had to be taken at the highest governmental levels, General Clay as military governor could not go any further. However, with hawkish Admiral Leahy as Truman's foreign-policy mentor, General Bedell Smith as ambassador in Moscow, and George Kennan in the State Department, it seems doubtful that Clay's farsighted warnings received the consideration they deserved. In any event, the suggested cost analysis was not made, and there was a decision to proceed with the fusion of the two zones at least on a tentative basis. Accordingly, unification was formalized in December 1946 by a Byrnes-Bevin agreement which provided for a pooling of all economic resources and imports in order to achieve a common standard of living. It also stipulated that the two zones were to be treated as a single area for economic purposes. The economic unification was to be accomplished by German administrative agencies scheduled to operate under the joint control of the American and British commanders-in-chief. While working out the details of the merger, the two military governors were under instructions to avoid even the appearance of a bipartite political action that might tend to reduce the chances for the unification of all of Germany. Accordingly, the Soviet Union and France not only were repeatedly invited to participate in the bilateral venture but also were kept informed as to American-British plans for the bizonal organization.

The instruction to avoid any move that could be interpreted as political caused some difficulties at the Military Government level. At the expense of efficiency Clay and Robertson were obliged not to establish one West German administration center where American-British and German offices could be located, but rather to put the newly established

43. Smith, *The Papers of General Lucius D. Clay,* Document 167, pp. 279–284.

bureaus into four different West German towns. The administration for food and agriculture therefore was set up in Stuttgart; for transportation in Bielefeld; for economics in Minden; and for communications, civil service, and finance in Frankfurt. The authority and responsibilities of the new German agencies were not clearly defined, however, and the orders to remain in the confines of economics often proved embarrassing for the military governor. By creating the Länderrat he had encouraged German initiatives which now were difficult to curtail.[44] The hoped-for spillover effect had become noticeable in the first part of 1946 when the chief German officers of the British and American Zones held several meetings exchanging information and mapping common policies. German feelers toward the East and the West, on the other hand, remained unproductive, and when, on October 4, a four-zonal meeting of German minister presidents was to take place in Bremen, neither the French nor the Russian Zones were represented. The inadequacy of the new directives and the need for Clay to veto any German moves which might be considered political led on occasion to acrimonious American-German debates. They also marked the limitations to further progress at the OMGUS level. Inasmuch as the next step had to be taken by the four governments, the forthcoming meeting of the foreign ministers in Moscow could be expected to produce the urgently needed political decision.

44. Gimbel, *American Occupation* . . . , pp. 87–100.

CHAPTER ELEVEN

THE CRITICAL CONFERENCE

Americans are not good at the observation of subtle gradations, the long-term calculations, the patient endurance of irremediable inconveniences that are part of the diplomatic substance. They want quick and definite solutions. But many international situations are not susceptible of quick and definite solutions, and this leads to a feeling of frustration. Patience is not a typically American quality, but it is one of the greatest diplomatic virtues.[1]

James F. Byrnes left the State Department in January 1947. He had tendered his resignation because of ill health six months earlier, but had decided to remain in office until the satellite peace treaties had been signed. President Truman, although not always in accord with Byrnes's handling of foreign affairs, wanted him to stay on, but when Byrnes persisted, he designated George Catlett Marshall as his successor. As Robert H. Ferrell, one of the general's biographers writes, the new secretary retired into the depths of his private office in his first weeks at Foggy Bottom and "went to school" on his new tasks.[2] It stands to reason that deteriorating American-Soviet relations were a priority subject at these briefings. During the eighteen months since Potsdam the American official and public attitude toward Russia had undergone gradual but drastic changes. There was no longer any need to overlook the objectionable features of a system on whose military cooperation America depended and whose accomplishments in every field therefore had to be built up for the public eye. Accordingly, the widely held anti-Communist feelings of Americans—merely suppressed after Pearl Harbor—again came to the fore. Moreover, the Soviet government had done its full share to hasten the process of disillusionment. Initially the

1. Sir William Hayter, *The Diplomacy of the Great Powers*, pp. 14–15.
2. Robert H. Ferrell, *George Marshall: The American Secretaries of State and Their Diplomacy*, p. 52.

focal point of the growing discord had been Poland. After breaking off relations with the London Government in Exile the Soviets had thrown their full support behind a Communist group, the Polish National Committee, supposedly representative of the true will of the people. They had rejected the dramatic pleas of Roosevelt and Churchill for assistance to the Polish resistance fighters and had stood idly by while the German army was permitted to suppress the Warsaw uprising. Later, when some Polish leaders, trusting Russian promises of free conduct, emerged from their hiding places, they were promptly arrested. At Yalta only a vaguely worded agreement on Poland could be reached, which led to further controversies. In July 1945, when a Polish coalition government could at last be formed as a result of Harry Hopkins's visit to Moscow, the authority of its non-Communist members was emasculated from the beginning. The promised free elections were never held.

Poland was not the only source of American and British disillusionment. In Romania, Hungary, and Bulgaria the American and British missions were confined to the role of impotent onlookers while the communization of the country progressed; in East Germany the Soviet army, disregarding the commitment of Potsdam, proceeded with the wholesale spoilage of the economy; the Greek Communist party was given Moscow's direct and indirect support in its efforts to evict the Athens government by force; and Turkey was faced with menacing demands for the border districts of Kaars and Ardahan and Soviet bases in the Dardanelles.

Against the background of a still ongoing and rather sterile debate as to whether these policies should be seen as aggressively expansive or merely defensive, it might be suggested that the Soviet rulers simply followed the example of their imperial predecessors to probe for soft spots and to push ahead whenever they would be found, while halting or even withdrawing when risks seemed to outweigh possible benefits. The case of Iran may serve as an example. According to the tripartite declaration of Teheran in November 1943, the three signatories were committed to maintain the independence, sovereignity, and territorial integrity of Iran. The result was that a deadline of March 2, 1946, was set after the end of the war for the evacuation of the country. In the meantime, however, Soviet troops had sealed off their area, released Communist sympathizers from prison, and encouraged the activities of the revolutionary Tudeh party, which led to the formation of a separatist national government of Azerbaijan in Tabriz. When the Iranian government tried to send a small military unit to deal with the insurgents, the Soviets refused it entry. Secretary Byrnes's conversations on the subject with Stalin were inconclusive and the Iranian government consequently took the case to the United Nations. This step was followed by direct negotiations with the Iranian prime minister in Moscow and it was accompanied by American and British official protests indicating that the two powers would keep the issue before the Security Council even if Iran should withdraw its complaints. The possibility of American military action was also intimated. The Soviets continued to dicker with the Persian government for a while but eventually understood the consequences and withdrew.

Another example, that of Czechoslovakia, can be mentioned in a more conjectural vein. In retrospect it appears that the Czech Communists could have seized power as soon as the country was liberated. At that time they were in charge of the Ministries of the Interior, which controlled the police; of Information, which licensed newspapers and supervised the national radio; of Agriculture; and of Social Welfare. The prime minister, nominally a Social Democrat, was pro-Communist and the chief of staff was a fellow traveler. Moreover, in the free elections of 1946 the Communists emerged as the strongest party and about two of every five adults were registered Communists.[3] The people in general were socialist minded, and after the disillusioning experiences of 1938, a close relation with Soviet Russia appeared to be the best guarantee for the nation's independent survival. In other words, it seems clear that under the prevailing circumstances the Soviets could have taken over in 1945, had it not been for the unpredictable effect of such action on Soviet relations with its wartime allies. By the same token, it is only logical that the Kremlin moved promptly ahead when this caveat no longer applied.

A change in American-Soviet relations in the area of public diplomacy was also to be expected and, once it had become clear that no American loans and few reparations would be forthcoming, it was Russia that took the lead. In a radio address of February 9, 1946, Stalin told his countrymen that they should not be misled by the wartime alliance as to the basic antagonism between the Communist state and the Western world. In Marxist-Leninist terms, he explained that crises and wars were essential elements of the capitalist system, that the split within the capitalist world had caused two wars, and that consequently a new military conflict could not be ruled out. The Soviet Union, however, had

3. R. V. Burks, "Eastern Europe," pp. 99–101.

nothing to fear, he said, since it had a first-class army with modern equipment, experienced officers, and a high morale.

In the West the first public evaluation of the changed political climate came four weeks later at Fulton, Missouri, when Winston Churchill in the presence of the American president rose to condemn the Iron Curtain which had descended from Stettin to Trieste, and to accuse the Soviet Union of trying to build up a pro-Communist Germany in its zone. He said that the Soviets wanted an indefinite expansion of their power and doctrine and he cautioned against any policies of appeasement. It is not surprising that the speech hastened the ongoing process of shedding "war romanticism," as John Foster Dulles put it, "which had overidealized all of the Allies and their objectives." Accordingly, little heed was paid to Secretary Henry Wallace's warning that America could not handle successfully a "get-tough-with-Russia" policy because "the tougher we get, the tougher the Russians will get." Wallace's partisan reference in the same speech to the Republicans as "the party of economic nationalism and political isolationism" [4] was equally ineffective, as the results of the congressional elections of November 1946 showed. In contrast to a Democratic majority of 53 in the House and of 19 in the Senate before the elections, the new congress had respective Republican majorities of 58 and 6.

Concurrently with the public reappraisal of the political scene, a similar process was taking place within the confines of the decision-making apparatus where the influence of the American chargé in Moscow was in the ascendancy.[5] As George F. Kennan himself recognized, had his complex policy recommendation of February 22, 1946, been sent "six months earlier, the message probably would have been received in the Department of State with raised eyebrows and lips pursed in disapproval. Six months later, it probably would have sounded redundant, a sort of preaching to the convinced." [6] In other words, Kennan's "containment" program reached Washington at the appropriate time when policy was in transition. A year later, when the concept was presented to the general public in the form of an article in *Foreign Affairs,* it promptly started a public controversy which grew in intensity as the cold war progressed, centering on the question of whether Kennan had had military or merely political containment in mind. While the resulting

4. Henry Agard Wallace, *The Price of Vision: The Diary of Henry A. Wallace, 1942–1946,* ed. John Morton Blum, pp. 663–664.
5. George Curry and Richard L. Walker, *James F. Byrnes: The American Secretaries of State and Their Diplomacy,* 14: 202.
6. George F. Kennan, *Memoirs, 1925–1950,* p. 295.

arguments never will be fully resolved, an objective appraisal of Kennan's role ought to start by evoking the political climate in the United States at the end of the war, reflected on the one hand in the disastrous demobilization which Congress and the American people had demanded, and on the other in the traditional public reluctance to face complex problems abroad.

Thus, when Kennan told Washington: "The Soviet Union does not take unnecessary risks. Impervious to logic or reason it is highly sensitive to logic of force. For this reason it can easily withdraw—and usually does—when strong resistance is encountered at any point. Consequently, if the adversary has sufficient force and makes clear his readiness to use it, he rarely has to do so. If situations are properly handled, there need be no prestige-engaging showdowns," [7] he merely reminded his superiors of a fundamental aspect of Russian power politics, as valid in 1946 as today.

There was, however, a second, sometimes overlooked, element in Kennan's 1946 policy recommendations which can be summarized under the heading, "You can't do business with the Kremlin." It came to the fore in the passage that "Russian rulers sought security . . . only in patient but deadly struggle for total destruction of rival power, never in compacts and compromises with it" [8]—not a felicitous comment since it suggested the futility of American-Soviet negotiations. The same negative attitude had been reflected in Kennan's policy recommendation of May 1945 not to participate in "a Soviet-ridden regime" in Vienna; [9] and it was reemphasized when he later referred to possible cooperation with the Soviet Union in Germany as mere "pipedreams." [10] This posture was promptly challenged by Walter Lippmann, who wrote: "For a diplomat to think that rival and unfriendly powers cannot be brought to a settlement is to forget what diplomacy is all about. There would be little for diplomats to do if the world consisted of partners enjoying political

7. U.S. Department of State, *Foreign Relations of the United States . . . Eastern Europe; the Soviet Union, 1946*, 6: 707. The timeliness of Kennan's comment will be appreciated if compared with an entry of 28 May 1946 in Admiral William D. Leahy's Diary: ". . . our military situation in Germany is hopeless if we should be attacked by the Soviets. They [competent American military observers] do not believe it would be possible to evacuate any large number of our troops."

8. *Foreign Relations . . . Eastern Europe . . . 1946*, 6: 699. Admiral Leahy, who daily briefed the president on foreign policy developments, also subscribed to the view that "Soviet agreements had no value." See his diary entry of 17 April 1946. And Dean Acheson thought it was "a mistake to believe you can sit down with the Russians and solve questions." See Daniel Yergin, *Shattered Peace*, p. 296.

9. *Foreign Relations . . . European Advisory Commission . . . 1945*, 3: 110.

10. Kennan, *Memoirs . . . .* , p. 178.

intimacy and responding to common appeals." [11] It is indicative of Kennan's vulnerability in this regard that he reacted to this provocative remark only in an unconvincing paragraph: "No one was more conscious than I was of the dangers of a permanent division of the European continent. The purpose of the containment . . . was not to perpetuate the status quo . . . it was to tide us over a difficult time and bring us to a point where we could discuss effectively with the Russians the drawbacks and the dangers of the status quo." [12]

As mentioned earlier, the containment concept emerged at a time when the administration and Congress were ready and eager for a new foreign policy. In the White House President Roosevelt's inexperienced successor was briefed every morning by Admiral Leahy on the dangers of Russia's emergence as a world power. And at the State Department and at the Moscow Embassy the two generals in charge were equally willing to accept the professional diplomat's recommendations against further compromises. As to the deeper reasons for Kennan's negative attitude, the answer may lie in the psychological makeup of this excellent scholar, which makes him shy away from arduous negotiations with adversaries regarded as ethically inferior. Another policy proposal of his—published twenty-seven years later—to discontinue all further dealings with the countries participating in the oil embargo, would lend support to this interpretation. [13]

Kennan's direct contribution to the German question can be judged from a second dispatch which followed his "long telegram" and which analyzed the Soviet position regarding a centralized German government. [14] As he saw it, the Soviets were probably quite pleased to have several months after Potsdam to take stock of the situation in Germany. They presumably considered central agencies as indispensable devices for entering all three zones at an appropriate moment. Consequently, there was no reason for Soviet officials to take the onus of opposing the establishment of such agencies and they were pleased to have the French "run interference for them." As to the future, Kennan doubted that the Soviets would support the establishment of such agencies as the United States envisaged until such time when Moscow could be reasonably certain that they would substantially advance its chances for the control of Germany. Kennan therefore was skeptical whether centralized agencies

11. Walter Lippmann, "A Defective Policy," p. 51.
12. George Kennan, "A Rebuttal and an Apology," p. 82.
13. "And Thank You Very Much," *New York Times,* 2 December 1973.
14. *Foreign Relations . . . British Commonwealth . . . 1946,* 5: 516–520.

would be an effective tool "in averting the final communization of Germany." Accordingly, he saw only two alternatives: to leave Germany united and highly vulnerable to Soviet political penetration or to "carry to its logical conclusion the process of partition which was begun in the East and to endeavor to rescue Western Zones of Germany by walling them off against Eastern penetration and integrating them into an international pattern of Western Europe rather than into a united Germany." The reader will recognize that this plan of action for Germany was not only a logical step toward implementing Kennan's overall policy of containment, but also was one that preceded Secretary Byrnes's first move toward Bizonia by several months and even came before the Soviet attitude toward an all-German export-import plan had actually been explored.

The new secretary of state had on his desk some additional policy recommendations toward partition in the form of a telegram from Moscow.[15] Ambassador Bedell Smith had mentioned to Clay earlier that "Americans were too naive politically to cope with the Russians in the framework of a centralized German administration."[16] Accordingly, and contrary to clearly recognizable facts,[17] he now declared that the current experiences in Vienna were sufficient proof of the Soviet ability to prevent the effective functioning of a central government which had to operate under quadripartite control. He therefore considered it "inevitable" for the United States to accept the continued separation of the Eastern and Western Zones of Germany because any "hollow" unification would only open the door "to the accomplishment of Soviet purpose in Germany as a whole." And he concluded his message as one general addressing another with the recommendation that the United States could have only one policy, namely to "support and defend" Germany's democratic forces "in active sense as distinguished from moral support and defense we have so far provided."

The American officials who leaned toward partition found scholarly support in the writings of Eugene V. Rostow, who considered a unified Germany within a European Federation of States almost as undesirable as in the role of the balancing factor between East and West. Regard-

---

15. *Foreign Relations . . . Council of Foreign Ministers . . . 1947*, 2: 139–142.
16. Clay, *Decision . . .* , p. 131.
17. Actually, the Austrian Renner and Figl governments operated quite effectively as almost all their laws were enacted without Allied interference. (Michael Balfour and John Mair, *Four Power Control in Germany and Austria*, pp. 281, 325.)

ing the second alternative, he pointed out that "the Russians are much better equipped than we are to play the game in Germany. As in 1939 they would have the support of powerful groups of nationalist Germans. The Soviets could offer the Germans prizes . . . Silesia and East Prussia, for example. . . . Instead of a capitalist Germany facing East we might find a National Communist Germany backed by a neutral Russia facing West." As to the first alternative, Rostow regarded prewar Germany even as reduced at Potsdam altogether too large a unit to be allowed into a European Union. In his judgment, the danger of German domination would be too great. It might be construed by the Soviet Union as a hostile act and would seem like a plan "to give defeated Germany the fruits of victory." In contrast to official American statements, especially those from Clay's headquarters in Berlin, Rostow recognized that despite bombing and defeat Germany ended the war in a position of great potential strength. Recent official studies of the German economy have clearly established, he wrote, that Germany's industrial potential was not reduced 5 percent by bombing, although its cities were wrecked. "Germany's industry today has the capacity to support a German army within a few months, a German economic life on the old scale within a few years." Rostow considered a permanent disarmament of Germany as "inherently unworkable" and since a unified Germany would constitute "the most serious of all threats to East-West relations," he suggested the creation of three or four separate German states within the framework of a European Union.[18]

Neither Rostow's analysis, however, nor similar appraisals at the top level of the Department of State and by the American Embassy in Moscow, represented as yet a generally held American view. For instance, John Foster Dulles, the presumptive secretary of state in a Republican administration expected to take office in 1949, had a different plan for the future of Germany. In a major address before the National Publishers Association, he indicated that the economic unity of Europe was more important than the Potsdam dictum that Germany should be "a single economic unit." This did not mean, he said, that Germany should not be unified but that Germany's unification ought to go hand in hand with European unification. Dulles condemned "industrial disarmament," which he considered a euphemism for pastoralization and which would require continued military occupation and charity feeding. On the other hand, he felt certain that a Germany reestablished as a single economic

18. Eugene V. Rostow, "The Partition of Germany and the Unity of Europe," pp. 18–33.

unit subject only to German political control would again become highly centralized even if initially a decentralized form of government were imposed. In order to prevent the economic forces in Germany from again becoming centripetal, Dulles suggested a form of joint control of Germany's industrial heartland, the Ruhr, "which will make it possible to develop the industrial potential of Western Germany in the interest of the economic life of Western Europe including Germany . . . without making Germany the master of Europe." As to the dangers of continued Soviet expansionism, Dulles's views at that time also differed from the opinions cited above. He indicated that the Soviet Union in 1946 had encountered Western energetic resistance in Iran and "as competent observers had thought likely," Soviet leaders drew back. "That is to their credit," he said. "Soviet leadership showed itself to be intelligent and realistic rather than reckless or fanatical." [19] In other words, in contrast to many others, Dulles as well as Lucius Clay had not given up hope for better cooperation with Russia and they still envisaged a unified Germany and an international control of the Ruhr.

It will be recalled that the specifics of a bizonal pooling agreement had not yet been worked out, and the State Department's policy studies and briefing papers for the Moscow conference [20] therefore neither reflected the consequences nor the finality of this first tentative step. Nothing irrevocable had yet been done and there was still the opportunity for the United States to move in a number of directions. A "Report of the Secretary's Policy Committee on Germany" accordingly warned against partition as "a solution incompatible with the objective of a neutral Germany." The paper conceded that a neutral Germany would probably be a potential ally of the Western powers but it also mentioned the risk of a Germany able and ready to play off the occupying powers against each other. In such a contest the Soviet Union, by its ability to make concessions on Germany's Eastern borders, would be in a strong bargaining position. "If there ever should be a split," the paper warned, "it must be clear to the whole world that it was in spite of U.S. policy and not because of it." The high level document also concluded that in any event before accepting partition "one more major effort must be made to obtain unification." [21]

Another study analyzed the crucial problem of reparations from cur-

19. John Foster Dulles, "Europe Must Federate or Perish," pp. 234–236.
20. *Foreign Relations . . . Council of Foreign Ministers . . . 1947*, 2: 201–234.
21. Council of Foreign Ministers file, Moscow, Lot M 88, Record Group 43, Box 147.

rent production in some depth. It came up with a tentative figure of $5 billion, to be divided between Russia and the West and payable over a period of five years. It was a relatively manageable program, the paper said, while admitting that it probably could be improved upon if there were "a highly organized and energetic management of the program comparable to that of the Soviet Military Administration in the Eastern Zone of Germany." "The United States and Britain," the analysis continued, "are politically unable themselves to provide that management, and politically committed to turning responsibility for German industrial production to German hands." It was a valid appraisal in contrast to the concluding comment which unduly discounted the impact of production incentives and of German interest in unification. "It is not considered that German officials and managers are likely to apply the energy and leadership to a program of exports and reparations out of current production which would be necessary to make both succeed . . . ," the paper said. The final summary, which expressed concern that the United States might have to serve as an underwriter of a plan for reparations, reflected the department's understandable apprehensions concerning the anticipated negative reaction on Capitol Hill.[22]

The briefing papers for the Moscow conference included detailed plans for the establishment of a provisional German government, an outline of the United States position on unsolved territorial questions, a draft treaty on disarmament and demilitarization of Germany, a memorandum on the treatment of Germany as a single economic unit, an analysis of the reparations and coal production problems, and a study pertaining to the international supervision of the Ruhr economy. The State Department had also requested and obtained from the Office of Military Government for Germany its comments and reactions to the Washington policy papers. The solution of most of the problems evidently depended on the settlement of the two primary ones, Germany's unification and reparations. In this regard the briefing papers mentioned "broad Russian hints" that the Soviet Union might subscribe to treating Germany as an economic unit provided it received reparations out of current production. Accordingly, an American plan, in order to safeguard against a feared outside manipulation, provided for a federal state with considerable authorities reserved for the individual *Länder*. As to reparations, it was envisaged that the Soviet Union would propose an upward revision of the Level-of-Industry Agreement in order to facili-

22. "Principal Economic Issues on Current German Problems for CFM Moscow." Memorandum 2. CFM File, Moscow. Box 147.

tate reparations from current production, that there would be similar suggestions from the British side, and that France probably had no strong views on the subject. With regard to reparations from current production, the briefing paper recommended that the United States should resist on the grounds that exports were not sufficient to pay for imports and were not likely to prove so within the near future. As a fall-back position the department suggested allowing deliveries from capital equipment to be replaced within narrow limits by reparations from current production and without increasing the reparations burden on Germany.

The drafters of these recommendations did not go into the underlying legal controversy which arose when Molotov reopened the discussion of the reparations problem at the July meeting of the Council of Foreign Ministers in Paris, asserting that at Yalta Roosevelt had accepted the Soviet claim for $10 billion. While this statement provided Byrnes with an opportunity to lecture his Soviet colleague on the meaning of accepting a figure as a basis for discussion, neither he nor Molotov on that occasion had come to grips with the fundamentals of the problem. In his Stuttgart speech the secretary of state had specifically laid the ground for the American position, as reflected in the briefing papers. "In fixing the level of industry no allowance was made for reparations from current production," he said. "They would be wholly incompatible with the levels of industry now established under the Potsdam agreement. Obviously, higher levels of industry would have to be fixed, if reparations from current production were contemplated." Byrnes's remarks corresponded to the United States' subsequent statements that the Potsdam agreement had superseded the Yalta Reparations Protocol. Because of the pivotal significance of this interpretation, it will be discussed here at some length.

On the opening day of the Moscow Conference the National Planning Association had released to the press an extensive analysis of the reparations issue.[23] Written by David Ginsburg, a young lawyer who only recently had resigned from his position as deputy director of Clay's Economic Division and as the United States alternate at the four-power Economic Directorate in Berlin, it showed some of the views held at that time in America's policy-making circles. Ginsburg was sympathetic to the wartime sufferings of the Soviet Union as he conceded that reparations at best would pay for a fraction of the material damages suf-

23. David Ginsburg, *The Future of German Reparations*.

fered by the Russians [24] and acknowledged that there was nothing immoral or wrong in the Soviet reparations claim.[25] On the other hand, he repeated the popular thesis that the United States had paid German reparations after the first war [26] and expressed the overriding concern of military administrators about whether Congress would remain amenable to appropriations for deficit expenditures in Germany.[27] "With a change in the economic and political climate in the country," he wrote—apparently referring to the new congressional majorities—"Congress may quickly conclude that further expenditures are unwarranted. . . . *This is a fact of American political life which Secretary Marshall cannot afford to ignore*" (emphasis added). Like so many of his colleagues at OMGUS, Ginsburg considered reparations from current production in the amounts demanded by the Russians as economically disastrous, and he too failed to recognize the great potential of the German economy. There was no reference in the paper to the important conclusions of the United States Strategic Bombing Survey, although the relevant data were available. An equally significant shortcoming of the paper was the apparent lack of understanding that German workers, farmers, manufacturers, and business people were engaged in a struggle for physical survival, without incentive and largely on the economic sidelines, rendering any judgment about the real state of the German economy fallacious. In a similar vein, the references to the absence of an internationally acceptable currency failed to recognize the temporary nature of this situation.

The paper also mentioned the debatable Morgenthau thesis that reparations would build up Germany to its dangerously dominant place in the European economy. It was more correct in stressing the risk of Soviet political and economic penetration into the Western Zones of Germany as a result of recurring reparations. Its conclusion, which was not without merit, was that "during a decade of such deliveries much could be done through banking, trade and cartel arrangements and the other paraphernalia of European commercial intercourse" to establish in Western Germany a more sympathetic climate for Communist ideas and policies.[28]

Apparently aware of the dim prospects of a settlement in Moscow, Ginsburg finally introduced the proposal of a loan for the rehabilitation and reconstruction of the Soviet Union. He pointed out that "the stimu-

24. Ibid., p. 30.   25. Ibid., p. 35.
26. Ibid., p. 4.   27. Ibid., p. 37.
28. Ibid., p. 29.

lus of Russia's vast needs may be compelling and an American loan would contribute to the satisfaction of those needs far more than even recurring reparations." Recognizing that a loan to Russia would be unpopular and impolitic, he nevertheless reached the common sense conclusion that "a Russian loan would be a small price to pay for relief from the crippling tensions arising from the fear of still another war. . . ." [29]

Ginsburg's legal analysis of the reparations controversy was based entirely on the Potsdam agreement, which did not mention reparations from current production, and consequently in Ginsburg's interpretation these were excluded. The ambiguities in the text, nevertheless, seemed compelling enough for him to try his hand at a vivid and realistic description of some aspects of diplomatic intercourse. Because of the context it is cited here in extenso:

> When the process of negotiating is approaching stalemate at the highest levels, and each delegation is anxiously searching for the elusive formula that may bring consent; when . . . the success of the entire conference turns on finding a substitute for an offending word or phrase or idea; when the negotiations have been tiring, and men are weary, and tempers ragged, and then suddenly a suggestion bursts on the conference which answers part but not all of a problem . . . the temptation to say "agreed" or "soglasen" without probing too deeply is a temptation almost too great to resist. . . .
>
> Sometimes an ambiguity is deliberately ignored because it is felt that the preferred interpretations may be made to prevail later under more propitious circumstances. All this is part of the tactic of negotiation. . . .
>
> Translators examine each other's texts and, lacking the knowledge of their superiors, occasionally overlook the verbal nuances which shade the meaning of important agreements. Differences in sentence construction add to the complexity of translation, and such differences are exaggerated when the languages are as dissimilar as Russian and English. So it was at Potsdam. So it must have been. . . . [30]

The reader will recall in this connection that Secretary Byrnes had reached the reparations agreement at Potsdam as a result of a "package

29. Ibid., p. 61.   30. Ibid., pp. 27–28.

deal" whereby the United States recognized Poland's de facto boundaries in the West against Soviet concessions in the reparations question. Russian negotiators naturally had been fully aware of the overriding importance of a long-term territorial concession in relation to a short-term economic agreement. At the same time neither Eastern nor Western diplomats wanted the conference to fail. Both sides were anxious at least to reach an understanding on paper, and, as Ginsburg so clearly perceived it, ambiguities were therefore ignored.

This explanation, however, still does not settle the legal aspects of the issue. Ginsburg as well as a number of writers who treated the subject in later years rested their case on the text of the Potsdam agreement. Oddly, they failed to take into consideration a number of official documents of the United States which demonstrate that the reparations settlement at Potsdam actually was an *interim agreement*. The first statement in support of this thesis was contained in a "Status Report" prepared in Moscow in July 1945 under Ambassador Pauley's instructions: "Soviet proposal defers question [of recurring reparations] until determination of extent of capital removals and German minimum requirements." [31] The United States concurrence with this view was expressed by Pauley in a press statement of August 30, 1945,[32] as well as in his final report to the secretary of state in which he refers to "Current Deliveries as Reparations" as follows:

> The problem of current deliveries as reparations is one which cannot be settled until the Control Council has announced the results of its program for German deindustrialization and until its outline of the export-import program for Germany are [*sic*] in hand. As soon as these two programs are available, it will be necessary to decide whether current production will be available to pay reparations and if such production is available it will be necessary to decide over what period of years production for reparations account will be required.[33]

Finally, the fourth reference is contained in Ambassador Pauley's official "Report on German Reparations to the President of the United States February to September 1945." Its concluding statement—that "this [Yalta] agreement is still unchanged, except that a deferment has been

31. Scandrett Papers, Cornell University.
32. *Department of State Bulletin* 13, no. 323 (2 September 1945): 309.
33. Letter, E. W. Pauley to the secretary of state, 14 September 1945 (740.-00119 EW/9–1445, National Archives.)

agreed in determination of the amount of, and time limit for, such current reparations until the schedule of capital removals is made . . ."—could not have been more explicit in clarifying the critical issue.

From the evidence cited above the present writer was obliged to deduce that some time between August 1945 and September 1946 the United States government had raised the ante, a conclusion subsequently confirmed by the discovery of a State Department memorandum, "Reparation Out of Current Output—The Legal Position," which expressly acknowledges the change in the United States position. The paper not only refers to Ambassador Pauley's above-mentioned statements but it also cites an Allied Control Authority document of September 15, 1945, which exempted reparations out of current production from first charge as follows:

All goods, merchandise and raw materials shipped to other countries for this purpose *except those goods, merchandise and raw materials applied in payment of approved reparations,* shall be deemed exports.

Moreover, the State Department memorandum records a conversation with Emile Despres, who had been the United States representative on the committee which drafted the critical paragraph 19 and who a year later explained that *the statement, "The proceeds of exports etc.," excepts exports of reparation out of current output on the ground that such export yields no proceeds.* To this the drafters of the legal brief added that the Russian members of the Economic Subcommittee accepted the language of paragraph 19 at the last moment and only after it had passed through a number of successive drafts.[34]

When the present writer—assuming that the changed American position was the result of a formal decision—queried General Clay on this point he learned that "there was never a decision and the situation was always discussed on an 'if-and-when' basis. There was never a decision to provide reparations from production although it was discussed in great length in many places."[35] On the basis of this authoritative comment one arrives then at the final and historically important conclusion that the United States reparations position evolved gradually. Since it deviated from the Yalta text as well as from the intended meaning of the Potsdam Reparations Agreement, it will be recognized as an un-

34. "Principal Economic Issues on Current German Problems for CFM Meeting Moscow," Memorandum no. 2—Annex E, CFM Box 147 (National Archives).
35. Letter to the present writer, 20 February 1975.

derstandable, though unwise, reaction to the aggressive policies of the
Soviet Union.

It should be stated here that in the weeks preceding the Moscow
Conference growing antagonistic feelings toward Russia received new
impetus in the form of two British Notes; delivered on February 21,
1947, they advised the United States Department of State of the pre-
carious situation of the Greek government and of the inability of the
British to maintain its position in Greece and Turkey. Secretary
Marshall participated in the initial decision to fill the gap, but since
he was in the midst of preparing for his trip to Moscow, he asked Dean
Acheson to carry on in his place. His instruction to the under secretary
to proceed without regard to his chief or to the Moscow meeting in-
duced Acheson to the dramatic comment that "many years would go
by before an officer commanding in a forward and exposed spot would
call down his own artillery fire upon his own position to block an
enemy advance." [36] A more critical observer, however, might have
suggested that by that time General Marshall was quite aware that
neither of the main adversaries would make any concessions in Moscow
and that consequently whatever the White House said or did would
have no effect on the outcome of the conference. The relationship between the evolving American policies in Germany and in the Middle
East was not causal but rather mutually supportive, with "containment" serving as the connecting link. In the case of Greece and Turkey,
however, the necessity of "scaring the hell" out of a reluctant Congress
created an ideological rhetoric which eventually had nefarious consequences.

On his way to Moscow General Marshall stopped in Paris and
Berlin. During the course of his visit to President Auriol, he was told
that France was receiving only half of the minimum requirements of
German coal and if essential dispositions were not taken in time,
Germany would be restored more quickly than France. As the French
correctly evaluated it, the question of French and German reconstruction dominated the political picture. Consequently, if France were to
receive guarantees on coal "the French would find it possible to go
along with the United States views on other German problems." [37]
Additional French comments about the dangers of German centralized
power actually reinforced the prevailing State Department views.

36. Dean Acheson, *Present at the Creation*, p. 220.
37. *Foreign Relations . . . Council of Foreign Ministers . . . 1947*, 2: 190–
195.

In Berlin General Marshall held a policy conference attended by General Clay, Ambassador Murphy, Ben Cohen, and John Foster Dulles, who had been invited to accompany the secretary. It seems that the minutes of the meeting were not recorded, but Clay's position can be deduced from his hand-carried memorandum for Secretary Byrnes cited above. Dulles's recommendations, on the other hand, are contained in a paper dated March 7, which he had prepared for the occasion and which is now on hand in Princeton's Seeley G. Mudd Manuscript Library. It is significant that both men were still thinking in terms of a unified Germany. But whereas Clay suggested a thorough investigation of Germany's economic potential before a crucial political decision was made, Dulles was critical of the department's concentration "on technical problems involved in the restoration of German political and economic life" and of the absence of "a basic policy of the United States." Because he feared the bargaining power of a unified independent Germany and also envisaged the alternative risk of a Soviet-dominated Germany, he proposed as a safeguard "the integration of the Ruhr area into Western Europe." He later reported that there was general acceptance of his view that Germany should not be dealt with as an isolated problem; [38] and General Marshall, who understandably evaluated the situation in military terms, remarked that when planning a military campaign he also had found "localitis" one of the most difficult problems to deal with. As one would expect, no "basic policy" was formulated at the meeting and the negotiating position for the United States remained unchanged. In view of the priority to strengthen Western Europe, France would be given the promise of additional coal and the economic and political control of the Saar. France's other territorial demands would not be conceded, but a Western supervision of the German steel and coal industry would remain on the agenda for future negotiations. The detailed plan for a federalized German constitution which had been drawn up by the State Department and OMGUS would be submitted to Moscow in the hope that it would help to alleviate French fears of a rejuvenated Germany while making Soviet manipulation of a unified Germany more difficult. As to the crucial reparations issue, however, Soviet expansionist policies had blocked any inclination toward further concessions. As Philip Mosely later wrote, "The pendulum had swung so far that anybody who admitted the possibility of ever settling any dispute with the Soviet gov-

38. John Foster Dulles, *War on Peace*, pp. 102–103.

ernment was likely to fall under suspicion of favoring appeasement." [39]

The Moscow meeting of the Council of Foreign Ministers lasted from March 10 to April 24, 1947. The first seven days of the conference were taken up by the issues of Germany's demilitarization, democratization, and denazification, as well as by the procedure for drafting a German peace treaty. The crucial question of Germany's economic and political unification was next on the agenda, with initial deliberations indicating that a reconciliation of the respective positions might succeed provided the reparations problems could be solved. In particular there was agreement that the level of German industry under Potsdam should be raised and that a German provisional government ought to be formed quickly. Whereas the Western representatives supported federalization, Molotov held out for centralization because "in a federalized Germany there will be no central German government capable of bearing responsibility for Germany's fulfillment of her obligations to the Allies. . . . It will be a different matter if the German people themselves declare in favor of federalization, if they decide this question by a free vote, without outside compulsion." [40] As General Marshall acknowledged, "There was much in common in the four views," [41] and even with regard to the reparations issue, Bidault could point out that there was no matter of principle involved, merely questions of fact which should be given realistic study. "There are," he said, "no insurmountable difficulties if the question is examined with a will to arrive at a practical solution." [42]

As the State Department had predicted, Molotov had taken a leaf out of Byrnes's Potsdam book by presenting a Russian "package deal" to the effect that the Soviet government would not proceed with a unification of Germany unless the question of reparations from current production were solved. "If we all agree that the establishment of the economic unity of Germany does not run counter to the payment of reparations but on the contrary must necessarily include a solution of the reparations problem, it should not be very difficult to reach agreement about the rest," he said. "The main point is that in settling the question of economic unity of Germany we must also settle the question of reparations." [43] The Soviet foreign minister's tone, more-

39. "Soviet American Relations since the War," p. 209
40. V. M. Molotov, *Speeches and Statements at the Moscow Session of the Council of Foreign Ministers 1947*, pp. 394–395 (22 March 1947).
41. CFM, Minutes of the Twelfth Meeting. 22 March 1947.
42. CFM, Minutes of the Eighteenth Meeting. 31 March 1947.
43. Molotov, *Speeches* . . . , p. 387 (19 March 1947).

over, was conciliatory, and he stressed that a German foreign trade program ought to be speedily prepared which would permit the increase of German exports, imports, and food rations. Although he asked for participation in the administration of the Ruhr and objected to a federalized constitution for Germany, Molotov repeatedly indicated that compromises would be possible provided the Soviet Union would be assisted in rebuilding its war-torn economy by means of German deliveries from current production.[44] John Foster Dulles in his last New York speech had mentioned the Soviet "pull-back" in response to a firm American and British stand in Iran, and an objective observer in Moscow might have sensed a similar Soviet willingness to yield in the face of Western resolve to proceed with a two-zonal unification. Stalin's subsequent remarks to General Marshall, that "it is wrong to give so tragic an interpretation to our disagreements . . . when people have exhausted themselves in dispute they recognize the necessity for compromise. . . . Compromises are possible on all the main questions,"[45] would lend support to such an evaluation. The strategic significance of the moment did not escape the attention of Adam Ulam, who commented in this connection with apparent regret, "Diplomacy consists in sensitivity to a favorable moment for settlement of a dispute, and statesmanship in the ability to transform a fragile agreement into reality through appropriate political and military measures as well as military vigilance. Neither of these arts could flourish under the conditions of Soviet-American discourse after the war."[46] While this is a valid general comment, it also ought to be recognized that General Marshall had only limited choices left by the time he arrived in Moscow. As to the American basic diplomatic approach, the fear of Soviet leverage in manipulating a German government, as well as recent experience with the Kremlin's devious methods, had prompted a resolve to "contain" rather than to negotiate. Accordingly the weak American legal position on the critical reparations issue had to be propped up by shifting the blame and engaging in the aggressive rhetoric of "no retreat to Yalta"[47] and "the Soviets are trying to sell the same horse twice."[48] Factually the secretary's comments were not valid and as propagandistic as several subsequent State Department statements which ascribed to the Soviet Union the entire responsibility

44. Ibid., p. 273 (31 March 1947).
45. *Foreign Relations . . . Council of Foreign Ministers . . . 1947*, 2: 273.
46. Adam B. Ulam, *Expansion and Coexistence*, p. 446.
47. *Department of State Bulletin* 16, no. 404 (30 March 1947): 564.
48. CFM, Minutes of Eighteenth Meeting, 13 March 1947.

for the impending split. Molotov, in turn, did not handle his case too well since he continued to mention the $10 billion figure ad nauseam rather than emphasizing that it would have been nonsensical to discuss reparations from current production at a time when the industrial basis for such payments had not yet been determined.

As to the economic aspects of the problem, the secretary was in an equal bind because only a few weeks earlier General Eisenhower had been told by key members of the United States Senate and House that Congress was determined to cut drastically the amount of civil relief.[49] The War Department consequently had assured Congress that appropriations for German food subsidies could be eliminated three years after the activation of Bizonia. Marshall acknowledged this state of affairs at a luncheon meeting with Bevin on March 20, when he mentioned "the political impossibility of securing agreement by an American Congress to a course of action which involved the indirect payment of reparations." Accordingly, he "had opposed this with the view that the Soviet demand for some form of reparations out of current production during the next two years would be implacable." [50]

Among the American delegates it was mainly Lucius Clay who recognized that the reparations issue would be a deciding factor in "fixing American influence in Germany at the Elbe rather than along the Oder-Neisse" and who consequently suggested that "the United States should not take an adamant stand without a study of the availability of reparations from current production which would show the costs unwarranted." [51] Accordingly, at OMGUS some efforts had been made to find a way out of the largely self-created dilemma. Draper's office had come up with a promising plan whereby the Soviets might provide the raw materials which would permit a form of reparations from current production without delaying the creation of a self-supporting German economy.[52] An "Interallied Loan Agreement" to finance the purchase of raw materials was equally taken into consideration.[53] There was, however, little interest at the top governmental level in an objective economic analysis and, having made his point, General Clay could

49. Cable, Eisenhower to McNarney, 14 February 1947 (OMGUS records 148/1/3).
50. Foreign Relations . . . Council of Foreign Ministers . . . 1947, 2: 274.
51. CFM, Fourth Session, Moscow, "Summary of Discussion on Report of Allied Control Council," Box 154.
52. Foreign Relations . . . Council of Foreign Ministers . . . 1947, 2: 273. Don Humphrey to Draper, 2 November 1946, OMGUS 177–313, CFM File, National Archives.
53. "Draft Plan for Interallied Loan Agreement," CFM, Box 191.

not go any further.[54] Otherwise it would have been easily recognized that a substantial part of the original Soviet reparations demand had already been fulfilled [55] and that, since Molotov had offered a reduction of the Soviet claim by $2 billion at Potsdam, a compromise could be reasonably expected. Moreover, as far as Germany's capacity to pay was concerned, a factual appraisal would have had to take the original estimates of the Federal Reserve and the Office of Strategic Services, as well as the results of the Strategic Bombing Survey of the United States, into consideration. Had this been done, it would not have been necessary to come up with an "economic miracle" when industrial production in West Germany promptly jumped by 60 percent after the currency reform, when prewar levels were reached by 1950, and when close to $5 billion were invested in the Federal Republic in the first year after the end of the dismantling process. An unprejudiced analysis also could not have failed to recognize that once the negative incentives of suppressed inflation and of uncertain reparations burdens had been eliminated, tremendous economic energies would have been released by the reunification of East and West Germany with Berlin as a vigorous center. The beneficial effects of a return of Soviet-expropriated (SAG) trusts and of Ruhr coal and steel properties could also have been anticipated. Finally, in accordance with General Draper's earlier proposal to prime the German pump by means of an initial subsidy for the purchase of raw materials, a sensible economic evaluation would have suggested short-term credits in lieu of the three-year food subsidy which Congress had already accepted.[56]

However, because of the commitments to Congress and the administration's predilection for containment, no rational investigation was made and on April 1 General Marshall proceeded with his final

54. "Clay did not hide his disagreement . . . Clay's response was violent and a little insubordinate. . . ." Daniel Yergin, *Shattered Peace*, p. 299.
55. Emanuel Gottlieb, *The German Peace Settlement and the Berlin Crisis*, p. 138.
56. Ibid., p. 155: "Concern with this deficit, overestimated through minimization of German economic potential and the rehabilatory leverage of settlement took on something of the role in Anglo-American official thought which wartime losses had in Soviet thought. The deficit with its alleged burdens on Anglo-American taxpayers became an obsession. That the already accrued deficit grew out of the weakness of occupation policy more than out of a lagging German balance of trade was ignored. Insistence on sharing the deficit was propelled into the negotiations as the key issue." In this connection it is of interest that Germany's "economic miracle" provided the United States and its Western Allies subsequently with an unanticipated return in the form of the London Debts Agreement of 1953. Under its terms the Federal Republic of Germany assumed responsibility for the payment of 7 billion DM of pre-1932 debts and of 6 billion DM of postwar debts, i.e., a total of about $3 billion. At the time of this writing nearly all of these debts had been paid.

compromise offer which entailed some reparations from current production in lieu of dismantled equipment in connection with a proposed
raising of the German level of industry. It was an either-one-or-the-
other proposal which had been approved by President Truman only
with added restrictions [57] and which of course negated the Soviet position that they were entitled to both. Presumably the Russians also
recognized that the American proposal offered current production
reparations of less value than they could easily extract in six months
from their own zone.[58]

When the Soviet government failed to react, the foreign ministers,
following General Marshall's suggestion, turned to the remaining
agenda which pertained to the demilitarization treaty, to the Austrian
issue, and to boundary questions such as the future of the Rhineland,
the Ruhr, and the Saar. Since French control of the latter was conceded by the two Western powers and a three-power agreement of
April 19 provided for increased coal shipments to France, Bidault
emerged as the only winner from an otherwise abortive conference.
Moreover, a final consequence of the meeting—Germany's partition—
was the best long-range result the Quai d'Orsay could hope for.

The closing American comment on the conference was made at Berlin airport when General Marshall, stopping on his return trip from
Moscow, instructed General Clay to proceed vigorously with the
strengthening of the bizonal organization.[59] There was no doubt among
the American delegation that a protracted division of Germany had
been decided upon and, as one of its members wrote, it meant the
maintenance of troops in West Germany for an indefinite period of
time.[60] It also is apparent that when the War Department and the Appropriation Committees of Congress discussed the financial benefits
of the bizonal fusion, the additional expenditures of continued troop
maintenance in Europe were not taken into consideration. In any
event, had this been done, it is not likely that anybody would have
suggested the sum of $66 billion [61]—the total bill to the time of this
writing.

57. *Foreign Relations . . . Council of Foreign Ministers . . . 1947*, 2: 301–
303.
58. Gottlieb, *German Peace Settlement,* p. 158.
59. Clay, *Decision . . .* , p. 174.
60. Edward S. Mason, "Reflections on the Moscow Conference."
61. Statistics supplied by comptroller assistant secretary of defense, D.O.D.

CHAPTER TWELVE

CONCLUSIONS

In the preceding chapter the Moscow Council of Foreign Ministers Conference of 1947 was mentioned as the meeting that confirmed the division of Germany. It obviously could also be argued with considerable validity that the Moscow conference was not decisive, that the quadripartite Control Council for Germany continued to operate for another year; that there followed a Council of Foreign Ministers meeting in London which dealt primarily with the German problem; that the nucleus of a German government was formed only after this conference had failed; and that the final divisive act—the currency reform—did not take place until the summer of 1948. The Moscow meeting, on the other hand, was critical because the issue of economic unity in accordance with Potsdam had to be faced squarely by the four powers. The Soviets tied their belated acceptance of an all-German government to the receipt of reparations. The Yalta protocol as well as the Potsdam agreement—as originally interpreted by the United States—lent support to the Russian position. The Truman administration, on the other hand, concerned about congressional appropriations committees and fearful of communist expansionism, refused to pursue the suggested compromise and decided on a temporary division of the country. The recognized high risk that it might become permanent was accepted—probably because of the much-dreaded alternative of a Soviet-dominated Germany.

In conclusion then, instead of pinpointing any particular date or event as decisive, it is suggested that the preferred democratic strategy of incremental decision making was at work, a process which Braybrooke and Lindblom have described as decision making through small, or incremental, moves on particular problems rather than through a comprehensive long-range program. In their much-discussed study [1] four typical categories of political decisions were outlined: de-

1. David Braybrooke and Charles E. Lindblom, *A Strategy of Decision Policy: Evaluation as a Social Process.*

cisions that effect large change and are guided by adequate information and understanding, decisions that effect large change but are not similarly guided, decisions that effect only small change and are guided by adequate information, and finally decisions that effect small change but are not similarly guided and therefore subject to constant reconsideration and redirection. It is the last category, provocatively labeled "disjointed incrementalism," which seems to apply to the American occupational policies for Germany. They not only consisted —to use Braybrooke's and Lindblom's definitions—of an "indefinite series of policy moves" but actually represented "an exploratory process in which the goals of policy-making continued to change as new experience with policy threw new light on what is possible and desirable."

The American decision to convert from a peacetime to a wartime economy was suggested by the two scholars as an empirical example of "disjointed incrementalism." Normally such a decision would be considered one of the largest and most consequential a nation could make; in the case of the United States, however, it became a process of incremental transformation from the revision of the Neutrality Act in 1939 to governmental arrangements for cash-and-carry purchases of arms from abroad, to informal pressures to expand the machine-tool industry, to "educational contracts" leading industry step by step into war production, to the declaration of an Unlimited National Emergency, to night-and-day production of machine tools, to the establishment of an Office of Civilian Defense, to the lend-lease program, and so on. The incremental direction was taken because in the prevailing political climate it was least controversial and at the same time very effective.

As to the treatment of postwar Germany, the ultimate cause for the incremental steps which led to the division of the country will be found in the policy vacuum created by Roosevelt's unwillingness, and Truman's initial inability, to decide on a definite course of action. Starting with the agreement to establish four zones of occupation, these steps encompassed: the rejection by Roosevelt of the State Department's plan to strengthen the authority of the Control Council over the zone commanders; the decision to reduce Germany's peacetime economy to the average European level; the programmatic statements that the United States would not "again" finance Germany's reparations; the Potsdam reparations agreement, which established the controversial "first charge" principle while negating the creation of a joint reparations pool; the recognition that West Germany's population would have to be temporarily fed at American expense; General Clay's reaction to the economic and political constraints upon the Military Government, namely, the effort to pull Germany up by its own bootstraps; the abortive attempt to establish a quadripartite export-import plan; the first Level-of-Industry Plan; the blocking of reparations shipments; the tentative plan to unify the British and American Zones in order to obtain early economic self-sufficiency; the commitment to Congress that American food subsidies would end after three years; the emergence of the containment concept; the resulting decision to proceed with the economic fusion of Bizonia while rejecting a reopening of the reparations issue as well as Soviet overtures for a compromise; the establishment of German governmental institutions; and finally the creation of a new currency.

An examination of these incremental way stations shows instances when the logic of the situation had eliminated reasonable alternatives. The agreement on zonal boundaries as a result of military operations, the establishment of a Level-of-Industry Committee to determine a floor for the dismantlement process, and the creation of a feeding program for the American Zone of Germany would all fall into this category. Equally, there had to be a currency reform and a German government once the concept of a separate West Germany had taken hold. The State Department's memorandum of March 10, 1945, was a logical move to strengthen the Control Council's authority over the zone commanders in order to avoid the feared partition of Germany along zonal boundaries. Moreover, the positive side of the containment policy emphasizing national power and will was a rational reaction to domestic pressures for a return to normal prewar conditions and to the disintegration of the American army.

Idealogy, on the other hand, was the motivating element in Morgenthau's opposition to the above-mentioned State Department memorandum, although it is not clear whether FDR's disavowal of his original concurrence was prompted by the same emotional considerations or by the army's administrative objections. In an equally nonrational manner the negative side of the containment policy, "You can't compromise with the Russians," played a significant role in preventing a meaningful American-Soviet dialogue at the Moscow Conference.

The influence of American leaders' past experiences on the occupational policies for Germany does not require any further elaboration at this point. As Roosevelt interpreted history, World War II had come about because of Woodrow Wilson's benign treatment of a defeated Germany; moreover, he—and Truman as well—perceived American speculative investments in the twenties as an unfortunate program of economic support for Germany which was not going to be repeated. The two resulting fundamental doctrines—Germany's economy must remain weak and the United States must not be financially involved— caused a number of incremental decisions to be taken at the administrative level of the Military Government relating to Graham Allison's Model II.[2] In particular this pertains to General Clay's efforts to pull Germany up by its own bootstraps, to his abortive attempts to set up a quadripartite export-import plan, to the halt to reparations, to the emergency solution of Bizonia, and to the resulting financial commitment to Congress. While the containment policy was instrumental in producing a negative attitude toward any compromise at the top governmental level, it also seems clear that the Military Government's organizational predicament in trying to establish a self-supporting German economy and to live up to the War Department's promises to the appropriation committees actually prompted the outcome of the Moscow meeting.

That the incremental process in this case was a disjointed one will be readily acknowledged if one considers that the significance of the available and adequate information was either not understood or disregarded. This pertains particularly to the extensive data assembled by the United States Strategic Bombing Survey demonstrating that Germany's industrial capacity had been only slightly reduced. It also applies to the analytical studies by OSS and Federal Reserve economists which indicated that Germany would be able to pay between $2.5 to $3.5 billion annually in reparations. The failure of the policy makers to consider such data from recognized experts, as well as their disregard for an important consequence of containment—maintaining troops in Europe indefinitely—may seem puzzling, but such omissions are part and parcel of incremental decision making. As Braybrooke and Lindblom stressed, "The strategy's striking feature is that what is omitted is often quite as important as what is being considered."[3] Moreover, when a consequence is originally neglected, "the decision makers can make it the focus of subsequent policy analysis."[4] As of 1950, this was precisely what had to be done.

2. Graham Allison, *Essence of Decision.*
3. Braybrooke and Lindblom, *Strategy* . . . , p. 93.
4. Ibid., p. 125.

It is clear that the major thrust of the present study deviates greatly from the interpretations of traditionalist as well as revisionist writers who see governing grand designs where there were none. Some of the former have maintained that the division of Germany was an un-avoidable necessity in order to forestall the "setting up of a communist Reich as an unchallengable menace to Western democracy," [5] while others suggested a Soviet plan to keep the German economy in disarray in order to promote the cause of communism in Europe.[6] Marxist doctrine seems to be in accord with these interpretations, and it is therefore possible that similar schemes were entertained by some Soviet leaders. However, everything that has since been learned about the state of Russia at the end of the war indicates an exhausted, terribly mutilated nation close to starvation. No evidence has been produced in the last thirty years which shows that there existed in 1945 a Soviet long-range plan for conquest. As to the alleged "inevitability" of the split, the traditionalist school has never examined whether, between the irresponsible permissiveness which promoted the disintegration of the American army and a policy favoring the division of Europe, ma-ture statesmanship could not have found some middle ground.

Among the revisionists Gabriel Kolko [7] offers the reader important insights, but he too sees a definite resolve to drop the Russian ally and to build up West Germany as an anti-Communist bulwark at a time when these were merely hazy concepts in the minds of some political leaders. A more extreme branch of the revisionist school advanced the theory that the cold war in general, and the division of Europe in par-ticular, were caused by the American policies of economic expansion-ism—reinforced during the critical period by a unilateral control of the atomic bomb. Using alternate labels of economic imperialism, demands for an "open door," [8] and "multilateralism," [9] these writers suggested that such policies resulted from the belief that without international trade domestic American markets would be glutted, that there would be widespread unemployment, and that the American standard of living would suffer grievously. By the same token a worldwide system of multilateral trade would tend to ensure prosperity and rising living standards of all nations. Western economic theory not only favors multilateralism, but it also can point to the example of bilateral Euro-

5. Samuel Flagg Bemis, *A Diplomatic History of the United States*, p. 927.
6. Herbert Feis, *Churchill, Roosevelt, Stalin*, pp. 619–620.
7. *The Politics of War*.
8. William Appleman Williams, *The Tragedy of American Diplomacy*.
9. Bruce Kuklick, *American Policy and the Division of Germany*.

pean trade between the two wars as a forbidding alternative. More-over, the necessary proof that a basic economic doctrine actually triggered a powerful policy-determining crusade is still outstanding.

As far as the decision to divide Germany is concerned, there exists no evidence that *any* long-range economic policies—let alone a nebu-lous "multilateralism"—played a significant role prior to the Marshall Plan legislation. It goes without saying that there was an under-standable desire in the United States as well as in the Soviet Union to reorganize the world as closely as possible in accord with one's own society. But at the beginning of the Moscow conference the most sig-nificant aspect of America's official attitude toward Germany was still its ambivalence. As the present study has suggested, if long-range consequences had been adequately appraised, a different course of action might well have been chosen.

The question arises as to whether a more conciliatory and more constructive American attitude in Moscow would have changed the map of Europe. On one hand, one will recall George Kennan's com-ment that the thoughts of American-Soviet cooperation in Germany were mere "pipe-dreams," [10] an appraisal apparently shared by Charles Bohlen.[11] It would be presumptuous to cast aside the views of these eminent experts on the Soviet Union. Undoubtedly the mistrust and ill will created among American diplomats by the Soviet disregard for the Yalta agreements on Eastern Europe presented a formidable ob-stacle to effective cooperation. It also is clear that American repre-sentatives who must work within the constitutional confines of the United States find themselves at a disadvantage when facing the unified command structure of the USSR. Finally, neither patience nor perse-verance—essential prerequisites for successful negotiations with the Soviet Union—is an American characteristic.

On the other side of the argument, there are three points to be made: first, a German provisional government—as discussed at length at the Moscow Conference—would have had a life of its own. The great majority of its members would not have been Communists and the country's unification would have been its primary goal. It is not neces-sary to speculate whether, for instance, the Austrian example, which gave the government considerable elbow room, would have been fol-lowed, because Molotov himself indicated Soviet expectations in this regard.

10. Kennan, *Memoirs* . . . , p. 178.
11. Clay, *Decision* . . . , p. 131.

The Allies must not assume direct moral responsibility for everything that takes place in Germany. Appropriate responsibility should lie upon a German government, invested with the necessary powers. The situation in this respect may be illustrated by the example of Japan. As we know, there is a Japanese government, although supreme power rests with the Allied occupation authorities. Other examples could be cited as well.[12]

He added that the question of whether Germany should have a centralized or federalized government ought to be decided by a German free vote.

Second, a four-power currency reform following a successful Moscow conference would have drastically transformed the German economic scene, revealed the dormant productive vigor of the German people, and demonstrated its impact on exports and reparations from current production. Accordingly, American food subsidies soon could have been curtailed and replaced by shipments of raw materials. As economic developments in Germany after June 1948 showed, there is no conjecture in this part of the scenario. Moreover, faced with the alternative of partition, a German administration—regardless of its composition—would have willingly accepted a substantial and long-range reparations burden.[13]

Third, had a genuine attempt to solve the impasse been made at Moscow, the United States representatives would have had two trump cards in hand: the promise of a continued flow of reparations from current production, which would have been of pivotal significance in view of Russia's desperate economic plight,[14] and the threat of an imminent partition, which would have equally strengthened the American negotiating position. While these two factors combined assured a considerable leverage for the American side, the practical application would still have required a clear sense of purpose and considerable skill. Naturally, as General Clay suggested, the flow of reparations would have had to be made contingent on a Soviet observation of certain fundamental commitments, including, among others, free elections at a definite date, considerable freedom of action for an emerging German government, and a return of the SAG enterprises to German control. Moreover, reparations had to be a promptly reversible con-

12. Molotov, *Speeches* . . . , pp. 394–395 (22 March 1947).
13. Emanuel Gottlieb, in *The German Peace Settlement,* chap. 8, offers a detailed blueprint of a realistic reparations program from current production.
14. Strobe Talbott, ed., *Khrushchev Remembers,* pp. 233–244.

cession made dependent on a faithful observance of all negotiated points. Partition could always have been held in reserve as a viable alternative. It stands to reason that the suggested American-Soviet cooperation in Germany still might have failed. However, the point the present writer is advancing is that a constructive effort should have been made. Without doubt the Kremlin's aggressive posture had become a major irritant. But neither the legal nor the economic rationale for the United States position is convincing and the long-range consequences of the chosen policy were not duly appraised.[15]

This leads us to the final question, whether from the standpoint of the United States a unified Germany would have made for a better world. It is clear that we are now entering the area of sheer speculation. Nevertheless it is probably safe to say that a unified and disarmed Germany per se would have promoted greater American-Soviet cooperation with the particular aim of preventing Germany's rearmament. Accordingly, a quadripartite disarmament pact similar to the one suggested by Byrnes in 1946 might have emerged. Possibly there would have been no war in Korea nor in Vietnam. On the other hand, a united Germany would represent a tremendous economic force which—even without arms—would have seriously impinged on Soviet controls in the East and on American hegemony in the West. Evidently there is no way to tell whether the resulting international problems and dangers would or would not have been equal to those with which the present generation has been obliged to live.

15. Warren F. Kimball, in *Swords or Ploughshares,* p. 62, reaches a similar conclusion: "When the American government finally threw out the Morgenthau Plan for Germany, it threw out the baby with the bath water; for not only did the United States eschew a policy of revenge, but it also tossed away programs which could have established a truly neutral, disengaged Germany. That alternative might have, with relatively little risk, significantly diminished the tension and length of the Cold War."

APPENDIX 1

THE YALTA REPARATIONS PROTOCOL

On the Talks between the Heads of Three Governments at the Crimean Conference on the German Reparations in Kind.

(1) Germany must pay in kind for the losses caused by her to the Allied nations in the course of the war. Reparations are to be received in the first instance by those countries which have borne the main burden of the war, have suffered the heaviest losses and have organized victory over the enemy.

(2) Reparation in kind is to be exacted from Germany in three following forms:

    a) Removals within two years from the surrender of Germany or the cessations of organized resistance from the national wealth of Germany located on the territory of Germany herself as well as outside her territory (equipment, machine tools, ships, rolling stock, German investments abroad, shares of industrial transport and other enterprises in Germany, etc.), these removals to be carried out chiefly for destroying the war potential of Germany.

    b) Annual deliveries of goods from current production over a period to be fixed.

    c) Use of German labor.

(3) For the working out on the above principles of a detailed plan for exaction of reparations from Germany an Allied Reparations Commission will be set up in Moscow. It will consist of three representatives—one from the Union of Soviet Socialist Republics, one from the United Kingdom and one from the United States of America.

(4) With regard to the fixing of the total sum of the reparation as well as the distribution of it among the countries which suffered from the German aggression, the Soviet and American delegation agreed as follows:

"The Moscow Reparation Commission should take in its initial studies as a basis for discussion the suggestion of the Soviet Government that the total sum of the reparation in accordance with the points (a) and (b) of the paragraph 2 should be $20,000,000,000, and that 50 percent of it should go to the Union of Soviet Socialist Republics."

The British delegation was of the opinion that, pending consideration of the reparation question by the Moscow Reparation Commission, no figures of reparation should be mentioned.

The above Soviet-American proposal has been passed to the Moscow Reparation Commission as one of the proposals to be considered by the Commission.

Appendix 2

Instructions for the United States Representative on the Allied Commission on Reparations [Pauley]

[Washington, May 18, 1945]

1. It was agreed at the Yalta Conference that Germany must pay in kind for the losses caused by her to the Allied Nations in the course of the war. The primary purpose of the Reparation Commission should be the formulation of a general program for the exaction of substantial reparation and the establishment of the policies under which this program is to be implemented.

2. It is and has been fundamental United States policy that Germany's war potential be destroyed, and its resurgence as far as possible be prevented, by removal or destruction of German plants, equipment and other property.

While cooperating with the other powers in implementing the basic purposes of the Yalta Agreement, the U.S. representative will bear in mind that whatever plan is formulated by the Reparation Commission (hereinafter referred to as the Reparation Plan) should be in conformity with the economic and security objectives of this country with respect to Germany. The position of the United States on the various issues involved in this respect is summarized in the following paragraphs.

3. In determining the size and character of reparation in accordance with points a and b of paragraph 2 of the Reparation Protocol and the allocation thereof among the various claimant nations the following principles are advocated by this Government:

a. The Reparation Plan should assist in the elimination of industrial capacity in Germany considered to be dangerous to the security of the United Nations.

b. The Reparation Plan should aid in strengthening and developing on a sound basis the industries and trade of the devastated non-enemy countries of Europe and of other United Nations, and in raising the living standards of these countries.

c. The reparation burden should be distributed in so far as practicable so as to impose equality of sacrifice upon, and result in an equal general standard of living for the German populations of each of the zones under the control of the respective occupying nations.

d. This Government opposes any reparation plan based upon the assumption that the United States or any other country will finance directly or indirectly any reconstruction in Germany or reparation by Germany.

e. The Reparation Plan should not maintain or foster dependence of other countries upon the German economy.

f. The Reparation Plan should not be of such a nature as to promote or require the building up of German economic capacity.

g. To the maximum extent possible, reparations should be taken from the national wealth of Germany existing at the time of collapse, with primary emphasis upon the removal of industrial machinery, equipment and plants, particularly the shipbuilding, metallurgical, machine tool producing, electrical machinery, and chemical industries (including all industries producing oil and oil products, synthetic nitrogen and synthetic rubber), ships, rolling stock, patents, copyrights, and German foreign exchange assets including investments abroad. Capacity for the production of component parts that enter into the production of the industries noted above should also be eligible for removal. Reparation in kind should not include arms, ammunition, and implements of war. (This Government favors the inclusion of German ocean-going merchant tonnage in the shipping pool until the end of the war against Japan and its division on some fair basis thereafter, and negotiations with other governments are in progress on this subject.)

h. To the extent that for political reasons it may become necessary in the negotiations to agree that reparations be collected in the form of deliveries of goods from current production over a period of years, such goods should be of such a nature and in such amounts as not to require the maintenance of the German war potential or the continued dependence of other countries on Germany after reparations cease. Accordingly, recurring reparations, over a period of years, should be:

(1) As small as possible in relation to the reparations to be paid in the form of industrial plants and equipment; and

(2) Primarily in the form of raw materials and natural resources, and to the smallest extent possible in the form of manufactured products.

i. The removal of plants and equipment shall take place regardless of the fact that they are owned in whole or in part, directly or indirectly, by United Nations nationals. Where plants or equipment which are owned in whole or in part by a United Nation national are to be so removed arrangements shall be made, if practicable and desired by the government of such national, for the owner to retain his interest in such plant and equipment after removal. If not practicable or so desired, Germany shall furnish to the government of such national adequate reparation to cover the interest of such national.

j. It will be inevitable that the German standard of living will be adversely affected by the carrying out of the Reparation Plan. However, the reparation exactions should be held within such limits as to leave the German people with sufficient means to provide a minimum subsistence standard of living without sustained outside relief; but under no condition should this limitation operate to require the retention in Germany of means to support basic living standards on a higher level than that existing in any one of the neighboring United Nations.

k. The Reparation Plan should not put the United States in a position where it will have to assume responsibility for sustained relief to the German people.

4. It was agreed at Yalta that reparation in kind is to be exacted from Germany, partly through the "use of German labor." In negotiations on labor reparation with the other powers in the Reparation Commission, the United States representatives will be guided by the following principles:

a. The United States will not accept reparation in the form of labor services.

b. Both compulsory and voluntary labor services furnished as reparation should be used outside of Germany only for reconstruction and repair of war damage and not for current production operations except for fuel and food.

c. This Government is strongly of the view that persons other than those specified in d below as deserving of punishment should not be called upon to perform compulsory labor service outside Germany.

d. Compulsory labor service should be required only from those judicially convicted as war criminals, including individuals determined by appropriate process to be members of European Axis organizations, official or unofficial, which themselves have been adjudicated to be criminal in purpose or activities.

e. Agreement should be sought along the following lines with regard to compulsory labor service:

(1) Except for persons tried for specific crimes, and convicted and sentenced to lifetime punishment, the period of compulsory labor service should be limited to a definite span of years.

(2) The standard of living and conditions of employment should conform to humane standards.

(3) The Reparation Commission or Agency should periodically survey the living and working conditions of compulsory workers and the uses made of their services.

f. Apart from persons deserving of punishment as defined above, German labor for reparations should be recruited only on a voluntary basis.

g. The net value of the services of both types of labor shall be included as reparations.

5. The first charge on all approved exports for reparation or otherwise (other than removals of existing plant and equipment) shall be a sum necessary to pay for approved imports. Accordingly, to the extent necessary

to pay for such minimum German imports as may be determined to be essential, recipient countries should be required to pay for German exports, except removals of existing plant and equipment. Imports for which payment will be sought shall include supplies imported by the occupying forces for displaced persons and German civilians.

6. Without the approval of an appropriate Allied body there shall be no re-export to third countries of goods received on reparation account.

7. In order to prevent the treatment as war booty or as reimbursement for occupation costs of exports from Germany which should properly be considered as reparations deliveries, agreement should be sought on the scope of war booty and reimbursement for occupation costs. Agreement should also be sought on the scope of restitution in relation to reparation.

8. The governments participating in the Reparation Commission will retain control over the disposition of German property located within their respective borders. These nations will seek agreement with other countries in which German assets are located designed to eliminate continued German control of such assets and prevent their eventual return to Germans.

9. The United States will expect to assert a claim for reparations before the Reparation Commission in accordance with the principles of the Yalta Protocol in order to preserve its rights to its proper share of payment for losses caused to it by Germany in the course of the war. Pending the furnishing of a more exact claim at a later date the United States representative shall reserve the right to claim delivery of reparations in a total amount to be determined. The United States will desire to receive as much as feasible of its share of reparations in the form of foreign exchange assets including German investments abroad.

10. As an interim program, pending the formulation of more definitive arrangements, this Government would favor formulation of an immediate program by the Reparation Commission along the following lines:

a. During the initial period following the collapse of Germany each of the four occupying powers—Great Britain, Russia, France and the United States—may remove from its zone of occupation in Germany plants, equipment and materials (including current output) of such a nature and not in excess of such amounts as may be determined by the Reparation Commission. It shall be our policy to press for inclusion in such an initial removal schedule the categories of plant, equipment and materials (excluding ocean-going merchant tonnage) described in paragraphs 30, 31 and 32 of the "Directive to the Commander in Chief of the United States Forces of Occupation Regarding the Military Government of Germany" and in paragraph 3 g above.

b. The decision as to whether or not the removal of particular plants, equipment or materials out of a zone in Germany is consistent with the purposes of occupation would be made by the commander of such zone, subject to the following conditions:

(1) There would be constant consultation between zone commanders.

(2) In making a decision as to removal the zone commander would be responsible for carrying out any relevant agreed policies which may be formulated from time to time by the Control Council.

(3) The Control Council would have an opportunity to consider any particular removal and could veto it.

(4) Regular reports should be made to the Control Council of transfers for reparation account and the Control Council should keep appropriate Allied agencies currently informed.

c. During this initial period any one of the four occupying powers could allow, if it so desired, any other United Nation entitled to reparations in the form of removals from Germany to take out of its zone plants, equipment and materials of such a nature and not in excess of such amounts as may be determined by the Reparation Commission. Such removals would be subject to the policy and conditions specified in sub-paragraphs a and b above.

d. Records should be kept of all deliveries made on reparations account under such interim arrangements and such deliveries should be made without prejudice to the final allocation of reparation shares. The Reparation Commission should determine the principles for valuation of such deliveries.

11. The Reparation Plan should include provision for the early establishment of a reparation agency including representatives of such governments as have suffered devastation or substantial damage. This agency, after detailed study of Germany's capacity to pay and examination of claims to reparation by the various claimant nations, shall develop a long term plan for the delivery of reparations. This plan shall set forth a description of the reparations to be delivered and their physical allocation to the various claimant nations. It shall contain a time schedule indicating the rate at which deliveries are to be made to the several governments over a stated period of years. The reparation agency should be given continuing responsibility for drawing up at regular intervals detailed schedules of the amounts and kinds of reparations items to be delivered and should have authority to determine the allocation of specific items among claimant governments.

In lieu of the establishment of the reparations agency referred to above the Reparation Plan may provide that the Reparation Commission, appropriately expanded by the addition of representatives of other claimant governments, may be continued in existence and utilized for the same purpose.

The occupation authorities should be responsible for the execution of the plan within Germany. In the execution of the plan, the Control Council should have the authority to withhold from transfer as reparations specific items the removal of which in its judgment would reduce the available economic means below the minimum required to meet the other purposes of the occupation. After review by the Control Council and in the absence of agreement, the zone commander if he believes that any specific item should be retained within his zone may with the specific determination of his government that such item is essential for the purposes of the occupation withhold the removal of such item. The zone commander may, of course, withhold the removal of such items pending such determination.

The long term plan referred to above should not be approved by the U.S. representatives on the Reparation Commission or Agency until it has been submitted to and approved by the United States Government.

The Control Council should advise the Reparation Agency (or Commission) from time to time as deliveries are made. The Reparation Agency (or Commission) should keep a record of all such deliveries, and should place appropriate values on the respective amounts delivered.

POTSDAM REPARATIONS AGREEMENT
[PART IV]

In accordance with the Crimean decision that Germany be compelled to compensate to the greatest possible extent for the loss and suffering that she has caused to the United Nations and for which the German people cannot escape responsibility, the following agreement on reparations was reached:

1. Reparations claims of the USSR shall be met by removals from the Zone of Germany occupied by the USSR and from appropriate German external assets.

2. The USSR undertakes to settle the reparations claims of Poland from its own share of reparations.

3. The reparations claims of the United States, the United Kingdom and other countries entitled to reparations shall be met from the Western Zones and from appropriate German external assets.

4. In addition to the reparations to be taken by the USSR from its own Zone of occupation, the USSR shall receive additionally from the Western Zones:

   a) 15 percent of such usable and complete industrial capital equipment, in the first place from the metallurgical, chemical, and machine manufacturing industries, as is unnecessary for the German peace economy and should be removed from the Western Zones of Germany, in exchange for an equivalent value of food, coal, potash, zinc, timber, clay products, petroleum products, and such other commodities as may be agreed upon.

   b) 10 percent of such industrial capital equipment as is unnecessary for the German peace economy and should be removed from the Western Zones, to be transferred to the Soviet Government on reparations account without payment or exchange of any kind in return. Removals of equipment as provided in (a) and (b) shall be made simultaneously.

5. The amount of equipment to be removed from the Western Zones on account of reparations must be determined within six months from now at latest.

6. Removals of industrial capital equipment shall begin as soon as pos-

sible and shall be completed within two years from the determination specified in paragraph 5. The delivery of products covered by 4(a) above shall begin as soon as possible and shall be made by the USSR in agreed installments within five years of the date hereof. The determination of the amount and character of the industrial capital equipment unnecessary for the German peace economy and therefore available for reparations shall be made by the Control Council under policies fixed by the Allied Commission on Reparations, with the participation of France, subject to the final approval of the Zone Commander in the Zone from which the equipment is removed.

7. Prior to the fixing of the total amount of equipment subject to removal, advance deliveries shall be made in respect of such equipment as will be determined to be eligible for delivery in accordance with the procedure set forth in the last sentence of paragraph 6.

8. The Soviet Government renounces all claims in respect of reparations to shares of German enterprises which are located in the Western Zones of occupation in Germany as well as to German foreign assets in all countries except those specified in paragraph 9 below.

9. The Government of the United Kingdom and the United States of America renounce their claims in respect of reparations to shares of German enterprises which are located in the Eastern Zone of occupation in Germany, as well as to German foreign assets in Bulgaria, Finland, Hungary, Rumania and Eastern Austria.

10. The Soviet Government makes no claims to gold captured by the Allied troops in Germany.

REPORT ON GERMAN REPARATIONS
TO THE PRESIDENT OF THE UNITED STATES
FEBRUARY TO SEPTEMBER 1945
PART IX (III)

Reparations are to be payable not in German paper credits, or German currency, but in 'things' or services. Under this new payment formula, payments will be made as follows:

(a) Through the removal of existing physical plants, including factories, power plants, machine tools, transport equipment and the like;

(b) Through the removal of already available raw materials and inventories on hand;

(c) Through the removal of a part of current production over future years both of raw materials like coal and lumber, and also the products of agriculture and of peaceful domestic industries, such as textiles and consumer goods, in amounts to be determined after the capital removal and import-export programs shall have been set;

(d) Through the seizure of German foreign investments and assets; and

(e) Through forced German labor for service abroad under rigidly limited conditions to be determined when the occasion arises. (The U.S. has indicated that it does not desire German labor as reparations.)

Not all shipments out of Germany, particularly those arising under paragraphs (b) and (c) will be taken as reparations because it has been agreed that essential and approved imports required for the German economy shall be a first charge against exports in the development of the import-export program for Germany as a whole.

It should be pointed out that it was decided in the Crimean Conference that reparations would be exacted from Germany annually from current production, as well as through capital removals as stated in (c) above. This agreement is still unchanged, except that a deferment has been agreed in determination of the amount of and time limit for such current reparations until the schedule of capital removals is made in accordance with the standards fixed. It is therefore assumed that when the program of annual recurring reparations is formulated, the responsibility for determining the amount and character of current deliveries will likewise be entrusted to the Allied Control Council, and the allocation of same to the Allied Reparations Agency.

PRINCIPAL ECONOMIC ISSUES ON CURRENT GERMAN PROBLEMS FOR COUNCIL OF FOREIGN MINISTERS' MEETING, MOSCOW MEMORANDUM NO. 2, ANNEX E

Reparation Out of Current Output—The Legal Position

The proposed United States position against reparation out of current production is not supported by all plausible interpretations of the relevant past agreements. Support for the United States position is found in one construction of the Berlin Protocol, Article III, B, paragraph 19 and in the Level of Industry Agreement, March 28, 1946, by which German industrial capacity after reparations removals was fixed without any consideration of the possibility that capacity would be needed for reparation deliveries of output. Arguments against the proposed U.S. position are to be found in the Secret Protocol of the Crimea Conference, in two possible interpretations of the Berlin Protocol, one widely held on the American side, and in a formal agreement of the Allied Control Authority.

Yalta

The secret protocol of Yalta states specifically:
"2. Reparation in kind is to be exacted from Germany in three following forms:
  (a) Removals . . . from the national wealth of Germany . . .
  (b) Annual deliveries of goods from current production for a period to be fixed.
  (c) Use of German labour."
It may be argued that the reparation agreement of Yalta was superceded by the provisions on reparation of the Berlin Protocol. This is in fact the U.S. position on a number of points. It should be borne in mind, however, that the USSR has a habit of recurring to the Yalta Protocol, as for example in the question of the Russian claim for $10 billion out of $20 billion of reparation from Germany mentioned again in Molotov's speech at the CFM in July 1946.

Potsdam

It is now generally regarded by the United States that Article III, B, 19 of the Berlin Protocol rules out reparation out of current output. This article reads:

> "Payment of reparations should leave enough resources to enable the German people to subsist without external assistance. In working out the economic balance of Germany the necessary means must be provided to pay for imports approved by the Control Council in Germany. The proceeds of exports from current production and stocks shall be available in the first place for payment for such imports.
>
> The above clause will not apply to the equipment and products referred to in paragraphs 4 (A) and 4 (B) of the Reparations Agreement."

It should be mentioned, however, that this interpretation is one which was not prevalent at the time. In his "Report on German Reparations to the President of the United States, February to September 1945" Ambassador Pauley refers many times to the fact that reparation out of current output remains to be decided upon even after the Potsdam Agreement (I, p. 16; IX, pp. 2 and 3; X, p. 5; Appendix 30, p. 13; Appendix 40, p. 3). Ambassador Pauley in all cases assumes that such reparation can be arranged only after exports have grown to the point where they are sufficient to pay on imports. He nevertheless everywhere assumes that reparation out of current production of all Germany will take place. To be sure, the statements made in this connection preceded the agreement on the level of industry reached in the Allied Control Authority on March 28, 1946, having for the most part been written in August and September 1945. Moreover, they were made at a time when there was little or no realization of the problems to be encountered in securing the economic unification of Germany, and the difficulties imposed thereby in balancing German exports and imports. It is significant to note, however, that the first-charge principle stated in Article III, para. 19 is not by itself a bar to reparation out of current output, and was not taken for such at the time of its adoption.

There is moreover, one interpretation of Article III, para. 19 of the Berlin Protocol which would prevent its being a barrier to reparation out of current output even while German exports against foreign exchange payment were insufficient to pay for imports. This view has been advanced by Mr. Emile Despres then a member of the Department of State delegation to the Potsdam Conference in his capacity as Adviser on German Affairs to Mr. Clayton, and a U.S. representative on the committee which finally drafted Article III, para. 19. This view is that the statement "The *proceeds* of exports etc." excepts exports of reparation out of current output on the ground that such export yields no proceeds. Mr. Despres since resigned from the Department has set forth this view in no memorandum known to exist in the Department, and in fact communicated it verbally to the writer approximately a year after the Potsdam Agreement. The merit of the position, however, is attested by the fact that the Deputy Director of the Economics Division, OMGUS, understands that the Russian members of the Economic Subcommittee accepted the language of Article III, para. 19 only after it had passed through a number of successive drafts; and that Ambassador Pauley's report states: . . . "The Soviet Delegation at the last moment . . . accepted the principle of imports as a first-charge on exports." (op. cit. V p. 12).

Whatever the merit of the theory that the statement of the first-charge principle in the Berlin Protocol was agreed to on a basis that excepted reparation out of current output, it has been made clear in the year or more following the Potsdam Conference, that the United States interpreted Article III, para. 19 to exclude this form of reparation so long as the German balance of payments was in deficit. The point may therefore be no longer relevant. It is interesting to observe in this connection that one German source, in commenting upon an alleged Soviet intention to retain Soviet owned plants in Germany not subject to German laws, says:

> "The reason for the formation of this mammoth concern was the realization among the Russians that continuous and difficult debates with the western Allies were unavoidable unless the 'proceeds of exports from current production and stocks' clause of the Potsdam agreement could be circumvented." (SSU DB-1275).

Allied Control Authority

Two actions of the Allied Control Authority bear upon the problem of reparation out of current output. The first of these is a preliminary agreement on principles to govern foreign trade, pending what was expected to be a forthcoming agreement on the economic unification of Germany. This agreement is represented by a document referred to as CONL/P (45)32, dated September 15, 1945, which contains a statement of the first-charge principle (Article III, para. 19 of the Berlin Protocol) in terms which specifically exempt reparation out of current output from the first-charge. The pertinent passage consists of a definition of exports as follows:

> "(b) All goods, merchandise and raw materials, shipped to other countries for this purpose, *except those goods, merchandise and raw materials applied in payment of approved reparations,* shall be deemed exports."

United States acceptance of this statement with the inclusion of the underlined expression is recognized as an error. The significance of the phrase was not seen at the time of its acceptance.

The second action, as already mentioned, was the agreement to the Level of Industry plan on March 28, 1946. This plan, designed to furnish a benchmark for measuring reparation removals in the form of capital equipment, is silent on the subject of reparation out of current output. Failing to allow for such reparation, it by implication excludes them. The strength of this U.S. position is clearly recognized by the Soviet negotiators who have offered to adjust the level of industry allowed for Germany upward, so as to make reparation out of current production feasible.

Stuttgart Speech

The Secretary's speech of September 6, 1946, adopts a position on reparation out of current output which represents the most recent public statement of official U.S. views on the subject. The speech states:

> "In fixing the levels of industry no allowance was made for reparations from current production. Reparations from current production would be wholly incompatible with the levels of industry now established under the Potsdam Agreement.
>
> Obviously, higher levels of industry would have to be fixed if reparations from current production were contemplated. The levels of industry fixed are only sufficient to enable the German people to become self-supporting and to maintain living standards approximating the average European living conditions. . . .
>
> That was the principle of reparations to which President Truman agreed at Potsdam. And the United States will not agree to the taking from Germany of greater reparations than was provided by the Potsdam Agreement."

It will be observed that this statement of policy, while it does not rule out reparation from current output, attempts sharply to limit it. The sense of the passage is that any large program of reparation out of current output is ruled out; but that the United States would consider an offer to exchange a certain amount of capital equipment designed to be removed under the level of industry plan for an equivalent, but no greater, amount of current production. It is not entirely clear, however, that the passage succeeds in stating this position unequivocally, since, as already pointed out, the Potsdam Agreement did not by itself exclude reparation out of current output. The fact that the United States will not agree to the taking from Germany of greater reparations than was provided by the Potsdam Agreement, therefore, does not exclude a program of reparation out of current output to a value exceeding the value of the capital equipment left in Germany in return for it, unless the words "Potsdam Agreement" are interpreted to mean Potsdam Agreement and Level of Industry Plan.

It should be noted that a limitation of a program of reparation out of current production to the value of the additional capital equipment exchanged therefore is unlikely to appeal to the USSR. It is generally accepted that a German plant at relatively full capacity production can produce the value of the movable capital equipment embodied in it in less than a year. To cite an extreme example the value of removable equipment in steel plants is relatively low by reason of the high proportion of fixed equipment of a construction rather than machinery nature. Thus if the Soviets were to ask for steel products in exchange for leaving the removable portions of a steel plant, they might only be entitled to receive seven or eight months output at full capacity.

BIBLIOGRAPHY

I. PRIMARY SOURCES

A. *Memoirs and Recollections*

Acheson, Dean. *Present at the Creation*. New York: Norton, 1969.

Baruch, Bernard Mannes. *The Making of the Reparation and Economic Sections of the Treaty.* New York: Harper, 1970.

Bohlen, Charles E. *Witness to History 1929–1969*. New York: Norton, 1973.

Brockdorff-Rantzau, Ulrich Karl Christian. *Dokumente und Gedanken.* Berlin: Verlag für Kulturpolitik, 1925.

Brüning, Heinrich. *Memoiren 1918–1934*. Stuttgart: Deutsche Verlagsanstalt, 1970.

Byrnes, James F. *Speaking Frankly*. New York: Harper, 1947.

——. *All in One Lifetime*. New York: Harper, 1958.

Catroux, Georges. *J'ai vu tomber le Rideau de fer, Moscou 1945–1948.* Paris: Hachette, 1952.

Churchill, Winston S. *The Second World War*. 6 vols. Boston: Bantam Books, 1962.

Clark, Mark Wayne. *Calculated Risk*. New York: Harper, 1950.

Clay, Lucius D. *Decision in Germany*. Garden City, N.Y.: Doubleday, 1950.

Deane, John R. *The Strange Alliance: The Story of Our Efforts at Wartime Cooperation with Russia*. New York: Viking, 1947.

Djilas, Milovan. *Conversations with Stalin*. New York: Harcourt, 1962.

Dulles, John Foster. *War or Peace*. New York: Macmillan, 1950.

John Foster Dulles Papers. Seeley G. Mudd Manuscript Library. Princeton University.

Eden, Anthony. *The Memoirs of Anthony Eden: Full Circle*. Boston: Houghton Mifflin, 1960.

——. *The Reckoning*. Boston: Houghton Mifflin, 1965.

Gruber, Karl. *Zwischen Befreiung und Freiheit*. Wien: Ullstein, 1953.

Harriman, Averell W. *Peace with Russia?* New York: Simon & Schuster, 1959.

House, Edward Mandell, ed. *What Really Happened at Paris: The Story of the Peace Conference 1918–1919, by American Delegates*. New York: Scribner's, 1921.

Hull, Cordell. *The Memoirs of Cordell Hull.* 2 vols. New York: Macmillan, 1945.

Kennan, George F. *Memoirs, 1925–1950.* Boston: Little, Brown, 1967.

Kennedy, Robert F. *Thirteen Days: A Memoir of the Cuban Missile Crisis.* New York: Norton, 1969.

Leahy, William Daniel. *I Was There.* New York: Wittlesey House, 1950.
———. Diary 1941–1946. U.S. Library of Congress.

Lloyd George, David. *The Truth about Reparations and War Debts.* New York: H. Fertig, 1970.

Maisky, Ivan. *Memoirs of a Soviet Ambassador.* New York: Scribner's, 1968.

Millis, Walter, ed. *The Forrestal Diaries.* New York: Viking, 1951.

Morgenthau Diary: Germany, U.S. Congress, Senate Committee on the Judiciary, Subcommittee to Investigate the Administration of the Internal Security Act and Other Security Laws. 90th Cong., 1st sess., Nov. 1967.

Murphy, Robert. *Diplomat among Warriors.* Garden City, N.Y.: Doubleday, 1964.

Ratchford, B. U. and W. D. Ross. *Berlin Reparations Assignment.* Chapel Hill, N.C.: University of North Carolina Press, 1947.

Roosevelt, Elliot. *As He Saw It.* New York: Duell, Sloan & Pearce, 1946.

Sherwood, Robert E. *Roosevelt and Hopkins: An Intimate History.* New York: Harper, 1948.

Smith, Walter Bedell. *My Three Years in Moscow.* Philadelphia: Lippincott, 1950.

Sorensen, Theodore. *Kennedy.* New York: Bantam, 1966.

Standley, William H. *Admiral Ambassador to Russia.* Chicago: Regnery, 1955.

Stettinius, Edward. *Roosevelt and the Russians: The Yalta Conference.* Garden City, N.Y.: Doubleday, 1949.

Stimson, Henry L. *On Active Service in Peace and War.* New York: Harper, 1947.

Talbott, Strobe, ed. *Khrushchev Remembers.* Boston: Little, Brown, 1970.

Truman, Harry S. *Memoirs.* Garden City, N.Y.: Doubleday, 1955–1956.

Vandenberg, Arthur H., Jr. *The Private Papers of Senator Vandenberg.* Boston: Houghton Mifflin, 1952.

Wallace, Henry Agard. *The Price of Vision: The Diary of Henry A. Wallace 1942–1946,* edited by John Morton Blum. Boston: Houghton Mifflin, 1973.

B. *Documents*

Abkommen über Deutsche Auslandsschulden vom 27 Februar 1953. 5 Köln 1: Deutscher Wirtschaftsdienst, June 1975.

Cornides, W., and H. Volle. *Um den Frieden mit Deutschland.* Vol. 6 of *Dokumente und Berichte des Europa Archivs.* Oberursel, 1948.

Degras, Jane. *Soviet Documents on Foreign Policy.* 3 vols. London: Oxford University Press, 1951–1953.

Die Deutsche Frage auf der Moskauer Konferenz der Aussenminister. Europa Archiv, Sonderheft 2.1947.
Die Reparationsleistungen der Sowjetischen Bèsatzungszone Deutschlands. Europa Archiv 4.
Die Sowjetische Reparationspolitik seit 1945. Hannover: Sopade Denkschrift no. 29, 1950.
IARA Bericht 1949 über Deutsche Auslandsvermögen. Bremen, 1950.
Interallied Reparations Agency. *Report of the Assembly.* Brussels, 1951.
JEIA (Joint Export Import Agency).
    Instructions
    Monthly Reports
Lubin Papers. Roosevelt Library, Hyde Park, N.Y.
Memorandum H. Hilldring to Asst. Sec. of War, 7 November 1945. ASW 370.8 Germany. Control Council. National Archives.
Ministère des Affaires Etrangères. *Documents français relatifs à l'Allemagne 1945–1947.*
Office of Military Government for Germany (US) Federal Records Center, Suitland, Maryland, OMGUS records, Record Group 260.
    "A Year of Potsdam: The German Economy since the Surrender." 1946.
    Colm-Dodge-Goldsmith Report. "A Plan for the Liquidation of War Finance and the Financial Rehabilitation of Germany." 14-3/5.
    "Comparative Readings in Basic U.S. Policy Directives on Germany." Prepared by Program Control Branch, OMGUS.
    "Food and Agriculture in the Bizonal Area of Germany." Manuscript. 1 October 1947.
    Handbook for Military Government in Germany. 15 August 1944.
    "History of Military Government: VE Day to June 30, 1946." Chap. 8. Economics. Pt. 6. Food and Agriculture Branch. Manuscript, 20-3/5.
    Hoover Report. "Food and Agriculture US-UK Zone of Germany." February 1947. Manuscript prepared by US-UK Bipartite Food and Agriculture Panel. 20-3/5.
    Hutton, Edward L., and D. Walter Robbins. "Post-war German Foreign Trade." Manuscript, 15 December 1947.
    Memorandum Charles Fahy, Legal Advisor. HQ. U.S. Group Control Council (Germany) to Assistant Deputy for Public Services, 9 August 1945. 4-35/16.
    OMGUS, "History of Economic Planning in the Bizone." Manuscript. 406-1/3.
    OMGUS. *Food and Agriculture.* Monthly Reports of the Military Governor, U.S. Zone.
    OMGUS. *Trade and Commerce.* Monthly Reports of the Military Governor, U.S. Zone.
    OMGUS. *Weekly Information Bulletin.*
    "Plan of the Allied Control Council for Reparations and the Level of Post-War German Economy."
    "Review of Industry, May 1945–September 1947." Unpublished manuscript. 358-1/5.

Verwaltungsamt für Wirtschaft. "The Effect of Envisaged Dismantling on Germany's Economic Situation and its Role in European Reconstruction." Frankfurt am Main, 1948. Manuscript.

Revised Plan for Level of Industry in the US/UK Zones of Germany. Berlin, August 1947.

Royal Institute of International Affairs. Information Department. *Memorandum on Foreign Short Term Loans in Germany, 1919–1932*. London, 1933.

Scandrett Papers. Cornell University, Ithaca, N.Y.

Schmidt, Hubert G. *Food and Agriculture Programs in West Germany*. U.S. High Commissioner for Germany, Office of the Executive Secretary, Historical Division, 1952.

―――. *The Liberalization of West German Foreign Trade*. U.S. High Commissioner for Germany, Office of the Executive Secretary, Historical Division, 1952.

Smith, Jean Edward, ed. *The Papers of General Lucius D. Clay*. Bloomington, Ind.: Indiana University Press, 1974.

Statistisches Jahrbuch für das Deutsche Reich. 1936 Statistisches Reichsamt, 1937.

U.S. Congress

Congressional Record. 78th Congress. 2nd sess. 8 May 1944.

―――. 79th Congress. 1st sess. 13 March 1945.

―――. 79th Congress. 1st sess. 10 April 1945.

―――. 79th Congress. 1st sess. 17 May 1945.

―――. 79th Congress. 2nd sess. 19 July 1946.

House. Committee on Appropriations. Hearings on *First Deficiency Appropriations Bill 1947*. 80th Cong., 1st sess.

―――. Committee on Appropriations. Hearings on *Military Establishment Appropriations Bill for 1947*. 79th Cong., 2nd sess.

―――. *Report of President Franklin D. Roosevelt to Congress*. Document no. 779. 77th Cong., 2nd sess. 11 June 1942.

―――. Special Committee on Post-War Economic Policy and Planning. *Economic Reconstruction in Europe*. 8th Report (Serial 10936). 79th Cong., 1st sess. 1945.

Senate. *Accessibility of Strategic and Critical Materials in Time of War*. Report of Committee on American and Insular Affairs. Appendix 4, Report no. 1627. 83rd Cong., 2nd sess.

―――. Committee on Appropriations. Hearings on *European Interim Aid and GARIOA*. 80th Cong., 1st sess.

―――. Committee on Appropriations, Armed Services and Banking and Currency. *Hearings on Occupation Currency Transactions*. 80th Cong., 1st sess.

―――. Committee on Banking and Currency. Hearings on *President Truman's Request to Increase Lending Authority of Export-Import Bank*. 79th Cong., 1st sess. July 1945.

―――. Committee on Finance. *Sale of Foreign Bonds or Securities in the United States.* Hearings Pursuant to Senate Resolution 19. 72nd Cong., 1st sess. December 1931.

U.S. Department of State
  Bulletin 13, no. 323 (2 September 1945).
  Bulletin 13, no. 338 (16 December 1945).
  Bulletin 15, no. 376 (15 September 1946).
  Bulletin 16, no. 404 (30 March 1947).
  Bulletin 16, no. 405 (6 April 1947).
  Bulletin 16, no. 406 (18 April 1947).
  Bulletin 16, no. 407 (20 April 1947).
  Bulletin 16, no. 408 (27 April 1947).
  Bulletin 16, no. 410 (11 May 1947).
  Foreign Relations of the United States. Diplomatic Papers.
    1943. The Conferences at Cairo and Teheran.
    1944. vol. 1. General.
    1944. vol. 4. Europe.
    1945. The Conferences at Malta and Yalta.
    1945. vol. 3. European Advisory Commission; Austria; Germany.
    1945. vol. 4. Europe.
    1945. The Conference of Berlin (Potsdam). 2 vols.
    1945. vol. 5. Europe.
    1946. vol. 2. Council of Foreign Ministers.
    1946. vol. 5. The British Commonwealth; Western and Central Europe.
    1946. vol. 6. Eastern Europe; the Soviet Union.
    1947. vol. 2. Council of Foreign Ministers; Germany and Austria.
  State Department Files. National Archives.
    Records Group 43. Records of Council of Foreign Ministers.
    Records Group 59. 740.00119 European War.
    Records Group 59. Notter Files.
    Records Group 59. 740.00119 Control (Germany).
U.S. Office of Strategic Services. National Archives.
  Research and Analysis Report 2350. "Problems of German Reparations."
  Research and Analysis Report 2060. "Russian Reconstruction and Post-war Foreign Trade Developments."
  Research and Analysis Report 1899. "Russian War Damage and Possible Reparations Claims."
U.S. Strategic Bombing Survey. Rare Books Collection. Library of Congress.
  "A Brief Study of the Effects of the Area Bombing on Berlin, Augsburg, Bochum and Leipzig."
  "The Effects of Strategic Bombing on the German War Economy."
  "The German Machine Tool Industry."
USSR. "Documents: The Crimea and Potsdam Conferences of the Leaders of the Three Great Powers." *International Affairs,* nos. 6–10. Moscow: June–October 1965.
von Oppen, B. R., ed. *Documents on Germany under Occupation.* New York: Oxford University Press, 1955.

C. *Speeches*

Boyden, Roland W. Speech on reparations before New England Society at Waldorf-Astoria. New York. 23 December 1923. National Archives. (46200 R 29/3324.)

Dulles, John Foster. "Europe Must Federate or Perish." *Vital Speeches of The Day.* 17 January 1947.

Faingar, Isakhar Moiseevich. "Germaniia i Reparatsii" [Germany and Reparations] 24 April 1947. Moscow: Ministry of Higher Education, 1947.

Molotov, V. M. *Speeches and Statements at the Moscow Session of the Council of Foreign Ministers 1947.* London: Soviet News, 1947.

————. *Problems of Foreign Policy.* Moscow: Foreign Languages Publishing House, 1949.

Stalin, J. Election Speech of 9 February 1946. *New York Times.* 10 February 1946.

D. *Newspapers, Journals, Public Opinion Polls*

Cantril and Struck, *Public Opinion 1935–1945.*

Current Digest of Soviet Press 3, no. 20.

Daily Digest of World Broadcasts, Pt. 2. 19 October 1943.

Germany and the Postwar World. National Opinion Research Center, University of Denver.

Landwirtschaftliche Zeitung 115, no. 1 (1948). Rheinischer Landwirtschaftsverband.

New York Times. 24 June 1941; 10 February 1946; 12 February 1973.

Public Opinion Quarterly 5. Fall 1941.

Wall Street Journal. 23 September 1944.

Washington Post. 24 September 1944; 26 September 1944.

E. *Interviews and Correspondence*

Bergson, Abram, Professor. October 1974.

Bohlen, Charles, Ambassador. 5 December 1972.

Clay, Lucius D., General. 21 March 1974 and 20 February 1975.

Cohen, Benjamin V., Ambassador. May 1974.

Ginsburg, David. January 1975.

Harriman, W. Averell, Ambassador. 8 October 1974.

Mason, Edward S., Professor. April 1974.

McCloy, John J. 30 November 1967.

Riddleberger, James W., Ambassador. January 1975.

Rubin, Seymour J. January 1975.

II. SECONDARY SOURCES

Acheson, Dean. "Dean Acheson's Version of Robert Kennedy's Version of the Cuban Missile Affair: Homage to Plain Dumb Luck." *Esquire* (February 1969).

Adler, Hans A. "The Postwar Reorganization." *Quarterly Journal of Economics* 63, no. 3 (August 1949).

Alexandrov, Vladimir. "The Dismantling of German Industry." In *Soviet Economic Policy in Post-War Germany*, edited by Robert Slusser. New York: Research Program on the USSR, 1953.

Allison, Graham T. *Essence of Decision: Explaining the Cuban Missile Crisis*. Boston: Little, Brown, 1971.

Alperovitz, Gar. *Cold War Essays*. Garden City, N.Y.: Doubleday, 1970.

Armstrong, Ann. *Unconditional Surrender*. New Brunswick, N.J.: Rutgers University Press, 1961.

Backer, John H. *Priming the German Economy: American Occupational Policies 1945–1948*. Durham, N.C.: Duke University Press, 1971.

Bader, William B. *Austria Between East and West, 1945–1955*. Stanford, Cal.: Stanford University Press, 1966.

Bailey, Thomas A. *The Man in the Street: The Impact of American Public Opinion on Foreign Policy*. Gloucester, Mass.: Peter Smith, 1964.

———. *Probing America's Past: A Critical Examination of Major Myths and Misconceptions*. Lexington, Mass.: Heath, 1973.

———. *A Diplomatic History of the American People*. Third Edition. New York: Crofts, 1946.

Baker, Ray Stannard. *Life and Letters of Woodrow Wilson*. Vol. 5. Westport, N.Y.: Greenwood, 1968.

———. *Woodrow Wilson and World Settlement*. Garden City, N.Y.: Doubleday, 1922.

Balabkins, Nicholas, *Germany under Direct Controls: Economic Aspects of Industrial Disarmament 1945–1948*. New Brunswick, N.J.: Rutgers University Press, 1964.

Balfour, Michael, and John Mair. *Four Power Control in Germany and Austria, 1945–1946*. London: Royal Institute of International Affairs, 1956.

Barber, Hollis. *Foreign Policies of the United States*. New York: Dryden, 1953.

Barnes, Harry Elmer. *In Quest of Truth and Justice: Debunking the War Guilt Myth*. Chicago: National Historical Society, 1928.

———, ed. *Perpetual War for Perpetual Peace*. New York: Greenwood, 1933.

Beard, Charles A. *American Foreign Policy in the Making, 1932–1940: A Study in Responsibilities*. Hamden, Conn.: Shoestring, 1968.

———. *President Roosevelt and the Coming of the War*. New Haven, Conn.: Yale University Press, 1948.

Bemis, Samuel Flagg. *A Diplomatic History of the United States*. New York: Holt, Rinehart, 1964.

Bennett, Jack. "The German Currency Reform." *Annals of the American Academy of Political and Social Science* 267 (January 1950).

Bergmann, Karl. *Deutschland und der Young Plan*. Berlin: W. Christians, 1930.

———. *The History of Reparations*. London: Ernest Benn, 1927.

Berkhofer, Robert F., Jr. *A Behavioral Approach to Historical Analysis.* New York: Free Press, 1969.

Bidwell, R. L. *Currency Conversion Tables and 100 Years of Change.* London: Rex Collins, 1970.

Blum, John Morton. *Roosevelt and Morgenthau.* Boston: Houghton Mifflin, 1972.

Boorsten, Dan. *The Image.* New York: Atheneum, 1971.

Braybrooke, David, and Charles E. Lindblom. *A Strategy of Decision: Policy Evaluation as a Social Process.* New York: Free Press, 1963.

Brueggeman, Felix. *Woodrow Wilson und die Vereinigten Staaten von Amerika: Betrachtungen zum Weltkrieg und Versailler Vertrag.* Doctoral dissertation, Giessen, 1933.

Buehrig, Edward Henry. *Woodrow Wilson and the Balance of Power.* Gloucester, Mass.: Peter Smith, 1968.

Burks, R. V. "Eastern Europe." In *Communism and Revolution,* edited by Cyril E. Black and Thomas P. Thornton. Princeton, N.J.: Princeton University Press, 1964.

Burnett, Philip Mason. *Reparation at the Paris Peace Conference from the Standpoint of the American Delegation.* 2 vols. New York: Octagon, 1965.

Carman, Harry J., and Harold C. Syrett. *A History of the American People.* New York: Knopf, 1952.

Carr, Albert Z. *Truman, Stalin and Peace.* Garden City, N.Y.: Doubleday, 1950.

Carr, Edward Hallett. *The Bolshevik Revolution, 1917–1923.* Baltimore, Md.: Penguin, 1966.

———. *Conditions of Peace.* London: Macmillan, 1942.

———. *The Twenty Years' Crisis, 1919–1939.* New York, Harper, 1964.

Castillon, Richard. *Les Reparations Allemandes.* Paris: Press Universitaires de France, 1953.

Caute, David. *Communism and the French Intellectuals, 1914–1960.* New York: Macmillan, 1964.

Cecil, Robert. "Potsdam and Its Legends." *International Affairs* (July 1970).

Chamberlin, William H. *America's Second Crusade.* Chicago: Henry Regnery, 1950.

Chambers, S. P. "Post-War German Finances." *International Affairs* 25, no. 3 (July 1948).

Chitwood, Oliver. *Short History of the American People.* New York: Van Nostrand, 1945–1948.

Clay, Lucius D. *Decision in Germany.* Garden City, N.Y.: Doubleday, 1950.

Clemens, Diane Shaver. *Yalta.* New York: Oxford, 1970.

Council on Foreign Relations. *The United States in World Affairs 1947/48: An Account of American Foreign Relations.* New York: Harper, 1948.

Curry, George. *James F. Byrnes,* vol. 14, pt. 1 of *The American Secretaries of State and Their Diplomacy.* New York: Cooper Square, 1965.

Dahl, Robert. *Congressional Foreign Policy*. New York: Harcourt, 1950.

Dennett, Raymond, and Joseph E. Johnson, eds. *Negotiating with the Russians*. Boston: World Peace Foundation, 1951.

Deutsch, Karl. *The Analysis of International Relations*. Englewood Cliffs, N.J.: Prentice Hall, 1968.

Divine, Robert A. *Roosevelt and World War II*. Baltimore, Md.: Johns Hopkins Press, 1969.

Dobb, Maurice. *Soviet Economic Development Since 1917*. New York: International Publishers, 1948.

Dulles, Eleanor. "The Evolution of Reparation Ideas." In *Facts and Factors in Economic History*. New York: Russell, 1967.

Erickson, Edgar C. "The Zoning of Austria." *Annals of the American Academy of Political and Social Science* 267 (January 1950).

Fay, Sidney B. *The Origins of the World War*. New York: Macmillan, 1938.

Feis, Herbert. *Between War and Peace: The Potsdam Conference*. Princeton, N.J.: Princeton University Press, 1960.

————. *Churchill, Roosevelt, Stalin: The War They Waged and the Peace They Sought*. Princeton, N.J.: Princeton University Press, 1957.

————. *The Diplomacy of the Dollar: First Era, 1919–1932*. Hamden, Conn.: Archon, 1965.

————. *From Trust to Terror: The Onset of the Cold War, 1945–1950*. New York: Norton, 1970.

Ferrell, Robert H. *George Marshall*, vol. 15 of *The American Secretaries of State and Their Diplomacy*. New York: Cooper Square, 1966.

Festinger, Leon. *A Theory of Cognitive Dissonance*. Stanford, Cal.: Stanford University Press, 1957.

Gaddis, John Lewis. *The United States and the Origins of the Cold War, 1941–1947*. New York: Columbia University Press, 1972.

Gardner, Lloyd C. *Architects of Illusion: Men and Ideas in American Foreign Policy, 1941–1949*. Chicago: Quadrangle, 1970.

Gay, Edwin F. "War Loans or Subsidies." *Foreign Affairs* 4, no. 3 (April 1926).

Gescher, Dieter Bruno. *Die Vereinigten Staaten von Nordamerika und die Reparationen 1920–1924*. Bonn: Roehrscheid, 1956.

Gimbel, John. *The American Occupation of Germany: Politics and the Military, 1945–1949*. Stanford, Cal.: Stanford University Press, 1968.

————. *The Origins of the Marshall Plan*. Stanford, Cal.: Stanford University Press, 1976.

————. "U.S. Post-War German Policy." *Political Science Quarterly* 87, no. 2 (June 1972).

Ginsburg, David. *The Future of German Reparations*. Washington, D.C.: National Planning Association, 18 February 1947.

Gottlieb, Manuel. "Failure of Quadripartite Monetary Reform, 1945–47." *Finanzarchiv* 17 (1957).

————. "The German Economic Potential." *Social Research* 17 (March 1950).

————. *The German Peace Settlement and the Berlin Crisis.* New York: Paine-Whitman, 1960.

————. "The Reparations Problem Again." *Canadian Journal of Economic and Political Science* 16 (February 1950).

Graefrath, Bernard. *Zur Geschichte der Reparationen.* Ost-Berlin: Deutscher Zentralverlag, 1954.

Graupner, R. *Inter-Alliierte Reparations Abkommen über die Liquidation des Deutschen Auslandsvermögens.* Bremen: Studiengesellschaft für Privatrechtliche Auslandsinteressen, 1950.

Grayson, Cary Travers. *Austria's International Position, 1948–1953: The Reestablishment of an Independent Austria.* Geneve: Librairie E. Droz, 1953.

Greer, Thomas H. *What Roosevelt Thought: The Social and Political Ideas of Franklin D. Roosevelt.* East Lansing, Mich.: Michigan State University Press, 1958.

Grimm, Friedrich. *Das Deutsche Nein: Schluss mit der Reparation.* Hamburg: Hanseatische Verlagsanstalt, 1932.

————. *Der Feind Diktiert: Die Geschichte der Reparationen.* Hamburg: Hanseatische Verlagsanstalt, 1932.

Gruber, Karl. "Austria Infelix." *Foreign Affairs* 25, no. 2 (January 1947).

Gulick, Edward Vose. *Europe's Classical Balance of Power.* New York: Norton, 1955.

Hacker, Jens. *Sovietunion und DDR zum Potsdamerabkommen.* Koln: Wissenschaft und Politik, 1968.

Halperin, Morton H., and Arnold Kanter, eds. *Readings in American Foreign Policy: A Bureaucratic Perspective.* Boston: Little, Brown, 1973.

Hammond, Paul V. "Directives for the Occupation of Germany: The Washington Controversy." In *American Civil-Military Decisions,* edited by Harold Stein. University, Ala.: University of Alabama Press, 1963.

Harmssen, G. W. *Am Abend der Demontage.* Bremen: F. Trüjen Verlag, 1951.

————. *Reparationen, Sozialprodukt, Lebensstandard: Versuch einer Wirtschaftsbilanz.* Bremen: F. Trüjen Verlag, 1947.

Hayter, William. *The Diplomacy of the Great Powers.* London: Ebenezer Baylis, 1960.

Helbich, Wolfgang J. *Die Reparationen in der Ära Brüning: Zur Bedeutung des Young Plans für die Deutsche Politik, 1930–1932.* Berlin: Colloquium Verlag, 1962.

Herring, George C., Jr. "Lend Lease to Russia and the Origins of the Cold War." *Journal of American History* 56, no. 1 (June 1969).

Hill, Russell. *The Struggle for Germany.* New York: Harper, 1947.

Hofstadter, Richard. *The Paranoid Style in American Politics.* New York: Knopf, 1965.

Holborn, Hajo. *A History of Modern Germany.* 3 vols. New York: Knopf, 1959.

————. *Kriegsschuld und Reparationen auf der Pariser Friedenskonferenz von 1919.* Leipzig: Teubner, 1932.

Holsti, Ole R. "The Belief System and National Images." In *International Politics and Foreign Policy*, edited by James N. Rosenau. New York: Free Press, 1969.

Hughes, Richard D. "Soviet Foreign Policy and Germany, 1945–1948." Doctoral dissertation, Claremont Graduate School, 1964.

Jervis, Robert. *Perception and Misperception in International Politics*. Princeton, N.J.: Princeton University Press, 1976.

Jonas, Manfred. *Isolationism in America, 1935–1941*. Ithaca, N.Y.: Cornell University Press, 1966.

Kecskemeti, Paul. *Strategic Surrender: The Politics of Victory and Defeat*. New York: Atheneum, 1964.

Kelmen, Herbert C. *International Behavior, A Social-Psychological Analysis*. New York: Holt, Rinehart, 1965.

Kennan, George F. "A Rebuttal and an Apology." In *Containment and the Cold War: American Foreign Policy Since 1945*, edited by Thomas G. Paterson. Reading, Mass.: Addison-Wesley, 1973.

————. *Russia and the West under Lenin and Stalin*. Boston: Little, Brown, 1960.

Keynes, John Maynard. *The Economic Consequences of the Peace*. New York: Harcourt, 1920.

————. "The German Transfer Problem." In *Readings in the Theory of International Trade*, edited by Howard S. Ellis and Lloyd Metzler. Philadelphia: Blakiston, 1949.

————. *A Revision of the Treaty*. Plainview, N.Y.: Books for Libraries, 1922.

Kimball, Warren F. *Swords or Ploughshares: The Morgenthau Plan for Defeated Nazi Germany 1943–1946*. Philadelphia: Lippincott, 1976.

Klein, Burton H. *Germany's Economic Preparations for War*. Cambridge, Mass.: Harvard University Press, 1959.

Kolko, Gabriel. *The Politics of War: The World and United States Foreign Policy, 1943–1945*. New York: Vintage Books, 1968.

Krueger, Peter. *Deutschland und die Reparationen, 1918–1919*. Stuttgart: Deutsche Verlagsanstalt, 1973.

Kuczynski, Robert R. *American Loans to Germany*. New York: Macmillan, 1927.

————. *Bankers' Profits from German Loans*. Washington, D.C.: Brookings, 1932.

Kuklick, Bruce. *American Policy and the Division of Germany: The Clash with Russia over Reparations*. Ithaca, N.Y.: Cornell University Press, 1972.

————. "The Division of Germany and American Policy on Reparations." *Western Political Quarterly* 23, no. 2 (June 1970).

Lenin, Vladimir I. *Sochineniya*. Third Edition, 24 vols. Leningrad: Partizdat, 1931–1937.

Levin, N. Gordon. *Woodrow Wilson and World Politics*. New York: Oxford University Press, 1968.

Lippmann, Walter. *The Cold War: A Study in U.S. Foreign Policy.* New York: Harper, 1947.

———. "A Defective Policy." In *Containment and the Cold War: American Foreign Policy Since 1945,* edited by Thomas G. Paterson. Reading, Mass.: Addison-Wesley, 1973.

———. *Public Opinion.* New York: Free Press, 1965.

———. *Public Opinion and Foreign Policy in the United States: Lectures.* London: Allen and Unwin, 1952.

———. *U.S. Foreign Policy: Shield of the Republic.* New York: Johnson Reprint, 1971.

Lodge, Henry Cabot. *The Senate and the League of Nations.* New York: Scribner's, 1925.

Macridis, Roy C. "French Foreign Policy." In *Foreign Policy in World Politics,* edited by Roy C. Macridis. Englewood Cliffs, N.J.: Prentice-Hall, 1958.

Maier, Reinhold. *Ein Grundstein wird gelegt: Die Jahre 1945–1947.* Tübingen: Wunderlich, 1964.

Mantoux, Etienne. *The Carthaginian Peace.* Pittsburgh, Pa.: University of Pittsburgh Press, 1952.

Martin, James Stewart. *All Honorable Men.* Boston: Little, Brown, 1950.

Mason, E. S. "Reflections on the Moscow Conference." *International Organization* 1, no. 2 (May 1947).

Mayer, Arno. *Political Origins of the New Diplomacy.* New York: Fertig, 1970.

———. *The Politics and Diplomacy of Peace Keeping: Containment and Counterrevolution at Versailles, 1918–1919.* New York: Knopf, 1968.

Meurer, Hubert. "U.S. Military Government in Germany: Policy and Functioning in Trade and Commerce." Manuscript, OCMH, U.S. Military Government, European Command. Karlsruhe, Germany, 1950.

Milekovsky, A. G., ed. *Meshdunarodnoe Otnosheniya posle Vtoroi Mirovoi Voini* [International Relations After the Second World War]. Vol. 1 (1945–1949). Moscow, 1962.

Millis, Walter. *Road to War: America 1914–1917.* New York: Fertig, 1970.

Mills, Judson, E. Aronson, and Hal Tobinson. "Selectivity in Exposure to Information." *Journal of Abnormal and Social Psychology* 54 (1959).

Mintz, Ilse. *Deterioration in the Quality of Foreign Bonds Issued in the U.S., 1920–1930.* New York: National Bureau of Economic Research, 1951.

Morgenthau, Hans. "John Foster Dulles." In *An Uncertain Tradition: American Secretaries of State in the Twentieth Century,* edited by N. A. Graebner. New York: McGraw-Hill, 1961.

Morgenthau, Henry. *Germany Is Our Problem.* New York: Harper, 1945.

———. "Our Policy Toward Germany." *New York Post,* 26 and 28 November 1947.

Mosely, Philip E. "Dismemberment of Germany." *Foreign Affairs* 28, no. 3 (April 1950).

————. "The Occupation of Germany: New Light on How the Zones Were Drawn." *Foreign Affairs* 28, no. 4 (July 1950).

————. "Soviet-American Relations since the War." *Annals of the American Academy of Political and Social Science* (May 1949).

————. "The Treaty with Austria." *International Organization* 4, no. 2 (May 1950).

Moulton, Harold G., and Constantine E. McGuire. *Germany's Capacity to Pay: A Study of the Reparations Problem.* New York: McGraw-Hill, 1923.

————, and Leo Pasvolsky. *War Debts and World Prosperity.* Washington, D.C.: Brookings, 1932.

Nettl, J. Peter. *The Eastern Zone and Soviet Policy in Germany, 1945–1950.* London: Oxford University Press, 1951.

————. "German Reparations in the Soviet Empire." *Foreign Affairs* 29, no. 2 (January 1951).

Neustadt, Richard E. *Alliance Politics.* New York: Columbia University Press, 1970.

Nevins, Allen, and Henry Steele Commager. *America, the Story of a Free People.* Boston: Little, Brown, 1942.

Notter, Harley. *Postwar Foreign Policy Preparation: 1939–1945.* Washington, D.C.: U.S. Government Printing Office, 1949.

O'Connor, Raymond C. *Diplomacy for Victory: Franklin Delano Roosevelt and Unconditional Surrender.* New York: Norton, 1971.

Opie, Redvers et al. *The Search for Peace Settlements.* Washington, D.C.: Brookings, 1951.

Osgood, Robert Endicott. *Ideals and Self-Interest in America's Foreign Relations.* Chicago: The University of Chicago Press, 1953.

Paterson, Thomas G. "The Abortive American Loan to Russia and the Origins of the Cold War, 1943–1946." *Journal of American History* 56, no. 1 (June 1969).

————. *Soviet-American Confrontation: Postwar Reconstruction and the Origins of the Cold War.* Baltimore, Md.: Johns Hopkins University Press, 1973.

————, ed. *Cold War Critics.* Chicago: Quadrangle, 1971.

————, *Containment and the Cold War: American Foreign Policy Since 1945.* Reading, Mass.: Addison-Wesley, 1973.

Penrose, E. F. *Economic Planning for the Peace.* Princeton, N.J.: Princeton University Press, 1953.

Petrov, Vladimir. *Money and Conquest: Allied Occupation Currencies in World War II.* Baltimore, Md.: Johns Hopkins Press, 1967.

Pick, Franz, and René Sedillot. *All the Monies of the World.* New York: Pick Public Corporation, 1971.

Potter, David M. *People of Plenty.* Chicago: University of Chicago Press, 1954.

Pratt, Julius W. *A History of United States Foreign Policy.* Englewood Cliffs, N.J.: Prentice-Hall, 1972.

Price, Harry Bayard. *The Marshall Plan and Its Meaning.* Ithaca, N.Y.: Cornell University Press, 1955.

Range, Willard. *Franklin D. Roosevelt's World Order.* Athens, Ga.: University of Georgia Press, 1959.

Reinsch, Paul S. *World Politics at the End of the Nineteenth Century as Influenced by the Oriental Situation.* New York: Macmillan, 1972.

Rosenau, James N. *Public Opinion and Foreign Policy.* New York: Random House, 1961.

Rostow, Eugene V. "The Partition of Germany and the Unity of Europe." *Virginia Quarterly Review* 23, no. 1 (Winter 1947).

Rudolph, Vladimir. "The Administrative Organization of Soviet Control." In *Soviet Economic Policy in Post-War Germany,* edited by Robert Slusser. New York: Research Program on the USSR, 1953.

Schacht, Hjalmar. *Das Ende der Reparationen.* Oldenburg: Stalling, 1931.

———. *Die Stabilization der Mark.* London: Allen & Unwin, 1927.

Schieber, Clara Eve. *The Transformation of American Sentiment toward Germany, 1870–1914.* New York: Russell, 1973.

Schmitt, Bernadotte. *The Coming of the War, 1914.* New York: Fertig, 1971.

Schwarz, Hans Peter. *Vom Reich zur Bundesrepublik.* Neuwied, 1966.

Scott, Andrew. *The Functioning of the International Political System.* New York: Macmillan, 1967.

Shulman, Marshal D. *Stalin's Foreign Policy Reappraised.* New York: Atheneum, 1969.

Snell, John L. *The War-Time Origins of the East-West Dilemma over Germany.* New Orleans: Hauser Press, 1959.

Snyder, Richard C., H. W. Bruck, and Burton Sapin. *Decision-Making as an Approach to the Study of International Politics.* Monograph 3 of the Foreign Policy Analysis Project Series, Princeton University, 1954.

Stearman, William Lloyd. *The Soviet Union and the Occupation of Austria: An Analysis of Soviet Policy in Austria, 1945–1955.* Bonn: Siegler, 1961.

Stolper, Gustav. *The German Economy, 1870–1940.* New York: Reynal, 1940.

———. *German Realities.* New York: Reynal, 1948.

Strauss, Harold. *The Division and Dismemberment of Germany from the Casablanca Conference to the Establishment of the East German Republic.* Thèse, Ambilly, 1952.

Toynbee, Arnold Joseph, and Veronica M. Toynbee, eds. *The Realignment of Europe.* 2 vols. London: Oxford University Press, 1962.

Ulam, Adam B. *Expansion and Coexistence: The History of Soviet Foreign Policy, 1917–1967.* New York: Praeger, 1968.

Varga, E. "Vosmeshchenije ushcherba gitlerovskoi germaniyei i yeyo soobshchnikami" [Reparations by Hitler's Germany and Its Accomplices]. *Voina i Rabochi Klass,* no. 10 (15 October 1943).

Verba, Sidney. "Assumptions of Rationality and Non-Rationality in Models of the International System." In *International Politics and Foreign Policy,* edited by James N. Rosenau. New York: Free Press, 1969.

Voznesensky, Nikolai A. *The Economy of the USSR during World War II*. Washington, D.C.: Public Affairs Press, 1948.

Wandel, Eckhard. *Die Bedeutung der Vereinigten Staaten von Amerika für das Deutsche Reparations Problem, 1924–1929*. Tübingen: Mohr, 1971.

Warburg, James P. *Germany: Bridge or Battleground?* New York: Harcourt, 1947.

Watt, Richard. *The Kings Depart*. New York: Touchstone-Clarion, 1970.

Wegener, Hertha. "Economic Relations between Soviet Russia and Eastern Germany." Master's thesis, Columbia University, 1951.

Weill-Raynal, Etienne. *Les Reparations Allemandes et la France*. 3 vols. Paris: Nouvelles Editions Latines, 1947.

Welles, Sumner. *Seven Decisions That Shaped History*. New York: Harper, 1951.

———. *The Time for Decision*. New York: Harper, 1944.

———. *Where Are We Heading?* New York: Harper, 1946.

Wheeler-Bennett, John. *The Wreck of Reparations: Being the Political Background of the Lausanne Agreement, 1932*. New York: Fertig, 1972.

White, Ralph K. *Nobody Wanted War*. Garden City, N.Y.: Doubleday, 1968.

Williams, Benjamin H. *The Economic Foreign Policy of the United States*. New York: Fertig, 1967.

Williams, William Appleman. *The Tragedy of American Diplomacy*. New York: Dell, 1972.

Willis, F. Roy. *The French in Germany, 1945–1949*. Stanford, Cal.: Stanford University Press, 1962.

Yergin, Daniel. *Shattered Peace: The Origins of the Cold War and the National Security State*. Boston: Houghton Mifflin, 1977.

Yershov, Vassily. "Confiscation and Plunder by the Army of Occupation." In *Soviet Economic Policy in Post-War Germany*, edited by Robert Slusser. New York: Research Program on the USSR, 1953.

Young, Roland. *Congressional Politics in the Second World War*. New York: Columbia University Press, 1956.

INDEX